The Complete Human Resources Writing Guide

Other Books by Diane Arthur

Success Through Assertiveness (1980)

Recruiting, Interviewing, Selecting & Orienting New Employees (1986)

Managing Human Resources in Small and Mid-Sized Companies (1987)

Recruiting, Interviewing, Selecting & Orienting New Employees,
Second Edition (1991)

Workplace Testing: An Employer's Guide to Policies and Practices (1994)

Managing Human Resources in Small and Mid-Sized Companies,
Second Edition (1995)

THE COMPLETE HUMAN RESOURCES WRITING GUIDE

Diane Arthur

American Management Association

New York • Atlanta • Boston • Chicago • Kansas City • San Francisco • Washington, D.C.
Brussels • Mexico City • Tokyo • Toronto

This book is available at a special
discount when ordered in bulk quantities.
For information, contact Special Sales Department,
AMACOM, a division of American Management Association,
1601 Broadway, New York, NY 10019

This publication is designed to provide accurate and authoritative in-
formation in regard to the subject matter covered. It is sold with the
understanding that the publisher is not engaged in rendering legal,
accounting, or other professional service. If legal advice or other expert
assistance is required, the services of a competent professional person
should be sought.

Library of Congress Cataloging-in-Publication Data

Arthur, Diana.
    The complete human resources writing guide / Diane Arthur.
        p.   cm.
    Includes index.
    ISBN 0-8144-0325-5 (hardcover)
    1. Communication in personnel management.   2. Business writing.
I. Title.
HF5549.5.C6A75   1997
808'.066658—dc21   *96-50445*
                                                               CIP

Printing number

10 9 8 7 6 5 4 3 2 1

Love to
Warren, Valerie & Victoria
who put up with my semantics

Contents

Preface and Acknowledgments

Human resources (HR) practitioners probably generate more paperwork than any other group of professionals. They produce countless forms, notices, requisitions, promotional packets, letters, memos, evaluations, references, orientation materials, policies, procedures, plans, announcements, surveys, and manuals on which organizations rely for their day-to-day operation.

Unfortunately, many HR professionals repeatedly demonstrate a lack of effective general writing skills, and more significant, effective HR writing skills. This deficiency becomes evident when ineffective note taking during an interview results in charges of employment discrimination, unclear information in benefits booklets results in confusion on the part of plan participants, inaccurate performance appraisal comments preclude managers from terminating below-average workers, and poorly worded employee handbooks result in charges of wrongful discharge.

Despite the fact that most HR professionals and managers "write" via computers, thereby generating written documents faster than ever before, they still run into difficulty. Computerization does not negate the need for accurate, carefully worded communications, which has never been greater. This increased need is due, in part, to frequent equal employment opportunity legislation changes, twenty-first century recruitment challenges, and an increasingly diverse workforce.

All of these requirements point to the need for this book, a comprehensive source of writing guidelines for all forms of HR communication. It is designed for use by everyone involved with HR activities—both HR professionals and non-HR practitioners. It is effective in any work setting, corporate and nonprofit, and both large and small businesses will benefit from its contents.

Human resources professionals and managers can use this guide to refine their general writing skills and learn the most effective means of generating specific HR documents. In addition, it will be useful to trainers and instructors in teaching general and HR writing skills in training workshops or college classrooms.

Busy HR practitioners and managers will appreciate the book's logical, easy-to-read style. It is divided into two main parts. Section One, which deals with general writing skills, is more than a guide to proper grammar, punctuation, and sentence structure. These aspects of writing are undeniably important, but they do not determine the effectiveness of an HR document. The emphasis is therefore on getting your message across clearly and effectively, even if this sometimes means deviating from standard rules of style and formatting.

The material in Section One serves as the foundation for Section Two, which examines specific HR documents. It contains over one hundred writing samples, which provide readers with useful tips for honing their writing efforts. Note that although many of these samples represent actual documents, individual and company names and addresses are all fictitious.

HR practitioners may not have much of a choice when it comes to the number and types of documents they must generate; however, they certainly can opt to make writing less time-consuming and burdensome and more effective.

Acknowledgments

I appreciate the expert editing and advice provided by Adrienne Hickey, Senior Acquisitions and Planning Editor, and Barbara Horowitz, Associate Editor, at AMACOM. Thanks to them, I continue to learn about, appreciate, and enjoy writing.

I am also indebted to those clients and colleagues who provided many of the samples for this book.

Section One

The Foundation for Effective Human Resources Writing

1
Keys to Effective Writing

Chances are you decided to read this book for one of two reasons: You consider yourself to be a fairly effective writer of human resources (HR) documents and want to hone your skills, or you basically dislike writing and would rather communicate by phone, in person, or via smoke signals. If you fall into the latter category, do not despair; you do not have to love writing (although some people really do!) or have a doctorate in English to generate effectively written communications. In addition, writing need not take an exorbitant amount of time or result in an outbreak of hives each time you have to send a letter or prepare a performance appraisal.

The Core of HR Writing

HR writing invariably emerges from a core of tangible information. Whether preparing a job description, documenting an employment interview, or soliciting responses to an attitude survey, you always have as the center of your writing concrete data from which to draw specific language and ideas. You are not expected to be creative, write sonnets, or strive for the Pulitzer Prize; the sole objective is to communicate specific information, the components of which you either know or are readily available to you.

Suppose you have been asked to prepare a blurb about your department's new customer service manager for the company newsletter. Consider the tangible information that provides the necessary ingredients: the employee's name, title, starting date, brief description of responsibilities, experience prior to joining your organization, and one or two interesting tidbits (e.g., she has a black belt in karate). You know all of these facts or can easily get them. Your task is to organize the data in a format that accurately conveys this information, flows smoothly, makes sense, and, as a bonus, is interesting to read.

There are a number of ways to accomplish this task. The most straightforward, least taxing method is simply to present the facts:

> Dolores Kelleher, Customer Service Manager, effective June 19, 199X, is responsible for ensuring maximum customer satisfaction. She was a senior customer service representative for two years at Valdart Associates before joining Avedon Industries and enjoys karate in her spare time.

Certainly this example conveys the necessary information, but it comes across as dry and dull. With some effort, it could be made more interesting:

> [Rewritten] Avedon welcomes Dolores Kelleher, our new Customer Service Manager. Dolores joined our team on June 19 after working at Valdart Associ-

ates for two years as a senior customer service representative. That experience will come in handy, since Dolores's new responsibilities include ensuring overall customer satisfaction and personally handling particularly "sticky" complaints. When Dolores is not making our customers happy, she can be found working out at the *dojo*, fine-tuning her karate skills and preparing for her second-degree black belt test. Welcome aboard, Dolores!

The second version offers the same information as the first, but the flow is smoother, the language more colorful, and the tone friendlier. And although it is nearly three times longer, it is less tiring to read. Significant, too, is the fact that it took just two minutes more to write—not a bad investment in time, considering the results.

A third approach to writing this blurb is the interview, or question-and-answer (Q&A) format. This may be the most lengthy, because it requires spending time with the new employee. On the other hand, it is the easiest to write. Preparing an introductory statement and a handful of questions constitutes your role; the rest is "written" by the employee:

This month Avedon welcomes Dolores Kelleher, who joined us on June 19 as our new Customer Service Manager.

Q: Dolores, what do your responsibilities at Avedon include?

A: I'm responsible for ensuring overall customer satisfaction. I also personally handle any particularly complex customer complaints.

Q: That sounds challenging. What did you do before coming to Avedon?

A: I worked for two years as a senior customer service representative at Valdart Associates.

Q: What do you like the most about customer service work?

A: What I like most is the variety of people I come in contact with.

Q: What do you find most challenging about customer service work?

A: I dislike it when a particularly irate customer really upsets one of my customer service reps.

Q: What do you enjoy doing when you're not working?

A: Right now I'm working toward earning my second-degree black belt in karate. My test is coming up in three weeks, so I'm at the *dojo* just about every night, training. Normally I work out two or three times a week.

Q: Is there anything else you'd like your fellow Avedon employees to know about you?

A: Just that I'm really glad to be working here. So far everyone has been very helpful and generous with their time. It looks like I made a smart move coming to Avedon!

We think you did too, Dolores. Welcome aboard! And good luck with your karate test!

This last approach is the most personal, especially when accompanied by a photograph of the new employee. The brief statements and questions provide the framework for the piece, and the employee's answers give it substance.

Regardless of the approach you select, keep this thought in mind: If you are being asked to write an HR document, it is either because you already have the necessary information at hand or you have access to it. This should take some of the sting out of the task and enable you to proceed.

The Blank Page Syndrome

Okay. So you are willing to acknowledge that access to concrete data should make it easier to accomplish the HR writing task at hand. But you still have to deal with actually getting started—that is, facing a blank page, which ranks right up there, for many otherwise fearless professionals, with telling the dentist to hold the Novocain. Reactions to a blank piece of paper or a blinking cursor on your computer monitor typically include sweaty palms, a dry mouth, tapping fingers, twirled hair, extra visits to the coffee machine, and overeating. All of this translates into excess stress and wasted time. If you wince at the prospect of getting started, try these six techniques:

1. *The minimalist approach.* At the outset of every writing task, immediately jot down or key in the facts that immediately come to mind. Do not do any research, do not fret about the wording, and do not try to organize your thoughts. This minimalist approach, of writing no more than a single no-strain statement per line, gives you a great sense of accomplishment. The newsletter assignment might start out looking like this:

Dolores Kelleher
Customer Service Manager
June 19, 199X
Two years: Sr. Customer Service Rep.
Valdart Associates
Spare time: karate

Now you have the basic framework for your document. The task that remains—filling in with verbiage and rearranging the thoughts to give your piece substance and a sense of sequence—is less overwhelming.

2. *The avoidance-with-a-purpose approach.* Avoid the blank page altogether; that is, never write on a blank piece of paper or key in on a blank screen. Make certain to begin writing on paper that already has something—anything at all—written on it. Once you get started, transfer your ideas to a clean slate, and continue working from there. If you view this as a duplication of effort, think about how long you typically stare at a blank piece of paper or monitor before unlocking your hands and starting working.

3. *The blank-but-scared approach.* If you prefer the idea of starting with a clean slate but then freeze when you actually see it, consider taking a blank piece of paper or a blank screen and immediately writing something—the date, the name of the person to whom you are writing, or anything else relevant to the topic to accomplish your objective of bypassing a blank page or blinking cursor.

4. *The parting-words-first approach.* Some people like to work backward by writing

their closing words first. This approach both combats the blank page syndrome and results in a wonderful (albeit, false) sense of accomplishment. Starting out with, "Welcome aboard, Dolores!" may be enough to get some writers started.

5. *The artistic approach.* Try creating a "writer's portrait": Write your opening and closing thoughts, leaving a blank canvas in between. Then draw a frame around the two paragraphs and sit back to admire what you have done. Now it is time to finish your work of art by filling in the body of your document. This artistic approach works especially well with memos, letters, and short documents.

6. *The take-a-deep-breath approach.* Let's say you have to document a disciplinary matter. It's the first thing you think of when you arrive at work in the morning, and the thought of doing it pesters you like an annoying gnat throughout the day. This is torture. Take a deep breath and force yourself to acknowledge that the employee is not going to quit or suddenly become a star performer. This task must be done—plain and simple. Look forward to the tremendous sense of relief that is guaranteed to follow after the task is completed and you are free to move on.

Focus on Your Objectives

Everything we do in life has a purpose, although that purpose may not always be clear. Students go to college out of an interest in certain subject areas or to earn a degree, applicants go on job interviews to land a particular job or just to see what's out there, and employees go to work to earn a living or because they love what they do (am I pushing it here?).

In the same way, everything we write has a purpose or objective. Once identified, objectives make staying on course easier, and your writing becomes clearer. It is particularly important to stay on track when preparing lengthy documents, such as employee handbooks, when it is easy to get lost amid a sea of employee do's and don'ts.

Writing down objectives at the outset of any assignment allows you to filter out distractions and stay focused. This small amount of time and effort spent instantly translates into less stress and greater productivity. What's more, these objectives can be saved and recycled each time you confront a similar writing assignment.

Begin with a broad-based objective that reflects the overall task to be accomplished:

HR Document	*Objective*
Recruiting	
Job requisition:	Communicates overall departmental needs and requirements for a given job
Job description:	Identifies primary and secondary duties, responsibilities, and requirements of a job
Job posting notice:	Specifies grade level, overall responsibilities, salary range, and reporting relationship of an available job
Job posting application:	Asks employees to identify their qualifications in relation to the requirements of a given job opening
Job advertisement:	Attracts qualified candidates

HR Document	Objective
Letter to applicants:	Invites applicants in for an interview or thanks them for their interest
Interviewing	
Application form:	Elicits pertinent job-related information about a candidate
Interview evaluation:	Records interviewer's assessment of a candidate's job suitability
Selection checklist:	Identifies key skills, abilities, traits, and characteristics relative to a given job
References:	Confirms information acquired during the interview; acquires additional job-related information to help interviewer make a hiring decision
Letter to rejected candidates:	Thanks candidates for their time and interest; welcomes future applications
Letter to selected candidates:	Informs an applicant that he or she has been selected for a given job; may include starting date and salary
New Employees	
Orientation material:	Identifies the organization's philosophy, structure, benefits, policies, and expectations of its employees
Benefits policies	Outlines all insurance-related information, including medical, disability, pension plans, and vacation and other days off
New employee announcement:	Informs existing staff of new employee's background and responsibilities
Performance management	
Performance appraisal	Identifies how an employee's performance has measured up against previously agreed-on objectives; pinpoints areas requiring improvement; identifies an action plan with a new set of objectives
Letter of commendation:	Praises an employee for performing a task particularly well or accomplishing a difficult assignment
Counseling session memorandum	Addresses a specific problem that is interfering with an employee's effective job performance
Disciplinary notice	Identifies the violation of a specific rule or policy and outlines the corrective steps to be taken
Exit interview	Determines what aspects of the job or company led to an employee's termination

HR Document	Objective
Letter of termination:	Advises an employee of the reason(s) for and effective date of termination
Employee Services	
Employee assistance program	Directs employees for help with matters such as alcohol and drugs that are affecting work performance
Dependent care program	Provides on-site services or referrals to programs that provide child or elder care
Company-sponsored activity or program	Informs employees of company-sponsored activities and programs, such as health club membership, smoke-enders programs, and weight-loss workshops.
Newsletter	Keeps employees informed about organizational changes, employee social functions, and personal news (e.g., births, marriages)
Suggestion program	Encourages employees to contribute ideas that will improve employer-employee relations or productivity; solicits employee comments and suggestions regarding various work-related matters
Letter of congratulations	Acknowledges outstanding employee accomplishments (e.g., promotion), as well as personal news (e.g., the birth of a child)
Letter to sick employees	Extends best wishes for a speedy recovery
Letter of condolence	Expresses sympathy for the loss of a loved one
Letter for retirement	Expresses thanks for the work an employee has performed
HR Guidelines	
Employee handbook	Identifies employer expectations and employee rights and obligations
HR policy manual	Assists managers and supervisors in handling day-to-day employer-employee relations matters

Now ask yourself a series of ten questions to fine-tune the generic objective:

1. Who are the recipients of this document?
2. How are the recipients likely to react to it?
3. What similar documents, if any, have they previously received?
4. What do the recipients already know about the subject matter?
5. What questions are they likely to need answered relative to this document?
6. What tone is likely to elicit a positive response from the recipients?

7. What action will be required as a result of this document?
8. Does the writing make clear who is responsible for taking action, including the time frame in which such action is to be taken?
9. Do the recipients know who to contact for additional information?
10. If I were the recipient of this document, how would I react?

Armed with a generic objective and the answers to these ten questions, begin writing. Suppose your task is to write a letter to a candidate who was interviewed but not hired. Your overall objective is twofold: to thank the applicant for expressing an interest in employment with your company and to encourage future applications. The answers to the ten questions will make your task virtually effortless:

1. *Recipient of the letter.* Rejected job applicant.
2. *Likely reaction to the letter.* Disappointment; possibly surprise, depression, anger, or resentment.
3. *Similar letters received in the past.* Probably, ranging from a few, in which case the recipient may be surprised or resentful, to many, making the applicant feel dejected.
4. *Applicant already knows.* Expecting a response, probably in the form of a letter.
5. *Questions likely to require answers.* (a) Did I get the job; (b) if not, why not; (c) should I bother applying for future jobs?
6. *Tone that is likely to elicit a positive response.* Understanding, support, and encouragement.
7. *Action required.* None.
8. *Responsible for taking action.* Not applicable.
9. *Who to contact for additional information.* Not applicable.
10. *Personal reaction.* Would want to feel as good as possible even though I had just been rejected.

Plucking the overall objective from the list on pages 6–8 and answering these ten questions took only a few moments. These two steps establish the framework of your letter and render the actual writing much simpler, as shown in Exhibit 1-1.

Know Your Subject Matter

Ask me to write about the steps for effective employment interviewing, and you will have trouble getting me to stop. Tell me to develop a benefits presentation for employees who are joining the company as a result of a merger, and my response would be, "How much time do I have to prepare?" Writing about a topic that technically falls within the realm of your area of expertise but is not one in which you are all that interested can be tricky. Answering the ten questions already listed becomes more difficult, as does knowing what to include and what to omit. The assignment becomes a chore, your focus becomes blurred, and blank page syndrome becomes harder to overcome.

Before you start writing, try to get out of the task. This is not meant to sound like a cop-out; it simply makes sense that someone who really knows the subject (say, benefits) should write about it. The basis of your argument is twofold: It will take less time and will probably be better written if a benefits expert does it.

Exhibit 1-1. Sample Letter to a Rejected Candidate.

September 11, 199X

Mr. Dell Richardson
38 Adobe Court
Garden City, NY 11530

Dear Mr. Richardson:

Thank you for taking the time to meet with me to discuss Avedon
Industries' opening for a marketing representative. I learned a great
deal about your accomplishments and aspirations, and appreciate the
interest you expressed in our company.

When filling an opening, Avedon looks at a number of factors, such as
experience, demonstrated skills, knowledge, and the ability to handle
key job-related situations. This can make the selection process difficult
when we are fortunate enough to attract many qualified candidates
like you. With only one opening, however, we are forced to turn away
many fine applicants. Accordingly, we regret that we are unable to
extend an offer of employment to you at this time.

Your credentials are impressive, Mr. Richardson. We hope you will
again consider us for employment in the future.

Sincerely,

Rebecca Picard
Senior Human Resources Representative

If this does not work, read on. There are a number of ways to become familiar
enough with a subject to write intelligibly and expeditiously.

▸ *Do not go it alone.* Approach experts in the area from within your organization,
asking not only for information but for their actual written input. They will probably be
flattered that you asked and appreciate the credit, and you will be getting the help you
need.

▸ *Build on what you know.* Start out with an area of the topic in which you are knowl-
edgeable (there has to be something!); intersperse this knowledge throughout the document, and, if possible, end with it.

▸ *Research the subject.* Better yet, delegate this task to someone on your staff. This
includes making phone calls to colleagues from other organizations and contacting members of professional organizations. When you are writing about something like dissemi-

nating benefits information to employees, originality is not of paramount importance. If others are willing to share their policies, offer to reciprocate and tailor what is relevant to your needs.

‣ *Think about what you would want to know.* This approach leads quite naturally to a question-and-answer format. By writing down all your questions, you are halfway home! Make an appointment to see a benefits expert and take the list of questions with you. Ask the questions verbally, and write down the answers. Before leaving, ask if there are any areas you did not cover. This approach ensures that your task will be accomplished in next to no time.

Target Your Audience

Knowing your audience is important, from the standpoint of what information they already have and anticipating questions the document is likely to generate. However, focusing on a person's characteristics, as opposed to what needs to be said, can distort the intended thrust of your document. For example, when preparing an employee's performance appraisal, tiptoeing around the person's likely reaction to criticism could prevent you from being frank about areas requiring improvement. The language in an appraisal should not be harsh, but it needs to be honest and accurate. The employee's feelings about what is being said are certainly relevant and should be addressed during the face-to-face meeting when you sit down together to develop an action plan for improvement. Feelings should not be a factor when writing the appraisal, however.

Also consider who else is likely to read the document. A performance appraisal, for example, will probably be read by salary administrators if performance is tied in with raises; other members from HR, in-house counsel, and union representatives if disciplinary matters develop; and managers from other departments should the employee opt for a transfer or promotion. In addition, the evaluation could become a source of reference during an exit interview or if the employee terminates and reapplies at some later date. Therefore, although the appraisal should be written for and about one primary reader, anticipate that it is likely to be scrutinized by other readers as well.

The one person *not* to be considered when writing an HR document is yourself. Write what needs to be said, not all that you know.

After you have completed a document, reread it, asking: "Have I covered all the germane points? Is the reader likely to understand their relevance? Have I anticipated and addressed questions that are likely to come up? Have I provided more information than is necessary?" The answer to the first three questions should be yes; if the answer to the final question is also yes, go back and edit. Do not overestimate your reader's need for information.

Organize Your Thoughts

Regardless of its nature or length, every document needs to be organized before being submitted or distributed. How it is organized is determined by the actual composition and complexity of the document.

Consider a long, multifaceted document like a policies and procedures manual. The contents might first be divided into several key categories; within each of those topics would be an *alphabetical* listing of related subjects. The alphabetical approach makes it easy for managers to locate what is needed expeditiously and effortlessly. A typical policies and procedures manual, then, might have the following main categories:

- Benefits administration
- Disciplinary action
- Equal employment opportunity (EEO) and affirmative action
- Employee grievances
- Employer-employee relations
- Employment practices
- Salary administration
- Training and development

Within each category would be an alphabetical listing of relevant topics. For example, the area pertaining to EEO might include these topics:

- Areas of responsibility
- Benefits
- Changes in job status
- Communications policies
- Compensation
- Legal considerations
- Posting requirements
- Selection procedures
- Sexual harassment
- Training

A *chronological* format lays out events in the order in which they occurred. This approach is suitable for documents such as a third-step disciplinary notice. Start by identifying the specific infraction; then recap the dates and highlights of the oral warning and the first and second written warnings. Conclude by stipulating what will happen if the offense occurs again within a specified period of time.

Another way to organize your thoughts is by the *situation and solution* approach. It first reports on the problem or situation and ends with the resolution or results achieved. Results of attitude surveys could be reported this way. Start by citing the areas identified by employees as needing improvement; next describe what currently exists; then summarize suggestions that were made; finally, list the steps that will be taken, with an accompanying time line, if appropriate.

The *reporter's technique* of highlighting who, what, where, when, why, and how was used in the newsletter blurb announcing a new employee earlier in this chapter. It also works well when writing letters to applicants, interview evaluations, and letters to selected or rejected candidates. This approach works best when the salient points are presented in order of descending importance.

When writing about a project for which you are seeking support, say, introducing an on-site dependent care program, an effective method is the *deductive reasoning approach*. Start by stating your theme: dependent care. Then provide facts, figures, and observations that show how it has worked out in comparable environments; the impact it is projected to have on employee morale, motivation, and absenteeism; and cost.

Support for a new program might also be achieved through an *inductive reasoning approach.* Start by citing a host of specific examples, leading up to the program your information logically suggests.

Priority ranking works well when there are a number of issues to discuss—some more important, complex, or of greater interest than others. A benefits packet would perhaps describe medical and dental insurance first and conclude with direct deposit privileges.

Finally, your HR document might be effectively written in a simple *list* format. A checklist for new employees, for example, could start out, "All employees must be issued the following twenty items on their first day at work." Then proceed to list the twenty items in one-two-three fashion.

Capture Your Reader's Attention

Face it: Regardless of how much time you put into writing an HR document, a reader is likely to zip through it at the speed of light. Unlike a novel read leisurely at the beach or a letter from an old friend, business writing is practical, necessary stuff that receives the minimum amount of attention. Capturing your reader's attention immediately is particularly important when you are trying to gain support for an idea or project, such as a dependent care program.

How do you hook your reader at the outset? Here are ten pointers:

1. *Make a startling statement.* A statement that shocks or surprises the reader can grab attention and hold it, but only if the content is relevant to the subject at hand. For example, making sexual inferences when writing to managers about employee orientation will undoubtedly generate reader interest at the outset, but this will quickly dissipate when it becomes evident that sex has nothing to do with this kind of orientation. In addition, the reader is likely to resent being duped and lose interest in continuing. Instead, try to use a lead-in statement like *Employees who attend orientation are likely to be 27% more productive than those who do not.*

2. *Tell something already known.* This technique immediately makes the reader feel a part of the message and thus acts as a lure into the rest of the document. Reading *No one has to tell you how rough it was last year when we had to downsize and tighten our belts* naturally makes the reader wonder if the next statement is going to say this year will be better, worse, or the same.

3. *Pose an intriguing question.* Starting a job advertisement with *Do you know how long it took us to hire our last marketing rep?* compels the reader to continue. It is only natural for someone to guess and compare his or her answer with the "correct" one in the ad.

4. *Make it personal.* Tell your readers in the opening paragraph that participation in the company's fitness program could win them a $250 gift certificate to the clothing store of their choice. You are effectively saying *This is about and for you*, thereby practically guaranteeing an attentive audience.

5. *Make it timely.* When you receive a memo that does not require an immediate response, no doubt you put it at the bottom of your to-do pile. Therefore, if you want your document to be read, say something timely: *Managerial training in the use of Avedon's new policies and procedures manual will begin two weeks from today. Please indicate, on the attached form, which of the two sessions you plan to attend, and return the form to HR by Friday of this week.*

6. *Make a promise.* Offering readers an incentive up front is likely to compel them to continue reading. Naturally it has to be one that you can keep: *Give Avedon a usable suggestion on how to increase productivity and we'll give you $500!*

7. *Give the reader good news.* Telling readers what they have been hoping to hear initially is guaranteed to capture their attention and hold it: *Effective immediately, Avedon employees are entitled to free membership at the New You Health Club.*

8. *Get the bad news over with.* If there is bad news, sometimes it is best to say it up front: *Effective May 1, Avedon employees will no longer be permitted to attend the New You Health Club free of charge.* Try to follow bad news with a positive statement: *While a fee of $5.00 per session will be charged, this is 40% less than what non-Avedon employees must pay.*

9. *Use the person's name.* Weaving the recipient's name throughout a letter not only personalizes it but catches the eye, drawing the reader to that part of the correspondence. Do not use this technique more than twice in an average letter; otherwise it starts to read like a lure to enter a contest.

10. *Echo your reader's concerns.* Let readers know at the outset that you appreciate the frustration over not knowing whether the company will be downsizing in the near future: *Lately, rumors have been flying about Avedon's downsizing by as much as 30% in the upcoming year. We understand how frustrating this has been for all of you, and how difficult it must be to work under these conditions.*

Stress the Four C's

Veronica was three months away from retirement when I first entered the field of human resources. She had held the position of personnel director for more than twenty years and was ready to embark on a new venture—travels to unknown destinations for an unspecified period of time—and she would be unreachable. Colleagues, especially her replacement, were in a state of panic. I quickly learned why: Veronica had twenty years of HR information in her head and rarely wrote anything down. There were hundreds of policies, procedures, and personnel changes that she could recite, but very little was in writing. When news of her retirement became known, staff members hovered around with pad and pen in hand, frantically writing down everything she said. It was an amazing sight and seemed to amuse Veronica. I asked if she had an aversion to writing, and she replied, "It's easier to remember things than to write about them. Besides, there are too many rules that go along with writing. I don't have time to worry about faulty grammar, misplaced modifiers, misleading references, or confusing sentence structure when writing an HR document."

What Veronica did not realize was that while there are numerous rules of grammar, sentence structure, and composition that improve one's writing, there are four simple guidelines to successful writing that any HR professional or manager can master with little effort. These are the four *C*'s: clarity, conciseness, consistency, and completeness.

Clarity

Clear messages are written in terms that are distinct, easily grasped, and free from confusion. This means steering clear of ambiguities or grandiose words. Remember that your objective is to communicate a particular message, not to impress your reader. Accordingly, select language that is reader friendly.

Try, too, to reread what you have written from the perspective of the recipient. The reader may not have your knowledge base and may therefore require additional information. Do not assume that what is clear to you is equally clear to others.

Clarity also means adhering to standard English word orders in your sentences. The most common word order is subject-verb-object: "Nathan [*subject*] submitted [*verb*] this month's winning suggestion [*object*]." This pattern, common in newspapers, is easy to read and understand. A second basic word pattern, subject-verb-complement, also conveys a clear message: "Nathan [*subject*] is [*verb*] this month's winner [*complement*]."

Getting to the point in the first paragraph will convey your point clearly as well. If you want the reader to begin writing an employee's performance appraisal three weeks before the scheduled face-to-face meeting, say so. Do not force a journey through a lengthy text to learn what could have been stated initially in a single sentence.

Strive to avoid redundancy. Using several words that mean the same thing slows the reader's ability to get to the core of your message and could give the impression that you do not have much to say. A sampling of redundant language and appropriate, single-word alternatives appears in Exhibit 1-2. Note that redundancy is not the same as repetition. Repeating the same message more than once in a document for emphasis can be effective and actually increases clarity if not overdone.

Conciseness

Readers of HR documents are busy and often impatient. They expect an economy of expression and have little tolerance for verbosity. Therefore, use the fewest words possible to communicate your meaning. Streamlining your choice of words and avoiding long phrases when a single word will do makes it more likely that your document will be understood. In Exhibit 1-3, you will find a sampling of wordy phrases and their single-word counterparts.

Conciseness also means avoiding unnecessary emphasis. Words such as *very, highly, definitely, totally,* and *absolutely* tend to be overused and dilute the impact of the intended message. Sometimes they can contradict the intended meaning, as in *practically impossible* and *somewhat essential*. Exhibit 1-4 offers examples of phrases that are better left alone.

Consistency

Consistency in voice and tense are important to the flow of a document. For example, *The more we learned about the policy, the clearer the issues become* presents an awkward shift in tense and makes reading and comprehension difficult. When *become* is changed to *became* the sentence is smooth, clear, and correct.

Choosing the appropriate words to convey your intent is another important aspect of consistency. Words should support your meaning, not get in the way of it. Suppose you are preparing a disciplinary notice. The topic is chronic lateness; the recipient is an outstanding employee who has recently developed an attendance problem. Your goal is to correct the behavior. You include a recap of the events that have led to this documentation, with reference to the verbal warning administered one month ago. Your lead-in statement is,

> During the verbal warning two weeks ago you acknowledged having trouble adjusting to the changed bus route and would find another way to get to work on time.

Exhibit 1-2. Redundant and Alternative Expressions.

Redundant	*Alternative*
actual experience	experience
advance planning	planning
any and all	any
as a general rule	as a rule
combine into one	combine
consensus of opinion	consensus
current status	status
different varieties	varieties
each and every	each
final outcome	outcome
first and foremost	first
first priority	priority
group meeting	meeting
hidden pitfalls	pitfalls
honest truth	truth
month of December	December
necessary requisite	requisite
one and only	only
one and the same	the same
overall plan	plan
past experience	experience
past history	history
personal opinion	opinion
point in time	time
postpone until later	postpone
range all the way from	range from
refer back to	refer to
repeat again	repeat
specific example	example
this particular instance	this instance
true facts	facts
whether or not	whether

Consider the following choices for your next statement:

[1] Since that time, however, it pains me to say that you have been late three times.

[2] Since that time, however, you have been admonished for being late three times.

Exhibit 1-3. Wordy Phrases and Concise Counterparts.

Wordy	*Concise*
at all times	always
at this point in time	now
can be in a position to	can
inasmuch as	since
in close proximity	near
in compliance with your request	as requested
in the event that	if
in the manner in which	how
in the very near future	soon
make a recommendation that	recommend
of a confidential nature	confidential
perform an analysis of	analyze
the reason for this is	because
the question as to whether	if
with regard to	regarding

Exhibit 1-4. Unnecessary Emphasis and Sufficient Wording.

Unnecessary Emphasis	*Sufficient*
absolutely exhausted	exhausted
carefully scrutinized	scrutinized
completely destroyed	destroyed
definitely superior	superior
highly confidential	confidential
incredibly obvious	obvious
terribly wrong	wrong
totally absurd	absurd
very unique	unique

[3] Since that time, however, you have been rebuked for being late three times.

[4] Since that time, however, you have been late three times.

Which of these makes the best choice? The first statement is apologetic and sympathetic; the second one expresses disapproval in a gentle way; the third reprimands; and the last example makes a statement of fact. Recall your purpose: to correct the recent attendance problem of an otherwise outstanding employee. With that in mind, examine your options. Notice that the first three personalize the situation and are therefore inappropriate. In addition, they are potentially damaging: Being sympathetic could lead to a continuation of the problem, and expressing disapproval of any kind is likely to elicit an emotional reaction from the employee that can interfere with a solution. The only appropriate statement is the last one. The language is factual and the tone neutral. It permits both you and the recipient to continue unhindered.

Consistency between thoughts is equally important. In the example, the lead-in statement is factual and free of emotion. The reader is set up to expect that the remainder of the message will be the same. Any change is going to have an impact on the flow and leave the reader focusing on the tone rather than the content of the message.

Completeness

HR documents must be complete to be effective; that is, each document must spell out the implications of the topic sentences with facts, illustrations, explanations, or definitions.

Consider the task of writing a vacation policy. Your topic sentences might read,

> All full-time employees are entitled to an allotted number of vacation days per calendar year according to their exemption status and tenure. Officers' vacations are calculated according to a separate schedule. Part-time employees will receive vacation days according to a prorated schedule. Unused vacation days may not be carried over to the following calendar year.

If the policy were to end at this point, there would be numerous unanswered questions. In addition, managers and employees would probably resent the abbreviated treatment of an important topic. To complete the vacation policy, support the topic sentences by anticipating and answering the following questions:

- What is the specific vacation schedule for exempt and nonexempt employees?—(*illustration*)
- What is the relationship between exemption status and tenure when calculating vacation entitlements?—(*definition, explanation*)
- How do officer vacation schedules differ from that of other exempt-status employees?—(*definition, explanation*)
- How are part-time vacation schedules prorated?—(*illustration*)
- When does a new employee begin to earn vacation time?—(*fact*)
- What is the relationship between vacation days and holidays, sick time, and leaves of absence?—(*explanation, illustration*)
- What role does seniority play in the granting of vacations?—(*fact*)
- Are employees required to take a minimum number of consecutive days off for vacation? Is there a maximum number of days that may be taken consecutively?—(*fact, explanation*)
- Can an employee request advance vacation pay? What is the procedure? (*fact, explanation*)
- When will employees who are promoted into a higher vacation classification begin to earn the increased vacation allowance?—(*fact, explanation*)
- Can employees receive payment for unused vacation time upon termination?—(*fact*)

Emphasize Key Points

Readers must be guided to the salient points of a document. Even in a short letter, individual ideas can get lost, and the reader may be left wondering how to respond. This difficulty commonly occurs when sentences consist of independent clauses strung together without a break to indicate emphasis. Since *independent clauses* are word units that can stand alone as sentences, grouping two or more together dilutes the emphasis of each unit. Consider the following:

> Excessive tardiness will not be tolerated and anyone who comes in late three times will be written up and a disciplinary notice will be placed in their HR file.

This sentence consists of three independent clauses. The impact of the overall message is lost because each thought is attached to two others. Separating the three sentences creates individual yet related statements. The end result is a strong and clear message concerning tardiness:

> Excessive tardiness will not be tolerated. Anyone who comes in late three times will be written up. A disciplinary notice will be placed in the person's HR file.

Using *dependent clauses* can also help writers emphasize key ideas. These are word units that cannot stand alone. They start with lead-in words like, *although*, *when*, and *while*. For example:

> Although there is construction underway on the expressway [*dependent clause*], employees are still expected to get to work on time.

> When tools are not put away [*dependent clause*], accidents occur.

> Although not all employees need to lose weight [*dependent clause*], Avedon is establishing a weight-loss program for anyone who wants to attend.

Note that in the last example the word unit that follows the dependent clause is an independent clause:

> Avedon is establishing a weight-loss program for anyone who wants to attend.

This order places a greater emphasis on the independent clause. If you wanted to stress that not all employees need to lose weight, you would rewrite the sentence to read:

> Although Avedon is establishing a weight-loss program, all employees do not need to lose weight.

Emphasis can also be achieved through brevity. The concept of "less is more" stresses a key point, especially if the emphasized message is surrounded by longer sentences. Consider this example:

Alcohol consumption on the job affects productivity and safety. *Don't mix drinking and working.* Employees who drink at work or arrive at work intoxicated will be severely disciplined.

Through the use of five simple words, the writer conveys a clear, strong message. The other two sentences serve to support it.

Another way of highlighting key ideas is to start a sentence with a word set off by a colon—for example, *note, important,* or *remember.* It is not necessary to capitalize the entire word. Be aware, though, that the impact of this technique will be diluted if you overuse it.

Summary

To write HR documents effectively, begin by accessing available data and extracting relevant ideas; then develop these ideas into comprehensive thoughts. Techniques that can help accomplish this include the *minimalist approach* of jotting down key words without organization, the *parting-words-first* approach of working backward by writing your closing words first, and the *artistic approach* of writing your opening and closing thoughts, leaving a blank canvas in between.

To help stay focused, identify a broad-based objective that reflects the overall task to be accomplished. Then thoroughly familiarize yourself with the subject so you can write both intelligibly and expeditiously. In addition, learn as much as possible about your audience's existing knowledge base so you can anticipate and address likely questions in the document.

When it is time to organize your thoughts, select one of eight approaches, depending on the nature and length of the document: alphabetical, chronological, situation and solution, the reporter's technique, deductive reasoning, inductive reasoning, priority ranking, or a list format. Regardless of the approach you select, be certain to capture your reader's attention at the outset. This may be done by making a startling statement, posing an intriguing question, giving the reader good news, or any of seven other techniques.

Always follow the four guidelines to successful writing for every type of document: clarity, conciseness, consistency, and completeness. In addition, emphasize key points through the use of independent and dependent clauses, brevity, and setting off key words with a colon at the beginning of a sentence.

Laying a solid foundation for effective writing allows you to turn your attention to the style and tone of a document, the subject of Chapter 2.

2

Writing Style and Tone

Style and *tone* refer to how a writer develops the contents of a document. Tone can vary depending on the purpose of the document being written. A disciplinary notice may be stern, a letter of condolence empathetic, and a policy on sick days factual. A person's attitude toward the subject, knowledge base, and relationship to the reader also influence the tone of the end product. A person's style, however, unless consciously changed, remains constant, as a reflection of our personalities and how we express our thoughts. It often coincides with how we talk. Style and tone are why three writers, all preparing the same document, using correct grammar and punctuation, will produce three different versions.

Titles Set the Tone

Titles and subtitles used throughout documents organize topics and capture the reader's attention. Because they have a line all to themselves, are often highlighted in some way, are set apart through the use of white space, and usually consist of just a few words, they stand out. Consequently, people tend to read titles and then decide if they want to continue reading the rest of the document. This decision, made quickly, is often a reaction to tone, in addition to the meaning of the words. Since titles are among the first words read, they send an immediate message that results in a mind-set on the part of the reader. The tone set by titles is strong, either solidifying your relationship with the reader or creating a chasm.

Some words inherently set a negative tone. Consider the word *no*. If it is the first word in a title, the reader is immediately set up for a negative message. Suppose you have to prepare a policy on personal phone calls. Your objective is to communicate the company's position that incoming and outgoing personal phone calls should be restricted to emergencies. You reason that this objective essentially translates into no personal phone calls during working hours and decide that this thought makes an appropriate title. "No Personal Phone Calls" is short, direct, and clear. It is so direct, in fact, that little more needs to be said. True. It is also offensive and unenforceable. What is the point of issuing a policy if employees are going to react with resentment and noncompliance? Better choices would be titles that are no less specific but far less threatening: "Use of the Phone," "Phone Calls," or "Personal Phone Calls." Other words in titles that convey a negative tone are illustrated in Exhibit 2-1.

Just as you should avoid words that convey a negative tone when writing HR documents, also stay away from soft language. I recently came across a dress code that was entitled, "Please Dress Properly for Work." It is nice to be polite, but words like *please*, and *we would appreciate it if* . . . do not belong in titles of HR documents.

Exhibit 2-1. Negative Words to Avoid in Titles.

banned	not condoned
barred	not permitted
disallowed	not tolerated
don't	prohibited
denied	ruled out
forbidden	taboo
never	unacceptable

Try also to avoid giving the impression of talking down to your readers. Headings like, "You Should Know Better," "From Now On Employees Will Be Expected to . . . ," and "10 Things We Don't Do at Avedon" are unlikely to result in changed behavior.

What is the best language to use in a title? There are several possibilities, depending on the nature of the document and the intended audience. You might choose a title to which the reader can relate, is familiar with, or has expressed an interest in. As an alternative, select wording that is intriguing or arouses curiosity, compelling the recipient to continue reading. Of course, descriptive titles are always safe and appropriate. Examples of suitable titles appear in Exhibit 2-2.

Writing Styles

Writing styles typically fall into one of three categories: formal, moderate, or conversational. Formal writers prefer sentences that are long and involved, favoring an extensive vocabulary, rarely using contractions, and avoiding slang expressions. The tone is impersonal, keeping readers at a distance. Moderate writers use sentences of medium length: around twenty words. Popular terms appear in these writings, along with occasional contractions. Reference to himself or herself as *I* and to the reader as *you* makes the moderate writer's tone close but not intimate. Short, simple sentences are used in conversational or informal writing. Diction is limited to simple words and popular phrases. The use of slang is frequent. The overall tone is that of informal conversation.

Exhibit 2-2. Suitable Titles for Documents.

Document	*Suitable Title*
suggestion program	Tell Us What You Think
dependent care programs	Child and Elder Care Services
employee assistance programs	Avedon Counseling Services
newsletters	Avedon News
orientation materials	Working at Avedon
recreational programs	Work and Play the Avedon Way

Formal style in a business setting should be reserved for technical writing and legal papers, just as the chatty messages of a conversational writer are more appropriate for letter writing between friends. Formal and conversational styles are so distinct that they call attention to themselves and get in the way of the message. Moderate writing projects a tone that is inviting to the reader but not overly casual. Since a moderate style of writing is direct and straightforward, it prevents misunderstandings. Readers are able to comprehend the intended message immediately without making assumptions, drawing conclusions, or guessing at the meaning. It is clearly the most usable and adaptable style for HR documents.

Moderate-style writers often sprinkle their work with personal pronouns. Words like *we* and *you* make the reader feel more involved. Moderate writing samples using personal pronouns appear in Exhibit 2-3.

Moderate-style writers also use familiar phrases, avoiding formal counterparts. For example, instead of saying, *pursuant to the request made on September 11*, say, *as you requested*. It is friendlier, less wordy, and to the point. Exhibit 2-4 offers additional moderate versions of formal phrases.

Another characteristic of moderate-style writing is use of the active voice, as opposed to the passive voice. In the active voice, the subject performs the activity; in the passive voice, the subject is the recipient of the action. *The manager wrote the memo* is written in the active voice. *The memo was written by the manager* is in the passive voice. Active-voice statements are more direct, sound more natural, and are less wordy. Examples of active-voice statements are in Exhibit 2-5.

Some writers deliberately use the passive voice to avoid taking responsibility. For example, if you wrote, *The status of your application will be checked at the appropriate time*, you are being vague as to who will do the checking and when. However, if you wrote, *I will check the status of your application by May 21*, it is clear that you are responsible.

Sometimes the passive voice is appropriate. Use it when the doer of the acting person is unknown: *Avedon was founded in 1961*. Use the passive voice, too, when the acting party is less important than the activity itself. In the following example, passive construction

Exhibit 2-3. Moderate Writing Using Personal Pronouns.

Without Personal Pronouns	*With Personal Pronouns*
Avedon is pleased to announce a new recreational program for its employees.	We are pleased to announce a new recreational program for our employees
The letter sent to Avedon employees on 2/17 outlined the recreational program.	The letter we sent you on 2/17 outlined our recreational program.
All employees are invited to attend the recreation program open house.	You are invited to attend our recreation program open house.
The management of Avedon wishes to thank its employees for setting up the recreation program.	On behalf of Avedon, I thank you for setting up the recreation program.

Exhibit 2-4. Moderate Versions of Formal Phrases.

Moderate Style	Formal Counterpart
call me	do not hesitate to call
allow enough time	render sufficient time
I am enclosing	the undersigned encloses herewith
if you need more information	should you require additional information
in six months	in no more than six months
as I said before	whereas previously stated
in the beginning	at the outset
about	in the matter concerning
we will try to give you	we will attempt to provide you with
please leave enough time	kindly allow sufficient time
if you use	if you utilize
if you can help us	if you can render some assistance
we will begin at 9:00	we will commence at precisely 9:00
please enclose your payment	enclosed please find your remittance
I understand that	it has come to my attention that
I am aware that	I am cognizant of the fact that

Exhibit 2-5. Statements in the Active and Passive Voices.

Active Voice	Passive Voice
Ted analyzed the report.	The report was analyzed by Ted.
David prepared the evaluation.	The evaluation was prepared by David.
You can request additional copies.	Additional copies may be requested.
Everyone enjoyed the retirement party.	The retirement party was enjoyed by all who attended.
Please complete this form and return it to HR by April 19.	The enclosed form should be completed and returned to HR by April 19.

correctly places emphasis on the activity: *Avedon was founded in 1961 by eight investment bankers.*

Style is also determined by the size of the words used. Big words can be fun. I love "enunciating" or "pontificating" instead of speaking, but I steer away from using such terms when writing HR documents. Ideas are conveyed most clearly using plain English. Saying *Jerome Fenwick no longer works here* is much more direct than, *Please be advised that, according to our statistical data, Jerome Fenwick has terminated his employment with this corporation.*

Of course, words are not deemed big by size alone. Words may be big in the sense of being pretentious. Hence, *relevance, disbelief* and *talkative* are better choices than *appositeness, minimifidianism,* and *loquacious.*

Style and tone are also weakened by unnecessary qualifiers—words or phrases that challenge a statement, diluting its validity. Saying, *I'll try to finish the project by tomorrow* lacks the impact and commitment of *I'll finish the project by tomorrow.* Exhibit 2-6 offers additional qualifiers.

Vary the Pace

Readers need variety to remain interested in a written document. In addition to content, variety derives from pace: the speed with which one can read a message. This pace should be slow when the information is complex and accelerated when the material is familiar or easy to understand.

The most effective method to regulate pace is to vary sentence and paragraph length. There are no rules regarding sentence length other than the one cited earlier: Moderate-style writers rely on sentences of about twenty words in length. This is only a guideline, however.

A sentence consisting of just three words can make a powerful statement, especially if it is flanked by longer sentences. Consider this sample:

> I have tried to reach you by phone on five occasions regarding your unexcused absence from work during the past two weeks. I left messages, two on your answering machine and three with your sister, Josie. Where are you? This letter is my final attempt to reach you. If you do not call me within 24 hours of receipt, I will have no choice but to terminate you, effective immediately.

Three simple words, *Where are you?* stand out as the most powerful among a total of seventy words because they are isolated yet surrounded by longer sentences. Consider the impact of these words if they were folded in as part of another sentence:

> I have tried to reach you by phone on five occasions regarding your unexcused absence from work during the past two weeks. I left messages, two on your

Exhibit 2-6. Unnecessary Qualifiers.

almost	likely
as I recall	may or may not be
as I understand it	might possibly have
for all intents and purposes	my best guess is that
hopefully	nearly
I would imagine that	practically
if	quite probably
in my opinion	to the best of my recollection
it has been my observation that	under these circumstances
it is my belief that	

answering machine and three with your sister, Josie, but I don't know where you are. This letter is my final attempt to reach you. If you do not call me within 24 hours of receipt, I will have no choice but to terminate you, effective immediately.

In this version the punch is gone and the impact is lost.

Lengthy sentences maintain a reader's interest as well. Sentences consisting of as many as fifty words can be effective, providing they do not contain excess rhetoric and redundancies. Of course, you should be able to read a sentence without running out of breath. The key is content: Each word in a sentence should make a contribution, either expressing or supporting an idea. Keep in mind the words written by William Strunk, Jr., in *The Elements of Style*:

> A sentence should contain no unnecessary words, a paragraph no unnecessary sentences, for the same reason that a drawing should have no unnecessary lines and a machine no unnecessary parts. This requires not that the writer make all his sentences short, or that he avoid all detail and treat his subjects only in outline, but that every word tell.

Varying the format in which you present information can also help regulate pace. Try using lists to organize and rank your ideas. Other techniques include making comparisons, asking questions, interjecting anecdotes and humor, and using quotations.

Varying the mechanics of your format can also help keep the reader alert. You can break up the text of a lengthy document with headings and subheadings. Use different type sizes and fonts, and weave in occasional underlining, boldface type, or italics. Depending on the document, you might also vary the use of white space and add color to highlight key points.

Sometimes pace can be varied by supplementing written documents with visual aids. Showing overheads, slides, or a film can enhance the quality of the written material and keep your audience attentive.

Write Positively

When writing, focus on what is favorable; stress what can be done, *not* what cannot be done. When you are writing about an unpleasant subject, positive wording softens the impact and makes the unpleasant message more acceptable. Suppose you are behind schedule and will not be able to meet a deadline. A negative approach would be: *Unfortunately, I will not be able to complete the progress report by the next board meeting.* Conveying the message in a more positive tone acts as a buffer: *The progress report will be completed one week after the board meeting.* The recipient obviously understands that the work will not be submitted on time, but the positive wording softens the bad news. Exhibit 2-7 presents additional samples of negative statements converted into positive statements. Other negative phrases to avoid include *you claim, your failure to, you neglected, your lack of, you should have, you forgot to, you fell short of, you overlooked,* and *you disregarded.*

Notice how negative phrases frequently begin with the word *you* or *your.* They point an accusing finger at the recipient, resulting in a defensive posture and dialogue, ranging from a debate to an argument. Any of these negative phrases can be reworded more positively, often beginning with the word *I.* The responsibility is now on the sender of

Exhibit 2-7. Negative Statements and Their Positive Counterparts.

Negative Statement	*Positive Statement*
You made a mistake.	There is a mistake.
Showing up late for work is unacceptable.	It is important for you to arrive at work on time.
We're only halfway there.	We're halfway there.
Your plan won't work unless we increase productivity by an additional 15%.	If we increase productivity by an additional 15%, your plan will work.
Don't reapply for this position until you've finished this semester's coursework.	When you've finished this semester's coursework, you can reapply for the position.

the message, thereby taking pressure off the receiver. For example, *You claim that you'd be able to get to work on time if the bus hadn't changed its route* can be changed to *I understand your belief that if the bus hadn't changed its route you'd be able to get in on time*. In the revision, not only is the burden removed from the recipient, a less accusing term is substituted for *claim*. These changes keep the tone and style of writing from being an issue and allow both parties to focus on the real problem.

Dropping the word *not* from your writing will also go a long way toward softening a negative message. Instead of saying *not satisfied*, substitute *dissatisfied*. True, both mean the same thing, but people are likely to react negatively to the word *not* and less so to an alternative word with the same meaning. Exhibit 2-8 offers additional samples of substitutes.

Another way of expressing a thought positively is to use the word *when* instead of *if*. Substitute *When your performance improves, you can apply for the senior analyst's position* for *If your performance improves, you can apply for the senior analyst's position*. The entire tone

Exhibit 2-8. Negative Wording and Softer Substitutes.

Negative Wording	*Substitute Wording*
not important	unimportant
did not remember	forgot
not honest	dishonest
not complete	incomplete
do not trust	distrust
did not pay attention to	ignored
did not understand	misunderstood
not correct	incorrect
not definite	indefinite
not checked	unchecked

changes with a single word: *If* connotes doubt and a lack of confidence, whereas *when* suggests optimism and confidence.

Positive messages should always appear at the beginning and end of your document because people first remember the last words they read; they next remember the first words they read. If your message contains both good and bad news, sandwich the bad news between the good. If it contains only bad news, place it up front, converted into upbeat terms, and end on a positive note.

The sample rejection letter in Exhibit 1-1 illustrates these points. Although the overall message of the letter is negative, the tone is not gloomy. The letter to Mr. Richardson begins with the writer's expressing appreciation to the applicant for his time and interest and commenting on how informative the interview was. *The tone is positive.* The next paragraph starts out by describing the company's process of selection and ends by lowering the boom: He did not get the job. *The news is bad.* Before closing, the writer comments on the quality of the applicant's credentials and invites him to apply again in the future. An added touch is the use of the applicant's name. *The tone is positive.*

Separating good and bad news with the word *but* or *however* can be effective, depending on what order the news is presented in. Here are two versions using *however* as a separator of good and bad news:

I don't have time to serve on the refreshment committee for the company picnic; however, I'd be glad to purchase the paper goods.

I'd be glad to purchase the paper goods for the company picnic; however, I don't have time to serve on the refreshment committee.

The first version gets the bad news out of the way and ends on an up note. With the second version the reader is going to remember one thing: This person cannot serve on the refreshment committee. Whatever task the writer is willing to undertake is diminished by the negative impact of the last statement.

Inform or Influence

All HR documents are informative. Many are also written to influence readers to act or think a certain way. Communicate your intent merely to inform or also to influence your reader at the outset. You will be setting both the tone and the direction of your document, affecting the contents and in some instances the outcome. The following list identifies common HR documents and their intent.

HR Document	Purpose

Recruiting

Job requisitions	Inform
Job descriptions	Inform
Job posting notices	Inform
Job posting applications	Inform
Job advertisements	Inform and influence
Letters to applicants	Inform

HR Document	Purpose
Interviewing	
Application forms	Inform
Interview evaluations	Inform
Selection checklists	Inform
References	Inform
Letters to rejected candidates	Inform
Letters to selected candidates	Inform
New employees	
Orientation materials	Inform and influence
Benefits policies	Inform and influence
New employee announcements	Inform
Performance management	
Performance appraisals	Inform and influence
Letters of commendation	Inform and influence
Counseling sessions	Inform and influence
Disciplinary notices	Inform and influence
Exit interviews	Inform
Letters of termination	Inform
Employee services	
Employee assistance programs	Inform and influence
Dependent care programs	Inform and influence
Recreational programs	Inform and influence
Newsletters	Inform
Suggestion programs and surveys	Inform
Letters of congratulations	Inform
Letters to sick employees	Inform
Letters for retirement	Inform
Letters of condolence	Inform
HR guidelines	
Employee handbooks	Inform
HR policy manuals	Inform

Inform

To inform is to explain. When you prepare an HR document, the overriding objective is to provide readers with information about a particular subject. The language should be objective, descriptive, factual, and impersonal. In recruiting, for example, requisitions communicate overall departmental needs and requirements for a given job; job descriptions identify primary and secondary duties, responsibilities, and requirements of a job; and job posting notices specify grade level, overall responsibilities, salary ranges, and reporting relationships of an available job. All of these documents should be prepared without the writer's imposing personal views or interjecting judgments.

Remaining objective about some documents is easier than with others—for example, preparing a courtesy letter that acknowledges receipt of a resumé (Exhibit 2-9). This letter informs the applicant of all the necessary information through four ideas:

Exhibit 2-9. Sample Courtesy Letter.

November 26, 199X

June Delgado
24-19 Whistler's Court
Princeton, NJ 08543

Dear Ms. Delgado:

Thank you for your resumé regarding the position of customer service representative.

We are in the process of reviewing the responses to our ad and expect to begin scheduling appointments with selected candidates during the week of December 8.

We appreciate your interest in Avedon Industries.

Sincerely,

Jonah Becket
Recruitment Coordinator

[1] Thank you for sending us your resumé.

[2] We are reviewing all the responses to our ad.

[3] We will begin scheduling appointments during the week of December 8.

[4] Thank you for your interest.

It is straightforward and devoid of any personal involvement.

The nature of other HR documents renders objectivity more difficult when the writer harbors a strong opinion about the subject matter. Suppose you are asked to prepare a policy on smoking. As a nonsmoker seeking a smoking ban on all company premises, you are delighted that senior management has decided to limit smoking to one lounge on the lower level. You have been given these facts to develop into a policy:

- No smoking will be permitted in offices, conference rooms, hallways, restrooms, or the cafeteria.
- Smoking will be restricted to the employees' lounge on the lower level.
- Employees may frequent the lounge before and after working hours, on breaks, and during their lunch periods.
- This policy is being implemented to comply with various safety codes.
- This policy will go into effect on June 23.

Sitting down at your desk, you come up with the following:

Smoking Policy

Effective June 23, 199X, smoking will all but cease to be permitted anywhere on company premises. This means no smoking in your office or at your work station, during meetings in the conference rooms, while walking in the hallways, in the restrooms, or in the cafeteria. Actually, the only place smoking will be allowed is the employees' lounge in the basement. If you must smoke, you are expected to restrict your habit to before and after working hours, during breaks, and on your lunch hour.

Avedon Industries is implementing this policy to comply with various safety codes and to accommodate nonsmokers.

The full cooperation of all smokers is expected.

This version is highly subjective and written in a dictatorial tone. Terms such as *cease to be permitted, if you must smoke,* and *restrict your habit* clearly show bias on the part of the writer. Even the use of the word *basement* instead of *lower level* illustrates the writer's contempt for smokers. Hence, what should have been an exclusively informative document has been inappropriately transformed into one that attempts to both inform and influence.

The writer should have put personal feelings about smoking aside and come up with a factual policy:

[Rewritten]

Smoking Policy

In compliance with various safety codes, employees of Avedon Industries are being asked to restrict all smoking to the employees' lounge on the lower level. This means no smoking in offices, at work stations, in conference rooms, or in the hallways, restrooms, and cafeteria. Smokers may visit the employees' lounge before and after working hours, on breaks, and during their lunch periods.

The effective date for this policy is June 23. We appreciate your cooperation.

This version explains the reason for the new policy and describes its contents. It is unbiased and factual—just what an informative document should be.

Influence

The goal of an influential document is twofold: to convince your readers to accept an idea not previously held and to change behavior. This reaction must be voluntary; the readers must conclude on their own that a certain idea or proposal has merit based on what you have written.

The most convincing way of bringing about a voluntary change in judgment is to show the readers how your conclusions were reached. Suppose your assignment is to prepare a report for senior management on the merits of on-site dependent care. Current positions on the subject range from not knowing what it is to a perception that it probably costs too much. A report that merely informs is not likely to gain support; therefore, your document must persuade senior management that dependent care is a worthwhile venture. You can go about this by following the ten steps to influential writing:

1. *Define the program.* Make a short, factual statement about dependent care to serve as the foundation of your report. Senior management cannot adopt a program it knows nothing about.

2. *Talk up the features.* Once you have defined dependent care, describe its components in greater detail. Create questions to which the reader is likely to seek answers, such as, "Looking for a way to keep top-notch employees from leaving?"

3. *Identify a need.* Sustain interest by convincing your readers that the company needs a dependent care program. Point out the success rate of a competitor's program.

4. *Offer an incentive.* Show a direct correlation between on-site dependent care and factors that are of primary importance to the company, such as improved employee performance and reduced turnover facts. Rely on facts and statistics to support your case. Use lead-in statements such as, *According to a study conducted by . . .* Cite sources supporting the information, especially if you believe it will be challenged.

5. *Be selective.* Facts and statistics are critical to your case, but do not overdo them. Overloading the readers with tons of data can make them bleary-eyed and cause a loss of interest. Be complete, but do not belabor a point.

6. *Time travel.* Offer projections by experts concerning the future of companies with and without dependent care facilities. Focus on bottom-line issues like productivity.

7. *Offer options.* Give your readers several plans from which to choose, citing the pros and cons of each. Compare the features of each option, such as operating costs, insurance figures, and levels of employee contributions. Avoid offering your opinion as to the best choice; let your readers draw their own conclusions from the data.

8. *Make it easy to read.* A report on dependent care is going to be long. Make it easy to read by breaking up the text with eye-catching headings, varying the length of sentences, and using graphs and charts.

9. *Say it again.* Isolate a key theme and weave it throughout the report. The statement *Dependent care tells our employees that they can depend on us* can be stated both overtly and subliminally several times to drive home the message.

10. *Back off.* If your readers feel pressured, they are likely to respond negatively. Hence, avoid phrases like *I'm sure you'll agree* and *As you can see.* They'll let you know if they agree soon enough.

Nonsexist Writing

Linguistic bias, however unconscious, is offensive. The *man* in compound words, the generic *man*, and distorted meanings caused by gratuitous modifiers are just a few of the ways language can offend.

One of the reasons so many continue to practice linguistic bias is that we learned certain rules of grammar and usage as children and don't tend to challenge their validity unless called upon to. Even when made aware of the sometimes degrading or biased references inherent in the English language, we resist change—not because we believe in the literal meaning of certain words but because it is easier to speak and write as we always have. Hence, we may shrug away the literal exclusion of all women employees when we say *workman's compensation* instead of *workers' compensation*. Similarly, although the term *chairman* has been replaced by a half a dozen words or more, including, *chair*, *chairperson*, *head*, *presider*, *moderator*, and *leader*, businesspeople continue to use it indiscriminately. The problem is compounded when commonly used reference sources, such as the tenth edition of *Webster's Collegiate Dictionary* (1993) defines *youth* as, among other things, "a young person; esp: a young male between adolescence and maturity." How ironic that those who deal with words professionally are among those resisting linguistic change.

Fortunately, the movement toward nonsexist language has gained momentum. Guidelines for linguistic equity have been published by major publishers of textbooks, and many organizations have developed nonsexist writing guidelines.

Use of Man

The word *man* has a double meaning in the English language. Obviously, it can refer to a particular male, just as *woman* refers to a female: *Every man on the committee voted in favor of the increase; the two women were opposed*. Unlike *woman*, however, *man* is also used in a generic sense as representative of the human species. When used generically, *man* is supposed to represent both sexes. This is the intention in the following samples:

[1] The average working man spends 60 hours a week on the job.

[2] It will take 48 man-hours to complete this project.

[3] Modern man has to deal with traffic and pollution when commuting to and from work.

Sentences such as these rarely stand alone; often they are followed by phrases containing the male pronoun *he*. Once this occurs, the generic translation of *man* becomes clouded, and a woman's role becomes obscure. Generic *man* imposes the image of maleness on the entire species.

Alternatives to the generic and compound *man* are easy. The three sentences above can readily be converted into nonsexist phrases:

[Rewritten]

[1] The average worker spends 60 hours a week on the job.

[2] It will take 48 hours to complete this project.

[3] Workers today have to deal with traffic and pollution when commuting.

Man can be replaced by any one of a number of words. In the singular, alternatives include *person, one, anyone,* or *someone*. In the plural, try writing *people, human beings, workers,* or *employees*. Of course you can also say *men and women* (or *women and men*). Exhibit 2-10 offers other options.

Pronouns

The pronouns *he, him,* and *his* have long been accepted as gender neutral when used to describe an unspecified person. Lately, presumably in an attempt to lend some balance

Exhibit 2-10. Nonsexist Alternatives to *Man*.

businessman	businessperson
layman	layperson, amateur
mankind	the human species, humanity, humans, humankind, people, human beings, human societies
man-hours	work-hours, labor time
manmade	handmade, hand-built, manufactured, machine-made, constructed
manpower	human resources, staff
middleman	go-between, intermediary, agent
spokesman	representative, spokesperson

to the unequal use of masculine pronouns, *she*, *her*, and *hers* are randomly used as well. At least the conscious intent is random use. What often happens, however, is that occupations or activities traditionally thought of as male receive male pronouns; the same holds true for female pronouns. Contrast these two examples:

[1] The average worker spends about 30 minutes getting ready in the morning. His daily ritual includes shaving and wolfing down a breakfast of coffee and doughnuts.

[2] The average worker spends about 45 minutes getting ready in the morning. Her daily ritual includes blow-drying her hair and eating a breakfast of coffee and doughnuts.

If male and female pronouns are randomly used to describe unspecified people, we should be able to swap the pronouns in these two statements. Let us try it and see what happens:

[1] The average worker spends about 30 minutes getting ready in the morning. Her daily ritual includes shaving and wolfing down a breakfast of coffee and doughnuts.

[2] The average worker spends about 45 minutes getting ready in the morning. His daily ritual includes blow-drying his hair and eating a breakfast of coffee and doughnuts.

Technically, these statements are gender free, but practically speaking, the second set is a bit disconcerting, for four stereotypical reasons:

1. We assume it takes men less time to get ready for work than women; hence, the average worker who takes 30 minutes to get ready in the morning is likely to be a man.
2. We associate shaving with men, even though women do shave. Accordingly, the daily ritual of shaving is assumed to be a male activity.
3. Although both men and women blow-dry their hair, we think of women performing this act more commonly than men.

4. The word *wolf* conjures up aggressive images of large, predatory animals, often thought of as fierce and destructive. To wolf one's food down is to devour or eat greedily. Therefore, the act is typically associated with men, not women.

Because of implications such as these, it is best to steer clear of attempts to use gender-neutral pronouns when describing unspecified people. What are the alternatives? Here are some suggestions:

‣ *Write in the plural form.* You need not worry about being grammatically correct if you stick to the plural form: *During the beginning of their senior year, college students are encouraged to attend job fairs and interview with prospective employers.*

‣ *Use double pronouns.* Using *his or her* to refer to an unspecified person is certainly equitable. It is also clumsy and interferes with the flow of a sentence: *Typically, an employee requires one hour in each direction for his or her daily commute.* One might also challenge the order of the two pronouns: By placing *his* before *her*, is the writer favoring the male reference?

‣ *Use slashed pronouns.* A variation of the double pronoun is to take the two gender-specific pronouns and separate them with a slash. This is equally awkward to read but inarguably fair.

‣ *Eliminate pronouns.* Rewriting a sentence to avoid using pronouns altogether takes a bit of creativity, but the results can be effective. Consider this: *An applicant with a physical disability will not be able to maneuver his or her wheelchair through the revolving doors without help.* Now consider the revised version eliminating pronouns: *An applicant in a wheelchair will need help maneuvering through the revolving doors.*

‣ *Address the reader directly.* Instead of using third-person pronouns, try addressing the reader directly. Hence, *After reviewing all the resumés, you should start calling in the candidates with the best qualifications.*

Modifiers

Avoid labeling someone with an incidental characteristic like sex, race, or national origin. Such labeling diminishes the person's level of competence and draws attention away from what is relevant, such as skill, knowledge, or ability. Describing someone as a black attorney, woman doctor, Mexican pharmacist, male nurse, or female truck driver is gratuitous and demeans the person's accomplishments.

Less direct, but just as disparaging, are comments that imply inferiority because of a particular characteristic. Referring to someone as doing an outstanding job in spite of a disability is inappropriate and insulting.

Job Titles

Being sensitive to gender-free language paves the way for changes in speech and writing. In the workplace, this includes how we refer to people's occupations. Job titles define us: In a single word, what we do tells others who we are. Fortunately, *man* as a suffix has been dropped in many job titles and substituted with gender-free words. The United States Department of Labor's *Dictionary of Occupational Titles* and the *Occupational Outlook Handbook*, published by the Bureau of Labor Statistics, both describe jobs in sex-neutral terms.

Titles may be converted from referring to men exclusively to both sexes in a number of ways:

- Drop the *man* from the word: *watchman* becomes *watch*.
- Change *man* to *person* or *people*: *salesman* becomes *salesperson*.
- Change *man* to *worker*: *craftsman* becomes *craftworker*.
- Change *man* to *representative*: *insurance man* becomes *insurance representative*.
- Shorten the word: *repairman* becomes *repairer*.
- Change the word entirely: *newsman* becomes *reporter*.

Additional title options appear in Exhibit 2-11.

Salutations

With so many women in professional positions today, it is no longer acceptable to send a letter to an unspecified person addressed to "Gentlemen" or "Dear Sir." Several alternatives are available:

- Dear Madam or Sir (the order is alphabetical)
- Dear [title, e.g., Director of Human Resources]
- To Whom It May Concern
- Gentlepeople
- Dear [company name, e.g., Avedon Industries]

Exhibit 2-11. Converting Sexist Job Titles.

Sexist Job Titles	Nonsexist Job Titles
cameraman	camera operator
copyboy	copy clerk
deliveryman	deliverer, delivery clerk
doorman	doorkeeper, doorkeep
draftsman	drafter
foreman	supervisor, leader
handyman	fixer
lineman	line repairer, line installer
mailman	mail carrier, letter carrier
newsboy	news carrier, paper carrier
policeman	police officer
pressman	press operator
seamstress	tailor, sewer
signalman	signal operator, signaler
stewardess	steward, flight attendant
tradesman	trades people
waiter	server

‣ No salutation at all. (If you drop the salutation, you should also omit the complimentary close of, say, "sincerely" and just write your name and title).

When you know the name of a woman addressee, you are faced with choosing Mrs., Miss, or Ms., all abbreviations for the now-outdated social title *Mistress*. From the eighteenth century on, the social title *Miss* was used to distinguish single women from married women, who were referred to as *Mrs*. The dissatisfaction of many women with this labeling system led to the widespread use of Ms.—a title intended to be analogous to *Mr.*, which, of course, does not reveal marital status. The plural of *Ms.* is *Mses.* or *Mss*.

Another option is to refer to a woman by her full name: *The project could not have been completed without the generous support of Holly Van Brink.* Of course, you must drop the social title of *Mr.* when referring to men in the same correspondence.

Summary

The tone of a document can vary depending on its purpose, as well as the writer's attitude toward and knowledge about the subject matter. Tone is often set by titles, which may be descriptive, intriguing, or familiar to the reader. Avoid titles that are negative or condescending.

A person's style of writing reflects his or her personality and coincides with how he or she talks. Writing styles usually fall into one of three categories: formal, moderate, or conversational. Formal writers rely on lengthy sentences and avoid contractions or slang expressions. Moderate writers develop sentences of around twenty words in length and are comfortable using popular terms and occasional contractions. They also write in the active voice and weave in personal pronouns. Conversational or informal writers use short, simple sentences and rely on popular phrases and slang. Moderate writing is the most usable and adaptable style for HR documents.

Varying the pace, or speed it takes to read a message, is necessary to keep readers interested. This can be accomplished by varying sentence and paragraph length, changing the format in which you present information, or supplementing written documents with visual aids.

Readers are more likely to respond to a message if it is written in a positive tone. If the overall message is negative, place positive messages at the beginning and end of your document, or place the bad news up front and end with something positive.

All HR documents are informative; that is, they attempt to explain something through objective, descriptive, and factual language. Many also are intended to influence readers to accept a new idea or change behavior. Let your readers know at the outset if your intent is to merely inform or also to influence them.

HR documents should be free of linguistic bias and reflect nonsexist, gender-neutral phrases. Job titles too should be gender free.

Having developed the style and tone of your document, you are ready to move on to the next level by tackling the seven stages of writing.

3
Stages of Writing

Few people can sit at their desks or in front of a computer and write without a plan. Just about everyone thinks they can, however, and most try. After all, they reason, how hard can it be to write a letter of congratulations or fill in the blanks of a performance appraisal? But even seasoned writers get sloppy sometimes and try to proceed without a plan. The result inevitably is a document that is unfocused, disorganized, and usually too long.

It is difficult to come up with ideas that instantaneously make sense. Moreover, words must be coherent in relation to other thoughts on a page. Producing clear, concise, and complete documents that achieve the desired goals takes considerable work and time, most of which should be expended at the outset, with planning.

The essentials described in Chapter 1 will get you started: focus on your objectives, know your subject matter, target your audience, and organize your thoughts. Chapter 2 stresses the importance of style and tone. Now it is time to start pulling it all together by moving on to the next level and tackling the seven stages of writing:

1. Prepare an outline.
2. Develop key ideas.
3. Write the opening.
4. Compose the main body.
5. Select correctives.
6. Write the closing.
7. Revise.

Prepare an Outline

Do I hear groans? Are you one of those people who believes an outline is an evil device created by teachers to torture students? If you were taught how to write an outline in school, consider yourself lucky; it is one of the most valuable writing tools available. An outline enables you to organize ideas in an orderly manner, keeps you focused on important ideas, and ensures that the document will be complete, with an introduction, main body, and conclusion.

Types of Outlines

Since you are no longer in school, no one is going to comment on whether your outline is correct or properly mapped out. Furthermore, you are free to choose from among a variety of outline formats. Some work best with letters and short forms; others are better suited for policies and procedures. You may also simply prefer one approach over another. Regardless of the type of outline selected, remember your objectives: (1) to achieve a balance between the contents of each portion of the outline and (2) to develop a logical progression of ideas.

Formal Outline

You probably learned how to develop a formal outline in school. A formal outline consists of headings or major units identified by roman numerals, and subheadings or minor units set off with capital letters. These minor units are further subdivided and marked by arabic numerals. The arabic numeral subdivisions are broken down and identified by lowercase letters. Hence, a formal outline may look, in part, like this:

III. Stages of writing
    A. Preparing an outline
        1. Types of outlines
           a. Formal outline

Typically there are two ways to proceed with a formal outline. First, complete the same level of each division before starting on the next lower level; that is, identify the roman numeral headings first, then the capital letter entries, and so on. This method enables you to get a view of the whole picture, gradually zeroing in on the details. The second approach is to complete each section, from roman numeral heading through lowercase letters, before proceeding to the next section. This method allows you to dovetail one section in with another, thereby ensuring continuity and flow.

You may opt to combine these approaches by identifying all the roman numeral headings first and then completing each section. Whatever approach achieves the desired results is effective.

Choose also whether to approach your formal outline with topics or sentences. The illustration above is topical. To convert the topics identified by arabic numerals and lowercase letters into sentences, I write:

III. Stages of writing
    A. Prepare an outline
        1. There are a variety of types of outlines from which to choose
           a. Formal outlines consist of roman numerals, capital letters, arabic numerals, and lowercase letters

Another choice, which lies between topics and sentences, is the use of phrases:

III. Stages of writing
    A. Preparing an outline
        1. Variety of types
           a. Formal: roman numerals, capitals, arabic numbers, and lowercase letters

Sentence or phrase outlines make the task of writing the document easier, since portions have already been completed in the outline. On the other hand, developing complete thoughts at the outline stage can be difficult or even overwhelming. Many writers therefore prefer the brevity of a topical outline, viewing it as a structured guide that can be fleshed out as the writing begins.

Topical outlines are effective when developing HR documents such as promotional packets, orientation materials, benefits plans, employee assistance programs, dependent care plans, recreational programs, suggestion plans, and HR policies and procedures.

Scratch Outline

At the other end of the outline spectrum is the *scratch outline*, or informal format that does not try to name major and minor divisions. Rather, it is intended to sort through an abundance of data, resulting in an organized scheme to be followed when writing. It offers direction without restriction. Throughout the entire process ask yourself two questions: What are my objectives? and How can I best communicate them to my reader?

Begin a scratch outline by assembling all the data that are to be culled into the final document—for example, notes taken during phone conversations and interviews; research from books, pamphlets, and magazines; and charts, graphs, or notes from brainstorming with colleagues. Now go through all the data, and eliminate anything superfluous. Sift through your materials again, grouping them into clusters with a common theme. Identify each cluster with a word, phrase, or number. Do not attempt to establish any sequence at this stage. Sit back and look at what you have. Perhaps what you thought were areas worthy of development are not, or you find that you need additional data. Other topics may have an abundance of information that could be broken down into two or more subgroups. Still other categories may overlap and warrant consolidation. Continue this examination process until you are satisfied that all of the clusters are relevant and either self-sustaining or supported by other sections. Once all of your information is grouped appropriately, arrange it in logical order. Continue to arrange and rearrange until you are satisfied with your choices. Ultimately you will end up with a scratch outline, typically consisting of from six to twelve main clusters. Each cluster can then be expanded into subcategories.

Scratch outline are useful when preparing a document requiring a great deal of research, such as benefits plans and new policies. Exhibit 3-1 contains an example of a scratch outline for a benefits program.

Sequential Outlines

How do you convince senior management to adopt a drug testing policy in spite of stated opposition? Can you convince an employee to try harder despite a recent decline in job performance due to problems at home? Has a top-notch applicant received two job offers in addition to yours and cannot decide which one to accept? In each of these instances, a sequential outline will facilitate your writing task and achieve more positive results.

Identify your objective and follow these five steps:

   I.   Get your reader's attention.
      A. Start off with a bang.
      B. Use anecdotes and examples.
  II.   Identify how the reader is affected by what you are promoting.
      A. Raise questions.
      B. Explain why change is needed.

Exhibit 3-1. Scratch Outline for a Benefits Program.

Objective: To convince senior management to adopt a revised, competitive, comprehensive benefits plan

Stage 1: Assemble the Data

> Buffet benefits plan
> Core cafeteria plan
> Alternative dinner plan
> Holidays
> Health care reform
> Vacations
> Leaves of absence
> Profit sharing
> Stock bonus plans
> Important to attract and keep qualified employees
> Unemployment compensation
> Benefits trends
> Important to improve employee morale
> Important to reduce turnover
> Benefits-related legislation: OSHA (Occupational Safety and Health Act), ERISA (Employee Retirement Income Security Act), PDA (Pregnancy Discrimination Act), ADEA (Age Discrimination in Employment Act), ADA (Americans with Disabilities Act), FMLA (Family Medical Leave Act)
> Cost of benefits
> How to choose an insurance carrier
> What's essential and what's optional
> Child and elder care
> Cafeteria
> Gym and health club memberships
> Tuition reimbursement

Stage 2: Eliminate Superfluous Data

1. Health care reform (not enough concrete information)
2. Legislation (too much information; most of it does not help sell the benefits plan; treat separately, if requested. Note: Keep OSHA and FMLA)
3. Benefits trends—since when? cannot be forever; pick a period of time, such as the past 20 years.

Stage 3: Group Data into Clusters

Cluster 1:	Types of benefits plans (buffet, core cafeteria, and alternative dinner)
Cluster 2:	Paid time off (holidays, vacations)
Cluster 3:	Leaves of absence (medical, personal)
Cluster 4:	Pension plans (profit sharing, stock bonus plans)
Cluster 5:	Primary objectives of benefits plans (attract qualified employees, maintain a competitive position, improve morale, reduce turnover)
Cluster 6:	Benefits trends over the past two decades
Cluster 7:	OSHA
Cluster 8:	FMLA
Cluster 9:	Cost of benefits
Cluster 10:	Choosing an insurance carrier

Exhibit 3-1. Continued.

Cluster 11:   Mandatory and flexible benefits (include workers' compensation and unemployment compensation)

Cluster 12:   Employee services (child and elder care, cafeteria, gym and health club, tuition reimbursement)

Stage 4: Arrange Clusters in a Logical Order

1. Primary objectives of a benefits plan
2. Benefits trends over the past 20 years
3. Mandatory and flexible benefits
4. OSHA
5. FMLA
6. Types of benefits plans
7. Choosing an insurance carrier
8. Pension plans
9. Paid time off
10. Leaves of absence
11. Employee services
12. Cost of benefits

III. Offer a solution
    A. Explain how and why your solution will work.
    B. Provide examples of how and where the solution has worked.
IV. Describe the impact of your solution.
    A. State the advantages.
    B. Take the solution into the future and demonstrate long-range impact.
V. Convince readers to adopt your solution.
    A. Tell them specifically what they should do.
    B. Direct them on how to proceed.

Exhibit 3-2 provides an example of a sequential outline for a letter to a graduating senior who cannot decide which job offer to accept.

Develop Key Ideas

Once your outline is completed, begin developing its contents. If you opted for either a sentence or phrase-formal outline or a sequential outline, this step is partially completed. Developing key ideas does not mean writing the document. At this stage your goal is to ensure that the outline encompasses the salient features of your topic. This is accomplished via two steps: (1) adding some substance to the outline, and (2) testing the validity of each item with a series of questions.

The first step of adding substance is accomplished by segregating each reference in the outline and converting it into a complete thought. For example, in Exhibit 3-1, we ended up with twelve clusters in stage 4 of the scratch outline for a benefits program. Each of those clusters should now be expanded to justify its placement in the document. Try doing this with the first cluster, *primary objectives of a benefits plan*. Go back one step,

Exhibit 3-2. Sequential Outline.

Objective: To convince Marisa Jacobi to work for Avedon Industries.

I. Attention
   A. Avedon was cited in the July 199X issue of *Future Trends* as one of the top ten companies in the Northeast for grads to join.
   B. 83% of graduating seniors who have joined Avedon in the past five years have been promoted at least twice and received an average increase of 40% during that time.

II. Effect
   A. How certain can you be that the skills and knowledge you've acquired over the past four years will not be wasted?
   B. Avedon believes a student's education shouldn't be left behind when he or she enters the job market.

III. Solution
   A. Avedon ensures new employees of a proper job match so they will have every opportunity to apply what they've learned in college.
   B. In the past five years all graduating students we've hired have been able to apply at least some part of their education to their job.

IV. Solution impact
   A. Avedon has job families that allow for the continuous application of skills and knowledge at higher levels.
   B. Avedon aggressively promotes from within.

V. Action
   A. Accept our job offer, and you will be ensured of the opportunity to expand on what you already know.
   B. Why not call me right now at 555-1523 and say yes?

to stage 3, to extract the topics grouped within this cluster: attract qualified employees, maintain a competitive position, improve morale, and reduce turnover. Then return to the research materials for backup data. What information is available for the first sub-topic, *attracting qualified employees*? Our data reveal that employees often look to benefits as a tie-breaker between companies; that is, if salaries are comparable, applicants decide between employers on the basis of the benefits offered. Consequently, employers who convincingly promote their benefits are likely to attract qualified candidates. How is this best accomplished? Based on phone surveys and readings, it appears that the most productive methods include detailed descriptions of benefits in ads, distributing CD-ROMs during campus recruiting, and handing out benefits pamphlets and brochures to prospective employees at job fairs and open houses.

Now think about whether there is any other way to attract qualified candidates to your company. How about verbally communicating your benefits package to employment agencies and search firms? Better yet, have them hand out benefits pamphlets to prospective employees. Take all of this information and assemble it. The result will be something like this:

Primary Objectives of a Benefits Plan

Goal: To convince qualified employees to work for our company

How can we accomplish this?

1. Provide highlights of benefits in job ads, including special benefits.
2. Send CD-ROMs to colleges and universities describing our benefits; show employees who are taking advantage of recreation program.
3. Print benefits pamphlets and brochures to hand out at open houses and job fairs; use color, drawings, and photographs to illustrate key benefits.
4. Send benefits information to employment agencies and search firms; instruct them to distribute to prospective employees while emphasizing how great the package is.

Now ask a series of questions to test the validity of this expanded cluster:

- Have I incorporated all of the relevant data from my research?
- Have I tried to come up with additional relevant information?
- Does the information tie in with my goal?
- Do I present plausible arguments?
- Is the information easy to understand?
- How is a reader likely to react to the information?
- Have I anticipated questions and tried to address them?
- Is there any excess verbiage that detracts from the message?
- Have I demonstrated the relevance of each point?
- Have I presented the information in as interesting a manner as possible?

The same procedure of adding substance and questioning the validity of the items will pertain to each cluster of the document. When you are done, wait a minimum of twenty-four hours and review the document as a whole. This time check for:

- Continuity and flow between the sections.
- A clear and consistent relationship among the parts.
- A logical progression of information.
- Assurance that each area can be developed in greater detail.

If you are under the pressure of a deadline and do not have the luxury of waiting a day to review your work, ask a colleague to do it for you. Do not taint your request with explanations or disclaimers; just provide the document and ask for feedback, focusing on the four criteria listed. If as a result of this review process changes are needed, take a deep breath and proceed: move blocks of information around, cut and paste, insert and delete. This is the time to make structural changes, before embarking on the remaining five stages.

Write the Opening

The purpose of an opening statement is twofold: to identify the document and to orient the reader. This is accomplished either by luring or "hooking" the reader or immediately getting to the point.

You can hook the reader with a number of techniques, such as starting off with an attention-getting statement: *You can convince good employees to stay, even if they get a better offer!* Avoid startling the reader or referring to irrelevant matters. The reader will soon feel duped and be reluctant to continue once it becomes apparent that the document has nothing to do with winning a free trip to Hawaii.

Another way of hooking your reader is to pose one or more intriguing questions at the outset. Consider this opening:

> How do you feel when good employees say they're leaving to work for the competition? Do you think there's any way to convince them to stay, short of offering them the CEO's position?

Questions such as these will capture the attention of managers concerned with high turnover, compelling them to read on. Of course, you are now committed to provide answers to these questions in the main body of the document.

You can also begin by sharing a personal anecdote. I did this in the introduction to my book, *Workplace Testing* (AMACOM, 1994):

> Say the word *test* to anyone you know, from the youngest schoolage child to a senior citizen, and you will undoubtedly hear a favorite horror story. My own tale concerns a high school French teacher named Miss Mealy. Diminutive in stature and soft-spoken, she was always available to her students for questions and patiently tolerated our persistent butchering of her beloved French. Despite all her positive traits, she still managed to evoke terror in the hearts of even the best students in the class whenever she murmured in French what translated into thirteen simple English words: "Take out a little piece of paper; we're going to have a test. ". . . Her directive terrified us because she believed absolutely in . . . a test's ability to reflect accurately an extensive degree of knowledge and comprehension.

I then proceeded to link my experience with employment testing:

> Many employers also believe this to be true, relying on tests to measure skill and ability . . . But can tests accurately predict how individuals are likely to perform in any given job?

A catchy story will hook your readers and hold their attention. (A number of people have asked me about Miss Mealy!)

Another option is to start off with an eye-opening statistic. Consider this introduction to a proposed policy on elder care:

> Today, 80 percent of all caregivers are women, and more than 20 percent of that group have had to quit their jobs to provide elder care. Those who continue working full or part time devote an additional forty hours a week providing care to an elderly relative (according to *Helping Yourself Help Others*, by Rosalynn Carter, as reported in *Newsday*, November 8, 1994, p. B3). Since nearly 70 percent of our company's staff consists of women, these figures have a direct impact on short-and long-term productivity. Therefore, it makes good dollars and "sense" to offer elder care to our employees.

Getting directly to the point is the second method of introducing a topic. This may be accomplished by starting with a number of lead-in phrases, such as these:

[1] The purpose of this document is . . .

[2] I am writing to inform you that . . .

[3] This letter is about . . .

[4] This policy will describe . . .

[5] This is a report on . . .

[6] The reason I am writing to you is . . .

[7] Here are ten reasons that you should . . .

[8] This letter will help you . . .

[9] In the following pages I will describe . . .

[10] After reading about the proposed recreational program, you will be able to . . .

[11] This letter will explain . . .

[12] After reading this proposal, you will be able to . . .

Many people have difficulty writing the introduction. Certainly it can be hard to condense reams of data into a few sentences that establish the focus of your subject. If you find yourself in this situation, try postponing the opening until the end of writing. At the very least, wait until you have developed the main body. Then you will have a clearer sense of the direction of your document and have less difficulty stating it.

Compose the Main Body

Having prepared an outline, developed key ideas, and drafted the opening, you are well on your way. Now it is time to compose the main body. This is the longest segment of your document, but it also tends to be the easiest to prepare, particularly if you developed a sentence or sequential outline. The basic information is all there, just waiting to be fleshed out.

The key to an effective main body is proper paragraphing. A paragraph is a collection of related sentences working together to develop a single idea. Each paragraph functions as a unit of development by organizing and advancing the writer's objectives.

Paragraphing is helpful to both the writer and the reader. Writers rely on paragraphs to organize and present information and to control how much emphasis to lend to an idea. Readers need paragraphs to keep key points separate, as well as to remain attentive. In this regard, writers are advised to vary the length of their paragraphs.

An effective paragraph has four key characteristics: focus, completeness, sequence, and unity.

Focus

The sentences of a paragraph must be integrated and focused. Sentences that lack a relation to the intent of the paragraph will blur the focus and confuse the reader. Accordingly, determine how you want to develop a paragraph before beginning so you avoid contradicting or digressing from your objective.

A paragraph can be focused by beginning with a topic sentence. A topic sentence states the main idea, with each succeeding sentence contributing to the development of that idea. It sends a clear message to the reader: "This is the main idea that I will develop in this paragraph. All subsequent sentences will support, explain, or expand this idea."

An example of a topic sentence from a policy dealing with bulletin boards could be,

> All notices, job openings, and announcements are posted on bulletin boards throughout the office for a specified period of time.

Subsequent sentences should tell the reader where these bulletin boards are located and how long the document will remain posted:

> "In Building 1, the bulletin board is located opposite the conference room; in Building 2, one board is in the reception area, and another is across from the HR director's office, Room 7. All notices will remain posted for one month.

Not all paragraphs must begin with a topic sentence in order to be focused. You may opt to place a topic sentence midway, where it supports sentences that both precede and follow it in the paragraph. The first sentence may suggest a topic that is affirmed in the topic sentence that follows. Placing the topic sentence at the end of a paragraph is another option. In this way, you build up to an idea and confirm it at the end. Also, not every paragraph requires a topic sentence. If a point can be inferred, readers will not require an explicit statement.

Since readers of HR documents are busy and want to focus on the point of a document right away, it is advisable to start most of your paragraphs with a topic sentence, with an occasional midway or end placement for variety. Omitting topic sentences altogether is tricky business that risks misleading your reader.

Completeness

Deciding how much information to include in a paragraph depends primarily on the purpose of the document. Letters and announcements that only inform will not require as much detail as those that inform and seek to influence.

The amount of information in a paragraph depends too on your knowledge of the readers. If they are conversant about the subject or have previously received communications on the topic, do not include data they already know, other than as background or to serve as a foundation.

To avoid giving too much information or not enough, use the topic sentence as your point of reference. Make certain the remaining sentences in the paragraph spell out the implications of that topic sentence with facts, illustrations, explanations, definitions, or whatever else is needed to make the thought complete.

Sequence

Sentences within a paragraph must follow some reasonable order that your readers can recognize and trace. There are four common sequences from which to choose:

1. *General to specific.* The most common order in paragraphs is one that moves from a general statement (typically, the topic sentence) to specific explanations of that statement. The meaning becomes increasingly clear as the paragraph progresses. The paragraph may conclude with a restatement of the topic sentence.

2. *Specific to general.* A paragraph written in this order reverses the sequence of the preceding pattern. It begins with specific information and leads to a general conclusion. If there is a topic sentence, it appears at or near the end of the paragraph.

3. *Partitive or enumerative.* Paragraphs sometimes show the parts or divisions of a topic. The opening sentence announces the number of parts of the topic, and the rest of the paragraph identifies and defines each of these parts. Partitive or enumerative paragraphs are typically used when a writer wants to introduce the issues that will be discussed or as a conclusion to sum up what has been covered.

4. *Question to answer.* A paragraph may begin with a question and devote the remainder of the paragraph to the answer. A variation on this sequence is *effect to cause*, in which case the paragraph begins by stating an effect and explaining the cause in the remaining sentences.

Unity

The sentences in a paragraph should be woven together in such a way that readers can move easily from one thought to the next and read the paragraph as an integrated whole rather than as a series of separate sentences. Typically, paragraphs lack unity or coherence when the writer thinks about the implications of each individual sentence (or worse, each individual word) instead of the paragraph as a whole. The flow or continuity is interrupted, and the result is a herky-jerky style.

One way of ensuring unity is to repeat key words, phrases, or sentence patterns. This technique can help connect sentences into a coherent pattern, but it should not be overdone.

Select Connectives

Connectives are words or phrases placed at or near the beginning of a sentence to signal the relationship between a new sentence and the one before it. They are typically short, simple words that clearly communicate their function: providing examples, expanding a point, pointing out a contrast, or drawing a conclusion.

Providing Examples

Providing examples is a common method of clarifying the purpose of a document. Whether you are seeking a specific sensory response to a description or compiling evidence for an argument, examples help readers understand your objective. A paragraph may contain a single illustration, say, a relevant statistic, or a series of examples. In either case, the examples should be presented and arranged in a logical pattern, with each one supporting the purpose.

This pattern can occur only if the examples are clearly linked to the point being illustrated—hence, the role of connectives. Consider the following passage, and note the single illustration introduced by the phrase *for example* (which I italicize):

> All organizations require benefits administration, but some of the benefits offered by larger companies simply do not exist in small and mid-sized organizations. . . . *For example*, many large companies offer business travel accident insurance, which provides benefits for employees required to conduct business for their organization somewhere away from their usual worksite. (Diane Arthur, *Managing Human Resources in Small and Mid-Sized Companies*, AMACOM, 1995)

The first sentence says that small companies do not offer the same benefits as larger companies. The statement is informative but does not have much of an impact as it stands. Adding the connecting words, *for example*, followed by an illustration, gives the reader specific information, making the passage more tangible. Exhibit 3-3 lists some connectives.

Expanding a Point

Some ideas stand well on their own; others require expansion. In order for readers to understand how certain sentences support others, an expansive link is required. Examples of such words appear in the following letter concerning problems associated with 360-degree performance appraisals (I have italicized the connectives):

> Many raters, such as peers or clients, may be reluctant to provide feedback, either because they lack the appropriate skills or in anticipation that it will strain their relationship with the employee. There is *also* the problem of varying expectations by the raters: some rate low, while others are generous in evaluations. *In addition*, the input of the raters should not necessarily be weighted

Exhibit 3-3. Common Connectives.

as an illustration

for example

for instance

such as

this is evidenced by

this is exemplified by

this point is illustrated by

to elaborate

to exemplify

to illustrate

equally, in view of their different levels of knowledge about the employee. *Furthermore,* culling data from as many as ten raters is a time-consuming and complex process.

This passage offers three statements that support the topic sentence. The reader understands this because the writer used connecting words: *also, in addition,* and *furthermore.* The result is a smooth-flowing paragraph consisting of sentences that all connect with one another. Exhibit 3-4 offers some options for expanding points.

Pointing Out a Contrast

Points are often emphasized when contrasting statements immediately follow. The following three examples illustrate this point:

[1] It is recommended that employees be permitted to apply for as many positions as they choose and as frequently as they choose. *However,* certain conditions should be met before an employee may apply for a posted job.

[2] Mandatory drug testing of all applicants has resulted in an 18 percent drop in drug use by new employees over the past year. *In contrast,* drug use by existing staff has increased by 5 percent.

[3] The Americans with Disabilities Act of 1990 prohibits employers with fifteen or more employees from discriminating against employees or applicants with disabilities. *Despite this fact,* individuals with disabilities report that they continue to be discriminated against in employment matters.

Exhibit 3-5 offers a selection of contrasting connectives.

Drawing a Conclusion

When writers use concluding connectives, such as *hence, therefore,* and *in other words,* they are sending two key messages to readers: (1) there is no additional information forthcoming, and (2) in case there is any doubt about the conclusion the readers should reach, the writer is spelling it out for them.

Exhibit 3-4. Connectives for Expanding Points.

again	in this regard
also	moreover
and	more specifically
at the same time	naturally
furthermore	next
in addition	second
indeed	similarly
in the second place	then
in this connection	to continue

Exhibit 3-5. Contrasting Connectives.

alternatively	meanwhile
but	nevertheless
by way of comparison	nor
conversely	on the other hand
despite this fact	or
here again	rather
however	still
in comparison	to compare
in contrast	to the contrary
in spite of this	yet
instead	

Let us examine these two points more closely. First, do readers need to be told that nothing more will be said about a given topic? Does this not become evident as the recipient reads on? And second, if the materials are organized and presented in a clear, consistent fashion, will readers need to be told what to conclude? Indeed, if the material is well written, highlighting the conclusion by concluding connectives will overstate the obvious, which can be annoying to a busy reader. On the other hand, if the material does not naturally point to a given conclusion, phrases such as *to sum up* will be confusing.

Concluding connectives should be used sparingly. Appropriate uses include periodic summaries throughout and at the end of lengthy documents. A list of concluding connectives appears in Exhibit 3-6.

Write the Closing

The purpose of a document's closing is to leave readers with a sense of completeness. All of your points should have already been made and explained, all questions anticipated and addressed. Your tone and style should remain constant. There should be no surprises, no new material or new issues introduced. It is a time for wrapping up.

Exhibit 3-6. Concluding Connectives.

accordingly	in short
as a result	now
consequently	so
finally	therefore
hence	to close
in conclusion	to conclude
in other words	to sum up

Your choice of closing words is crucial for three primary reasons: (1) The last words read are often the first to be remembered, (2) if the document is a page or less in length and the reader is rushed, the closing may be the only statement read, and (3) this is the last chance to get the message across. That said, here is a list of ways to make your closings strong and purposeful:

- Make your closing a separate paragraph so that it will stand out.
- Paraphrase your opening paragraph.
- Highlight what has been said throughout the document.
- Draw conclusions from previous paragraphs.
- Emphasize main points.
- Include dates and times that might otherwise be forgotten.
- Provide instructions.
- Take a definitive stand.

Let us look at some examples of strong closings:

The last three pages have shown statistically that drug testing has an impact on reducing the rate of drug use in the workplace. In view of this, I recommend that Avedon adopt a drug testing program, effective January 1 of next year.—(*highlights, draws conclusions, takes a definitive stand*)

Therefore, if you want to improve employee performance, provide a motivating environment and offer ongoing coaching and counseling as needed.—(*draws conclusions, emphasizes main points*)

Again, thank you and congratulations on doing an excellent job as a customer service representative for the past five years.—(*paraphrases the opening paragraph*)

It is crucial that you call or otherwise contact me by April 30, to avoid termination effective May 1.—(*includes dates, provides instructions*)

Hence, if you are able to arrive at work on time over the next six weeks and avoid unexcused absences in accordance with the plan described above, the warning notice issued on February 4 will be removed from your HR file.—(*highlights, draws conclusions, emphasizes main points*)

I look forward to seeing you at the job fair on July 17 at 10:00 A.M.—(*includes date and time*)

I hope you will accept our offer of employment and look forward to your favorable reply by November 18.—(*includes date*)

Due to the positive impact on employee morale, attendance, and productivity, as identified by your June 8 statistical study, I am prepared to support the proposal for on-site child care. Please come to my office on the 15th at 9:00 A.M. so that we may begin planning the project in detail.—(*draws conclusions, includes date and time, provides instructions, takes a definitive stand*)

Otherwise strong documents are often ruined by weak closings. When writers flounder around, repeating themselves or resorting to stock phrases, they dull the readers' interest they have worked so hard to develop. Here are some examples of weak closings:

Thanking you in advance . . .

If you have any questions, please do not hesitate to call.

I look forward to hearing from you in the near future.

I'm sure you'll agree that . . .

Thus, I have shown that . . .

After reading this letter, I'm sure you can understand . . .

I'm sure you can see why I feel so strongly about this issue.

Please call me at your earliest convenience.

I hope the contents of this letter meet with your approval.

Please call me with a meeting date and time that is convenient for you.

Revise

Revising is the final stage in writing a document: a procedure for checking over your work, making any substantive changes and otherwise polishing it.

If you have been diligent in following the stages of writing described thus far—preparing an outline, developing key ideas, writing the opening, composing the main body, and selecting connectives—then the revisions should be minor—for example, rearranging phrases, substituting words, deleting excess verbiage, correcting dates, and checking for proper spelling. Revising also includes checking for improper word usage and incorrect grammar, as well as punctuation (see Chapter 4). Occasionally new information or a change in circumstances may require a complete rewrite.

If time permits, put your final draft aside for several days before the final review. As with the procedure for finalizing the outline, this break in time will allow you to view the contents objectively and make any necessary changes. Asking colleagues to review your final draft can also be helpful, eliciting comments about the tone and style, as well as overall impressions.

Revising is not as time-consuming as the outline stage, but it is equally important. The outline is where your ideas originated; the revision is the end result. Hence, the two are closely linked. Checking the final draft against the outline is a good way to ensure that your message is on target.

It helps also to read the final draft from the perspective of your readers. How are they likely to react to the topic, your approach, the language, the tone, and the specific contents?

While reviewing the document for changes, ask yourself three key questions:

1. What did I set out to accomplish?
2. What are the document's strengths and weaknesses?
3. Can I eliminate the weaknesses or convert them into strengths?

The outline will help you answer the first question; reviewing the document from the perspective of your reader or having an objective third party read it will enable you to answer the second one. And the answer to the third question is always yes. The reason is simple: You may not have complete control over what goes into the document, but it's your call as to how the material is presented. Hence, even if you cannot eliminate certain information, you can always reword it.

If you are revising a letter or some other relatively short document, say, three pages or fewer, reviewing it as a whole should be sufficient. If the document is lengthy, however, such as a policy or orientation packet, then it is helpful to break down the revision process: Check first for style and tone; next for organization and use of language; and finally for proper grammar, spelling, and punctuation.

The revision process can go on endlessly, as you continuously rearrange information, rewrite paragraphs and sentences, and substitute new words. The more you review the work, the more you will see the need for revision. But at some point, your changes lose purpose. Excessive revision can even destroy good writing as original insights are replaced with self-conscious, trite phrases. When is it time to stop revising? When a change fails to produce a significant improvement.

Summary

Effective writing has seven stages. Stage 1 is the outline: formal, scratch, or sequential. Regardless of the type selected, the purpose of an outline is to achieve a balance between the contents of each portion and to develop a logical progression of ideas.

The second stage is the development of key ideas. Your goal is to ensure that the outline encompasses the main features of your topics by adding some substance to the outline and testing the validity of each item by a series of questions.

Next, write the opening statement. The purpose of the opening is to identify the document and orient the reader. This is done by hooking the reader with an attention-getting statement, posing intriguing questions, sharing a personal anecdote, or presenting eye-opening statistics. Immediately getting to the point also allows you to introduce a topic. This may be accomplished by starting with various lead-in phrases.

Now it is time to compose the main body. The key to an effective main body is proper paragraphing. A paragraph is a collection of related sentences working together to develop a single idea. Effective paragraphs have four key characteristics: focus, completeness, sequence, and unity.

The fifth stage of writing concerns the use of connectives: words or phrases placed at or near the beginning of a sentence to signal the relationship between a new sentence and the one before it. Connectives are typically short, simple words that clearly communicate their function: providing examples, expanding a point, pointing out a contrast, or drawing a conclusion.

Writing the closing is the sixth stage. The purpose of a closing is to leave readers with a feeling of completeness. Choosing appropriate closing words is important for three reasons: the last words read are often the first to be remembered, the closing may be the only statement read, and this is your last chance to get a message across.

Revision is the final stage in writing a document: a procedure for checking over your work and making any final changes. These changes may consist of rearranging phrases, substituting words, deleting excess verbiage, correcting dates, and checking grammar, word usage, and punctuation.

Once the writing process is complete, you are ready to check for writing pitfalls, the subject of Chapter 4.

4
Writing Pitfalls

Regardless of how well you have followed the guidelines described thus far, there are still a handful of writing pitfalls to guard against before declaring a document finished. These pitfalls may be derived from the specific words or expressions chosen, how they are used, and—yes—those three nasty words: grammar, punctuation, and spelling. (You knew they had to appear somewhere in this book.) Checking for errors in these areas will distinguish the finished document from those that are not as polished.

Denotations and Connotations

Words either name things or express views about them. Those used merely to refer to things—papers, employees, computers, meetings, or clients—are *denotations*. The word *applicant* denotes a person looking for a job. A denotation for *job* is work. When a particular view or attitude is associated with a word, it acquires a *connotation*. By writing *the impressive applicant*, you are inviting readers to share your opinion of the candidate. Hence, connotations go beyond the naming quality of denotations by attaching a favorable or unfavorable attitude.

Keep this distinction in mind. When you write documents that inform, objectively choose words that denote. If your purpose is to influence as well, select words that clearly connote your views. Sometimes this is an effortless process, with words coming so easily that your fingers can scarcely keep pace with your brain. The thoughts you want to express flow readily to paper or screen. Then at other times you struggle to find the word that will best convey the intended meaning. When this occurs (and it does, even to the best writers), remember that what makes a word effective is the impact it has in a particular sentence or paragraph. Readers of HR documents rarely focus on single words (unless there is an error in usage, spelling, grammar, or punctuation); rather, they react to words in a context provided by other words. Keeping this in mind should allow you to get past fretting over the connotation of a single word.

Clichés

Call them clichés, stock phrases, trite words, antiquated phrases, threadbare terms, or hackneyed expressions, they all mean essentially the same thing: once fresh, colorful, and original words that have been overused, losing their appeal. True, business writing does not require the same degree of originality as creative writing, nor am I suggesting that you write with originality every time you pick up a pen or face the computer monitor.

Certain phrases, while overused, still say it best (I shamelessly admit that for a long time one of my favorite phrases has been, "in accordance with your request.") However, repeatedly relying on a string of stock phrases conveys a lack of effort, as evidenced by this paragraph:

> Attached herewith please find the information as per your request. I trust that it meets with your expectations and that you will find it to be of assistance. Please call me at your earliest possible convenience so that we may discuss its contents.

A rewritten version of this paragraph, minus the stock phrases, might read:

> [Rewritten] Here is the information you requested. I hope you find it helpful. Please call me by July 17 so we can review it together.

Rephrasing your work to avoid tired expressions is not difficult, once you acknowledge that an overreliance on triteness can taint the way you come across and learn to recognize phrasing to avoid. Unfortunately, what is recognized as trite or tired by some may seem original and clever to someone starting their first professional job. Exhibit 4-1 identifies a partial list of clichés that are commonly used in business.

Exhibit 4-1. Common Business Clichés and Shopworn Phrases.

above-mentioned
acid test
acknowledge receipt of
according to our records
affix your signature to
aforementioned letter
as luck would have it
as of this writing
attached please find
attached herewith
back to square one
ballpark figure
be good enough to
beyond a shadow of a doubt
bottom line
brainstorm
contact me by telephone
contents noted
cost-effective
each and every
earliest convenience
enclosed herewith
enclosed please find

few and far between
first and foremost
give the matter our immediate attention
have before me
have duly noted the contents of
hit the nail on the head
hoping for the favor of a reply
I am in receipt of your letter
If I can be of further assistance, please do not hesitate to call me
in accordance with your request
in a timely manner
in receipt of
interface
in view of the fact that
it has been brought to my attention
it is incumbent upon us
last but not least
make every effort
multifaceted
near future
nip the problem in the bud
once-in-a-lifetime opportunity
parameters
pending receipt of
permit me to take this opportunity to
pursuant to our recent conversation
put on a back burner
state-of-the-art
take this opportunity
take the ball and run with it
take the liberty of sending you
thank you in advance
time is money
to the fullest extent possible
trusting you will
under separate cover
until such time as
user friendly
water over the dam
water under the bridge
we appreciate your prompt compliance with
we are in receipt of your letter dated
we regret to inform you that

Jargon

Jargon means made-up words and the specialized language of a particular profession. Simple, direct words may be converted into industry-unique buzzwords or acronyms, and suffixes, such as *-ize* and *-wise,* are often added to verbs and nouns to create new words.

The first resumé I ever reviewed was for a data processing position. As a newcomer to human resources, I was having enough trouble learning the special language used by HR professionals, much less understanding the unique terms and expressions of computer experts. Staring at the resumé, I assumed that it was written in English, but only because I could read portions of it—the person's name, address, and educational credentials. The rest was written exclusively for experts in data processing, and I was unable to decipher the jargon. Consequently I did not have a clue as to the candidate's level of competence. I had to sit down with a colleague from data processing who translated the mysterious code into common terms.

Jargon can interfere with a clear, precise message. Readers may be confused by its meaning or find it pompous. In both cases, the effect is to slow the reader down.

Jargon is not altogether without merit. The need for a term more precise than any that already exists may justify a new word. Naming something in order to avoid a repetitive description can also justify jargon.

Interweave jargon throughout your work if you anticipate that at least 90 percent of the readers will understand its precise meaning. When *The Wall Street Journal* ran a front-page article on May 14, 1996, entitled, "Call It Dumbsizing," the reporter added a subtitle, "Why Some Companies Regret Cost Cutting." The authors wrote an entire piece around a made-up word that defined another bit of jargon: *downsizing.*

With terms that are ambiguous, provide a definition the first time the word or term appears in your document. It is also a good idea to review the document from the perspective of someone outside your field. For instance, can you safely assume that everyone knows the meanings of "career pathing" and "exempt and nonexempt status"? How about EEO, ADA, FMLA, ADEA, CRA, and AA? A non-HR practitioner may come across AA and, not knowing anything about affirmative action, wonder why you are writing about Alcoholics Anonymous. If you have the least suspicion that readers will not share the meaning that is intended for a term, either spell it out or make a clearer choice. Examples of jargon appear in Exhibit 4-2.

Exhibit 4-2. Common Jargon.

bureaucratese	HRese
compartmentalize	prioritize
competencewise	prioritization
corporatese	profitwise
downsize	sizewise
DPer	strategize
dumbsize	systemize
economywise	

Word Usage

The English language is full of words that are confused with one another. At some point in our education we all undoubtedly learned the difference between *affect* and *effect*, *all together* and *altogether*, and *adapt* and *adopt*. Yet when it comes time to use these words in a sentence, we often play a guessing game as to which one is correct.

How important is proper word usage when writing an HR document? You could take the attitude that you are not a professional writer and your readers are more interested in content than perfect English. Besides, chances are they don't know the difference between *ensure* and *insure* either. You might further reason that the documents *they* generate would never win any prizes, so they have no right to expect any better from *you*. Maybe so. But errors have a way of standing out, and even if readers cannot tell you how or why a word is improperly used, it will be evident. Incorrect usage disrupts the flow, thereby interfering with the reader's ability to absorb the information, and sends a message to the reader that you are careless in checking your work before sending it out. The impression that may be created is that you are sloppy in other aspects of your work. In addition, outsiders may assume that the error is reflective of the kind of work regularly generated by your organization.

Consider the reaction of an applicant who has just received an offer of employment through a letter that contains improper word usage. The applicant could ignore this or view it as representative of the organization, wondering if such mistakes are commonplace and acceptable. If other offers are being considered, your improper word usage could tip the scales.

Exhibit 4-3 offers a list of words that pose usage problems. Some are words that sound alike but have different meanings. Others are words that are commonly confused with one another.

Proper usage extends beyond selecting the correct word to include being aware of the images or pictures that words suggest. Although HR writing should not be filled with colorful pictorials, images can help readers understand your focus or point of view. The figures of speech most commonly used to create images are similes, metaphors, personification, and allusion.

A *simile* compares two different objects or situations by suggesting that one is like the other. Similes are usually introduced by the word *like, as,* or *so:*

> When Jacob received the letter from Avedon Industries offering him a starting salary that was $10,000 more than he had hoped for, he felt as if he had just won the lottery.

Metaphors compare two things by identifying one with the other. Unlike similes, metaphors do not say that one is like another but that one *is* the other. Hence,

> Jean was accustomed to being the star of the show; working as a team member was a difficult adjustment for her to make.

Personification is a figure of speech by which abstractions and nonanimals are given human or animal characteristics—for example,

> The words in the report leaped off the page like an angry tiger.

Exhibit 4-3. Words That Can Cause Usage Problems.

Word	Meaning
ability	to do something
capacity	to receive or contain
about	a rough estimate
approximately	implies accuracy
accede	to agree
exceed	to go beyond
accept	to receive willingly
except	to exclude
adapt	to change
adopt	to take on
adverse	acting against
averse	dislike
advise	to offer suggestions
inform	to communicate information
affect	a verb meaning "change" or "influence"
effect	As a verb, meaning "to bring about"; as a noun, meaning "result" or "outcome"
all ready	everything or everyone is ready
already	previously
all together	everything or everyone is together
altogether	completely
alternate	a substitute
alternative	a choice between two or more possibilities
appraise	to determine the value of
apprise	to inform
assure	to convince
ensure	to make certain that
because of	by reason of, on account of
due to	attributable to
beside	at the side of
besides	in addition to
can	implies ability
may	implies permission
complement	to fit together with
compliment	to praise
continual	recurring frequently
continuous	without interruption
disinterested	impartial
uninterested	indifferent
e.g.	for example
i.e.	in other words, that is

farther	refers to physical distance
further	to a greater degree or extent, or something additional
fewer	refers to units or individuals
less	refers to quantities of mass, bulk, or volume
like	similar to
as	in the same way or manner
people	refers to large groups
persons	refers to small groups
percent	per hundred
percentage	a proportion or share in relation to a whole
practicable	appears to be feasible
practical	usefulness
precede	occur at an earlier time
proceed	to continue
stationary	not moving
stationery	writing paper
than	used for comparison
then	indicates time
who	substitute for *he, she,* or *they*
whom	substitute for *him, her,* or *them*

Personification should be used with restraint. The reader may view your attempts to be descriptive as excessively dramatic.

Allusion refers to some historical or literary event or person seen to resemble in some way the subject under discussion. When the Prudential Insurance Company urges people to "own a piece of the rock," they are suggesting that their company is solid and permanent like the Rock of Gibraltar. Likewise, the director of HR may summarize a disciplinary matter involving employee theft by stating,

> This Watergate-like event will necessitate hiring a security guard to patrol between 6:00 P.M. and 8:00 A.M.

Grammar, Punctuation, and Spelling

Relax. This section does not contain an exhaustive set of rules for proper grammar, punctuation, and spelling. There are volumes devoted to these subjects, written by experts who enjoy dissecting parts of speech, dangling modifiers, and split infinitives (Two particularly fine sources are *The Elements of Style,* 3d ed., by Strunk and White (Macmillan, New York) and *Words Into Type,* 3d ed. (Prentice Hall, Englewood Cliffs, N.J.). Some writers of HR documents may be interested in the nuances of every principle of grammar (yes, really!), but they only need to know the basics. Accordingly, in this segment you will learn how to avoid those grammar, punctuation, and spelling errors most commonly made in business writing.

Grammar

Grammar is a system of arranging words in sentences so that the intended meaning is clearly communicated. Much of what is considered "good" grammar comes naturally to us as we learn to use English formally in school and informally while going about daily activities. We also respond to English as used by other people. We know, for example, that the following sentence is grammatically correct: *She wrote an excellent report.* We may not be able to explain why that sentence constitutes good grammar; we just know that it does. If those same words were arranged differently so that the sentence read, *Wrote she an excellent report*, we would know that some rule of grammar had been violated. We would also find it disconcerting if the sentence did not begin with a capital letter or end with a period. Also, if the word *write* were substituted for *wrote*, we would find the tense awkward and want to change it.

Give yourself credit, then, for already knowing a good deal about the fundamentals of grammar. Know, too, that even the best authors and editors occasionally have problems with grammar.

There are eight areas of grammar that are most troublesome:

1. *Subject and verb disagreement.* Most people know that singular subjects and singular verbs go together and that plural subjects pair up with plural verbs. We are thrown off, however, when a phrase comes between a subject and a verb. If the subject is singular but the phrase contains a plural, the subject and verb should still be singular—for example: *In reference to your recent letters, the address in our files is correct.* The correct verb is *is*, not *are*, since *address* is singular.

2. *Improper use of pronouns.* Selecting the correct pronoun is easy if you follow one simple rule: Say the sentence as if the pronoun were the only recipient of the action. In the following sentence, omit *Peter* and decide if *I* or *me* is correct: *Sammy invited Peter and [I/me] to the office picnic.* The construction *Sammy invited I to the office picnic* is wrong without Peter: hence, the correct pronoun is *me*.

3. *Sentence fragments and run-on sentences.* A sentence fragment is a group of words that does not express a complete thought. It can be avoided by giving each thought a subject and a verb. A run-on sentence is two complete sentences separated with a comma. Separate the two sentences with a period.

4. *Dangling modifiers.* A modifier should clarify or limit the word it modifies. When a phrase does not modify the subject of the sentence, then the modifier is said to be dangling. If you wrote, *When choosing an employee, skill should be your priority*, it is unclear as to who is choosing the employee. This sentence should read, *When you choose an employee, skill should be a priority*.

5. *Misplaced modifiers.* If a modifier is placed too far from the word it is supposed to modify, or placed where it might modify either of two different words, it is said to be misplaced. Misplaced modifiers leave the reader guessing what you mean. *I need a new computer for my assistant, preferably with a large memory*, should be reworded to read, *I need a new computer, preferably with a large memory, for my assistant*.

6. *Capitalization.* Capitalize titles of books and articles. Official names and titles of business and government entities are also capitalized. Do not capitalize words such as *company*, *division*, or *department* when they stand alone. These are capitalized only when part of an official name. Also, avoid arbitrarily capitalizing words to emphasize their importance.

7. *Parallel structure.* Parallelism clarifies meaning, creates symmetry, and lends equality to each idea in the series. According to *The Elements of Style*, "The likeness of form enables the reader to recognize more readily the likeness of content and function." The principle of parallelism refers to the construction within a sentence, as well as the wording of a list. Following is an example of parallelism: *The interviewer met with the candidate, evaluated his test scores, and offered him a job.*

8. *Split infinitives.* An infinitive is a simple verb form, often preceded by the word *to*. In the sentence *Katy likes to go to work,* the verb *to go* is an infinitive. If putting a number of words between the *to* and the verb disrupts continuity, avoid splitting the infinitive. But do not try to avoid splitting an infinitive at all costs.

Punctuation

The word *punctuate* comes from a Latin word meaning "point." Latin writing was marked by dots and other "points" to show where sentences began or ended and to give other information. English writing continues to be marked by periods, commas, semicolons, hyphens, quotation marks, question marks, and other forms of punctuation to make the meaning of written material clear.

Punctuation usually follows vocal inflections and gestures that clarify meaning when we speak. For example, a comma is the written equivalent of a brief pause; a semicolon represents a longer pause. Exclamation points are the same as shouting! And a dash is like—stopping suddenly in the middle of a sentence.

While errors in punctuation may not be perceived as aggrievedly as poor organization and unclear wording, they can detract from the quality of the finished product. Here, then, are eight punctuation guidelines that will improve your finished document:

1. *Commas.* The proper placement of commas is a problem for many writers. Generally, if you would naturally pause when reading a sentence aloud, then a comma is appropriate. Here are some other guidelines for using commas:

- If confusion in a short sentence would otherwise result: *To review, commas are sometimes needed in short sentences.*
- To separate elements in a series: *I enjoy recruiting, conducting interviews, preparing evaluations, and writing policies.*
- To separate independent clauses that are joined by *and, but, or, nor, for,* and *yet: I waited for an hour, but the applicant did not show up.*
- To set off a parenthetical expression: *The HR department, located in Room 17, is where the interviews will be held.*
- To separate two or more adjectives when each modifies a noun: *It was a short, productive meeting.*
- To indicate omission of words that are understood: *Vivian is in charge of recruiting; Monica, benefits.*
- To set off geographic terms and to separate the date from the year: *The meeting will take place on September 11, 199X, at company headquarters in San Francisco.*

2. *Colons.* In addition to being used after the salutation of a business letter, colons are used to direct attention to something that follows, such as a list, an explanation, or a quotation: *You will be responsible for the work of three people: a clerk, an assistant, and a supervi-*

sor. They are also used to separate independent clauses when the second clause explains or amplifies the first: *He had one goal: to become president.*

3. *Semicolons.* Semicolons separate independent thoughts that relate closely to each other: *I will be in New York on January 23; however, I will not be able to attend the meeting.* They also separate phrases or items in a list in which the phrases and items themselves contain commas: *While on the East Coast, I will visit three cities: Princeton, New Jersey; Darien, Connecticut; and Boston, Massachusetts.''*

4. *Apostrophes.* Use an apostrophe and an *s* to form a possessive of a singular noun or name: *Jed's boss.* To form the possessive of a plural noun, add just an apostrophe: *employees' benefits.* Apostrophes also mark the omission of letters in a contraction, as in *She can't come to the meeting.*

5. *Hyphens.* Hyphens should be inserted in compound numerals (e.g., forty-eight). Also, when two or more words are compounded to form an adjective, they are hyphenated: *Long-range goals include adding twenty employees.* Excessive use of hyphens is distracting and should be avoided.

6. *Parentheses.* Parentheses are used to enclose and set apart a word or group of words in a sentence: *The HR policies manual (revised last year) clearly describes the performance review process.* Periods and commas usually appear outside the parentheses. The only time a period is used within parentheses is when the parentheses contain a complete sentence. Question marks or exclamation points appear inside the parentheses if they pertain to the parenthetic expression.

7. *Quotation marks.* Double quotation marks enclose the actual words of a speaker: *"Justine," I said, "you can't do that!"* Single quotation marks are used to mark quotations within quotations. Periods and commas are always placed inside quotation marks; colons always appear outside.

8. *Exclamation points.* Exclamation points can be used to express a strong conviction or order: *There will be no smoking on company premises at any time!* Overuse of exclamations renders them ineffective.

Spelling

Spelling is simply a matter of arranging the letters of a word in the correct order. Documents that are organized and otherwise written well may not be taken seriously if they contain spelling errors. Since we all have easy access to dictionaries and computer spell checks, spelling errors should rarely occur. Nevertheless, be cautious about spell checks: They cannot distinguish between sound-alike words such as *principle* and *principal*; *their*, *there*, and *they're*; or *it's* and *its*. The spell check will report that a word is correctly spelled but not whether it is correctly used.

Remembering a few rules can help you spell correctly:

1. *Final silent e.*

- A word ending in silent *-e* drops the *-e* before a suffix beginning with a vowel, such as *-able* and *-ing.* Examples: *admirable, movable, arranging, writing.* Some exceptions: *eyeing, mileage.*
- A word retains the *-e* before a suffix beginning with a consonant, such as *-ful*, *-ment*, and *-ness.* Examples: *careful, movement, likeness.* Some exceptions: *argument, acknowledgment, truly.*

Exhibit 4-4. Most Commonly Misspelled Words in HR Documents.

abbreviate	benefited	especially	performance
absence	brochure	excellence	perseverance
academic	budget	exceptionally	personnel
accessible	bulletin	exemption	predominant
accidentally	business	exorbitant	preferable
accommodate	calendar	extremely	prejudice
accompanying	candidate	familiar	programmed
accomplish	career	familiarize	qualitative
accordance	category	favorable	quantitative
accrued	changeable	feasibility	questionnaire
accumulate	characteristic	financial	recommend
accurate	circumstances	flexible	reference
achievement	commitment	focused	referred
acknowledge	committee	gamut	regrettable
acquaintance	comparatively	gauge	reimbursement
acquire	compelled	grievance	relevant
address	competence	guidance	representative
adequately	competition	harassment	responsibility
adjustment	conceivable	hierarchy	schedule
advantageous	confidential	hindrance	semiannual
advertisement	conscientious	illegal	separate
advisable	consequence	illiterate	significant
allotment	cooperate	immaterial	sincerely
allotted	criticism	immediately	skeptical
always	definitely	inaccessible	statistics
announcement	description	incidentally	subordinate
annually	desirable	indefinitely	subsequent
apparatus	development	insignificant	technician
apparent	discernible	intercede	temperament
appearance	discrepancy	interfere	temporarily
applicable	dismissal	judgment	tendency
applicant	dissatisfied	knowledgeable	testimonies
appointment	echelon	liaison	transferred
appreciate	eligible	management	truly
appropriate	eliminate	mandatory	ultimately
arrangement	emphasize	mediocre	undoubtedly
article	employee	memorandum	unforeseen
assignment	encouragement	misinterpreted	unfortunately
assistance	enthusiastic	necessitate	unusually
association	entrepreneur	negligence	valuable
attendance	environment	negotiable	versatile
auxiliary	equipment	occasionally	waive
available	equivalent	occurrence	warranted
basically	erroneous	omission	yield
beneficial			

‣ The -*e* is retained in some words to keep the soft sound of *c* and *g*. Examples: *advantageous, noticeable, outrageous*.

2. *ie or ei*. Put *i* before *e* except after *c* or when sounded like *a* as in *neighbor* and *weigh*. Examples: *achieve, believe, brief, conceive, deceive, perceive*. Exceptions: *either, financier, neither*.

3. *Words ending in y*. If the *y* is preceded by a consonant, change the *y* to *i* except before a suffix beginning with *i*. Examples: *flies, skies, studying*. If the *y* is preceded by a vowel, the *y* is usually retained, as in *attorneys*. Some exceptions: *laid, paid, said*.

4. *Cede, ceed, and sede*. Words ending with the sound *seed* are usually spelled -*cede*. Examples: *concede, precede, recede*. Only one word ends in -*sede: supersede*. Only three words end in -*ceed: exceed, proceed, succeed*.

5. *Doubling final consonants*. One-syllable words, or words of several syllables accented on the last syllable, double the final consonant before adding a suffix beginning with a vowel if they end in a single consonant preceded by a single vowel. Examples: *getting, admitted, concurring*. Exceptions: *excellent, transferable*.

6. *Plurals*. To make a regular noun plural, add an *s*, as in *books, buildings, employees*. With irregular plurals, add *es* if the noun ends in *o* preceded by a consonant. Examples: *tomatoes, embargoes*. There are numerous exceptions when converting a word into its plural form. Following is a sampling, with the singular form of the word listed first:

Addendum Addenda	Criterion Criteria
Analysis Analyses	Datum Data
Appendix Appendixes	Medium Media
Basis Bases	Parenthesis Parentheses
Crisis Crises	Phenomenon Phenomena

Spelling rules are helpful; however, because there are so many exceptions, it is a good idea to memorize those words that you misspell frequently. You can also refer to Exhibit 4-4, which lists the 175 most commonly misspelled words likely to appear in HR documents.

Summary

Always check for a handful of writing pitfalls before declaring a document finished: distinguishing between words that denote, or refer to things, and those that connote, or express a particular view or attitude; avoiding clichés; overusing jargon; avoiding improper word usage; and steering clear of grammar, punctuation, and spelling errors.

Errors have a way of standing out. They can affect the desired result of informing or influencing in two significant ways: they disrupt the flow, and they send a message to the reader that you are careless in checking your work before sending it out. Outsiders may also assume that the error is reflective of the kind of work regularly generated by your organization.

Checking for errors will distinguish the finished product from others that are not as polished.

This leads us to the final aspect of this section: the structure, format, and design of HR documents.

5

Structure, Format, and Design

I wish I could include in this chapter a copy of the most memorable resumé I have ever received. But if I had, this book would be nearly twice as long! All right, so that is a slight exaggeration. But the resumé was voluminous, running nearly one hundred pages in length, single spaced on legal-sized paper. Honest. In addition to describing his employment history as an engineer and educational credentials in minutia, the applicant provided information about aspects of his life that I had no business knowing: his current wife's employment status (she was his third), the majors each of his four children had pursued in college, and his political affiliation. He included copies of documents from every aspect of his life: educational diplomas, certificates and awards dating back to grade school when he was selected student of the month and made the honor role in middle and high school; employment offers during his lifetime of job searches; workplace notices of accomplishment for outstanding performance and employee of the month; marriage certificates; his children's birth records; letters written and responses received from presidential candidates and other famous people; and a list of references from twenty-seven people. Was he qualified for the available position? Who could tell? There was so much information it was hard to glean what was relevant. One hundred pages is a great deal to wade through to determine job suitability.

If this applicant's intention was to stand out, he succeeded, but not in a positive way. I am willing to bet that everyone else receiving his resumé (it must have cost him a fortune to duplicate and mail) reacted in the same way: disbelief and uninterest. I, at least, have been able to refer to it as an example of how appearances can count.

Deviating from what is considered standard and acceptable in the structure, format, and design of HR-related documents is tricky. Applicants, for example, want their resumés to capture attention. Sure, accomplishments are what ultimately result in a job offer, but resumés are not only intended to be read, but read more than another applicant's and remembered. Consequently, some resumés are printed on colored paper, appear in a report folder, arrive wrapped in a gift box, or come rolled up in a bottle like a cry for help tossed out to sea. Reactions to these attention-getting tactics are unpredictable. Some HR professionals may applaud the creativity and effort; others may label the originators as being nonconformists and troublemakers. The applicant is taking a chance by stepping outside the norm.

Since reactions to deviation from accepted standards of preparing HR documents can be unpredictable, it is advisable to adhere to an acceptable framework. The contents of your document should be the focal point, but appearances count. All the work put into planning, researching, and organizing will not matter if no one reads what you have written. After all, it can take as little as 4 seconds for the person receiving the document to react to what may have taken you hours, days, or longer to write. In the final analysis, success could depend on how the document is presented. (The sample numbers that follow refer to the sample forms in Section Two.)

Letters and Memos

[Samples 6-19–6-22, 7-14–7-20, 9-5–9-8, 9-16–9-17, 10-17–10-30]

HR practitioners write a multitude of letters and memos, not only to different people but to the same person, from the application process through termination. Jacqueline received her first letter from Avedon Industries after responding to an ad for a marketing representative. The letter invited her in for an interview. Following the interview, she received a letter advising her that a decision would be reached in about six weeks. In two months, Jacqueline received a verbal job offer, confirmed by letter. The day before starting her new job, she received a fourth letter, an official welcome. During her eight years with Avedon Industries, Jacqueline received two memos of commendation for outstanding performance, a letter of congratulations on her marriage and, later, on the births of her two children, condolences on the death of her father, good wishes for a speedy recovery when she broke her leg skiing, an invitation to a dinner honoring employees with the company five or more years, and a termination letter when she left Avedon.

The contents and appearance of these letters and memos, especially those she received as an applicant, made a favorable impression on Jacqueline, conveying professionalism through their format, structure, and design.

Format

HR letters may be written in one of two formats: full block or semiblock. In the full-block format, all the lines of the letter are aligned flush with the left margin. The sample letter in Chapter 1 was written in full-block form. The semiblock format allows for placement of the date, complimentary close, and signature closer to the right margin. In addition, paragraphs may be indented five spaces. Either format is acceptable. Memos may also be written in a full-block or semiblock format.

Structure

The structure of an HR letter should consist of the following ten components:

1. *Date.* The date can appear flush with the left margin or close to the right margin. As long as it aligns with the complimentary close and signature, the choice is yours. The standard order of month, day, and year is appropriate, with the month always spelled out.

2. *Address.* Typically the recipient's address appears four lines below the date line, flush with the left margin. If the letter is being sent to an applicant or employee at home, address the person as "Mr." or "Ms." If the letter is going to a person's office, include the professional title and company name. Numbered streets should be spelled out for streets numbered one through ten; arabic numerals should be used for streets numbered

eleven and above.

3. *Salutation.* The salutation appears two lines below the inside address and is typed flush with the left margin. Using "Dear" is standard, with the *D* capitalized, unless the person holds an academic title, such as "Dr." You may use the person's first name or last, depending on the relationship. Follow the name with a colon.

4. *Contents.* Begin the first paragraph two lines below the salutation. Single-space the contents of each paragraph, and double-space between paragraphs. Use either no indentation or a five-space indentation at the beginning of each paragraph. Numbered items should be indented five spaces.

5. *Consecutive pages.* If another page is needed, drop down six spaces from the top, and place the recipient's name flush with the left margin, the page number in the center, and the date at the right margin.

6. *Complimentary close.* The complimentary close is typed two lines below the last line of the contents, lined up with the date. The best choices are *Sincerely, Sincerely yours, Yours truly,* or *Cordially.* Additional options, such as *Most sincerely* or *Most cordially yours,* are also possibilities, although a bit flowery. If you are on a first-name basis with the recipient, a friendlier complimentary close is a good choice: *Regards, Best regards, Kindest regards,* or *Best wishes.* The first letter of the first word in the complimentary close should be capitalized, and the last word should be followed by a comma.

7. *Signature block.* Type your name and title four lines below the complimentary close, flush with the left margin. Sign your name the same way it is typed, between the two. A person signing the letter for someone else should initial below and to the right of the signature.

8. *Enclosures.* If you are including an additional document with the letter, drop two lines below your typed name and title and add *Enclosure, Enc.,* or *Encl.* (flush with the left margin). If more than one document is included, put that number in parentheses after the plural enclosure reference: *Enclosures (4).* If any of the enclosures are to be signed or returned, so indicate in parentheses: *Enclosure: Employment-at-will agreement (please sign and return).*

9. *Copy list.* The words *Copy to, Copies to,* or *cc* should appear under the enclosure notation, two spaces down, lined up with the left margin. Arrange the names of multiple recipients alphabetically, unless one person (e.g., the CEO) stands out as outranking the rest. Add the person's title, company name, or any other useful information in parentheses.

10. *P.S.* The rule about postscripts in HR letters and memos is simple: don't do it. They are fine for personal letters but do not belong in business. If the P.S. message is important enough, move it into the main body. Otherwise leave it out.

Design

The use of white space—the area where there is no writing—is important in letters and memos. White space allows you to set off important information and makes it easier for the recipient to read. This means having at least a 1-inch margin on all four sides.

Documents that contain more than three paragraphs or are longer than one page should be written in a semiblock format; the paragraph indentations provide additional white space.

Forms

HR professionals work knee-deep in forms: job requisitions, job posting notices, job posting applications, employment applications, interview evaluations, selection checklists, references, performance appraisals, and exit interviews, among others. A well-developed form clarifies the information needed, as well as its placement; a poorly planned form creates confusion, eliciting inaccurate or impartial information.

Job Requisitions

[Samples 6-1–6-3]

A job requisition is designed for management to communicate departmental needs and requirements for a given job to HR. To accomplish this, the form should provide the following information:

- Job title
- Department and division
- Location
- Number of hours regularly scheduled
- Work hours and days
- Reporting relationship
- Working conditions
- Primary duties and responsibilities
- Experience and education requirements
- Intangible requirements (e.g., ability to work as a member of a team)
- Special requirements (e.g., wearing of a uniform)
- Travel

HR can fill in additional information: exemption status, grade, salary range, position in a job family, growth opportunities, and so forth.

The originator of the job requisition should conclude by providing information concerning the current status of the position: Is there an incumbent? If so, when will the position become vacant? Is this a newly created job? If so, who is currently performing the duties? The more information HR has relating to an opening, the more effective will be the effort to find a qualified candidate.

Job Posting Notices

[Samples 6-7–6-9]

Job posting notices are modified requisitions informing employees of an available opening and providing them with information that will facilitate a decision to apply. Applicants are most interested in job functions and rate of pay. Hence, emphasize duties and responsibilities, grade, and salary range.

Job Posting Applications

[Samples 6-10–6-12]

Every job posting notice should be accompanied by applications for interested employees to complete and submit to HR. The application permits employees to identify their qualifications in relation to the requirements of a job opening. Applications should include a written statement concerning employee eligibility and required approval:

> Employees who have been in their current positions for a minimum of one year and have received a satisfactory or above rating on their annual performance appraisal are eligible to apply for a posted opening. Employees who have disciplinary matters pending are ineligible. Employees may apply for as many positions as they wish; however, the signature of their current supervisor is required on each application.

Be sure to state when the applications must be submitted and to whom.

Employment Applications

[Samples 7-1–7-3]

Employment applications elicit pertinent job-related information about a candidate, enabling HR professionals and managers to make effective hiring decisions. I have seen applications that range in length from a single page (too sparse) to sixty-seven pages (ridiculously long). Most run between two to four pages, with, ideally, the following categories:

- EEO statement
- Date application is completed
- Applicant's name, address, and phone number
- Position applied for
- Hours and days available to work
- Source of referral
- Former applicant or employee status
- Relatives or friends currently employed by the company
- Above minimum legal working age
- U.S. citizenship or legal work status
- Record of convictions
- Ability to perform the essential functions of the job with or without accommodation
- U.S. military service record
- Language skills relative to the available position
- Affiliation with professional organizations relative to the available position
- Employment experience
- Education and training
- Additional qualifications
- Professional references
- Special notice to veterans and individuals with disabilities
- Agreement regarding accuracy of application contents
- Agreement regarding at-will employment

When designing an employment application, ensure that all categories are job related. Also, make the form easy for the applicant to complete by using boldface type for headings, boxes to be checked off, clear and direct language, and plenty of white space. If you find that a number of applicants overlook a particular category, it may be that the question is wedged tightly between two other categories or placed off to one side. Perhaps it is difficult to read because of type size, lack of highlighting, or ambiguous wording.

Interview Evaluations

[Samples 7-4–7-6]

Interview evaluations record an interviewer's assessment of a candidate's job suitability and should begin with spaces for the applicant's name, position applied for, department or division, and date of application. The balance of the form should be devoted to assessing job-related qualifications. A legally sound and effective way of accomplishing this is to identify a specific position requirement first and then describe the applicant's qualifications in relation to the requirement. Do not work with a form that includes categories such as "appearance," "attitude," and "personality," accompanied by boxed choices ranging from "outstanding" to "poor." This approach is highly subjective and puts you at risk of EEO scrutiny.

Selection Checklists

[Samples 7-7–7-8]

Selection checklists identify key skills, abilities, traits, and characteristics relative to a given job. They are particularly useful when comparing the qualifications of several candidates. Setting up a chart with the names of the candidates across the top and a list of job-related topics down the side makes the information on the checklist easy to decipher.

References

[Samples 7-9–7-14]

References allow interviewers to confirm information acquired during interviews, as well as ascertain additional job-related data on which to base a hiring decision. The form should request basic information, including the date, applicant's name and position applied for, person contacted, and that person's title, company, phone and fax numbers, and address.

Do not overwhelm the recipient with dozens of questions that go on for pages. Start out with an easy question that asks for confirmation of the former employee's title and dates of employment. Then select a dozen or so key categories from the job description and develop relevant, open-ended questions. Allow enough space for the recipient to answer but not so much as to be intimidating. The task can usually be accomplished within two pages.

Performance Appraisals

[Samples 9-1–9-4]

Performance appraisals identify how an employee's performance has measured up against previously agreed-on objectives, pinpoint areas requiring improvement, and identify an action plan with a new set of objectives. The appraisal form should note the employee's name, department or division, job title, appraisal period, and date of the appraisal meeting.

Instructions for completion and use of the form should be clearly written, including an explanation of the rating terms (e.g., outstanding, above average, average, below average, and unsatisfactory). Ratings should always be supported by specific examples. Most forms also have an overall rating. The evaluation portion of the form should encompass the categories relevant to a given job or job level. In this respect, some companies have separate forms for exempt and nonexempt positions. Generic categories applicable to any performance appraisal form include areas of responsibility, knowledge of the job, demonstrated skill level, communication, quality of work, quantity of work, and attendance and punctuality.

In addition to evaluating past performance, appraisal forms should call for agreed-on steps for improving performance. Accordingly, sufficient room should be made available for the evaluator's comments. Employees should be encouraged to comment on the contents of the evaluation.

The type of form used depends largely on the organization's performance appraisal method. The commonly used methods for evaluating standards of performance are management by objectives, essay evaluation, graphic rating scale, weighted checklist, behaviorally anchored rating scale, forced choice, critical incident, ranking, and paired comparison. The choice of many companies over the past few years is the 360-degree performance appraisal, consisting of feedback from a number of people who deal with an employee on a regular basis. The form for this method is generally one to two pages with five to fifteen questions and room for additional remarks. The data and perspectives are then pooled, resulting in a final evaluation.

At the end of the form, leave room for the signatures of the appraising manager, employee, next level of management, and human resources.

Because of the space required in performance appraisal forms, such forms should have an appealing look that is easy to follow. This can be accomplished through the use of such design elements as heads, boldface type, and list formats.

Bear in mind that a well-designed appraisal form is worthless if the appraising manager is not well prepared for the face-to-face meeting with the employee and fails to practice effective communication skills during the evaluation.

Exit Interviews

[Samples 9-13–9-15]

The purpose of an exit interview is to determine what aspects of the job or company practices resulted in an employee's termination. Exit interview forms are essentially questionnaires that serve as guides during the interview to ensure that important areas are not overlooked. Sample questions include the following:

- What is your reason for leaving?
- Was your job accurately represented and described at the time of hire?
- What did you enjoy most about working for this company?
- What would you have changed about your employment if you could have?
- Do you feel that you were fairly compensated for the work you did? Please explain.

Allow enough room between questions to record the employee's responses. Where possible, record direct quotations. Be certain the form identifies the employee by name, department or division, dates of employment, and salary from hire to termination. Sign the form on completion, and ask the employee to sign as well.

Note: Questionnaires are often used as a guide during an exit interview to ensure that important areas are not overlooked. The questions should be posed verbally, and any notes taken by the interviewer should be verified by the employee before signing. In addition to responding to the questions on the form, departing employees should be encouraged to add comments. The completed exit interview questionnaire should be placed in the employee's HR file.

Job Descriptions

[Samples 6-4–6-6]

A job description is a formalized document of factual and concise information, descriptive of the identity of a job, its responsibilities, and the work it entails. This multipurpose tool can be used in virtually every aspect of the employment process: recruitment, interviewing, selection, job posting, training and development, performance appraisal, promotion, transfer, disciplinary action, demotion, grievance proceedings, employee orientation, work flow analysis, salary administration structuring, clarifying relationships between jobs and work assignments, exit interviews, and outplacement.

Since job descriptions can be used for so many different purposes, care should be taken to make them as comprehensive as possible. Initially, this task will require a fair amount of time but will prove well worth the effort.

The exact contents of a job description will be dictated by the specific environment and needs of an organization. The following list provides the twelve basic categories of job information required for most positions:

- Date prepared
- Name of the job analyst
- Job title
- Division and department
- Reporting relationship
- Location of the job
- Exemption status
- Salary grade and range
- Work schedule
- Job summary
- Primary duties and responsibilities
- Job requirements

Additional categories may be relevant:

- Physical environment and working conditions
- Equipment and machinery used
- Other (such as customer contact or access to confidential information)

The format of a job description should include a well-spaced listing of duties and responsibilities, beginning with the task requiring the greatest amount of time or carrying the greatest responsibility. Accompanying this list should be a column with corresponding percentages that represent the estimated amount of time devoted to each task. In addition, each duty should be labeled *E* or *N*, for essential and nonessential functions, respectively.

Most job descriptions run from one to three pages.

Advertisements

[Samples 6-13–6-18]

If you are seeking candidates for a highly competitive field, you must compete visually with other ads, using eye-catching display ads with boldface letters, varied type size, logos, and borders. Alternating the use of black and white (e.g., white letters against a black background in one section, and reversing this in another) can be effective. Color, clever job-related language, and tasteful humor can also draw attention and still project an appropriate image.

The appearance of an ad is a reflection on the organization. Consider the image you wish to project, and proceed accordingly. Whether you are looking for individuals with very specialized skills or scouting for talent, be direct and straightforward in your wording. Job hunters should not be expected to wade through cute, nondescriptive, or unprofessional jargon to determine what positions are available or the employee qualities being sought. Make certain, too, that all language is in accordance with applicable equal employment opportunity laws. A statement confirming nondiscriminatory intent such as, "equal employment opportunity employer, M/F/V/D" (which stands for male/female/ veteran/disabled) should always be included at the end.

Also, brag about your company's standing in the industry, outstanding benefits package, and any other perks offered. Comment on some key attractions within striking distance of your company to draw applicants' interest.

Brochures

The purpose of any brochure is to highlight. Promotional booklets distributed on campus (now being supplemented, and in some instances, replaced, by CD-ROM presentations) describe the company's history, products, services, customers, work environment, and culture, as well as addressing typical questions about the work environment. Orientation materials identify the organization's philosophy, structure, benefits, policies, and expectations of its employees. These areas are also detailed in the employee handbook. Benefit packets outline all insurance-related information: eligibility, medical and dental insurance plans, life insurance options, disability, pension plans, and any other benefits (e.g., vacation and other days off, employee assistance programs, recreational activities, and dependent care services).

These are key areas that draw employees' interest. Therefore, the language must be easy to understand and the brochure visually pleasing. With so much information, break up the copy with headings in boldface type, separated by double spacing. Use drawings and photographs to represent specific text. Intersperse pages with color or borders. Use diagrams, charts, graphs, and tables where appropriate—say, to compare statistics. Use lists to emphasize some ideas that may be lost in paragraph form.

Programs

Organizations sponsor numerous programs—for example, suggestion programs inviting employees to comment on various aspects of the work environment and to offer suggestions for change; employee assistance programs (EAPs) helping employees to resolve personal problems; dependent care programs offering child and elder care options, both on site and off site; and company-sponsored activities and programs ranging from company picnics to health club memberships. The success of these programs depends in part on how effectively pertinent information is communicated.

Suggestion Programs and Attitude Surveys

[Samples 10-13–10-16]

Suggestion programs function in two ways: open and directed. *Open suggestion programs* encourage employees to contribute ideas that will improve work-related matters. A memo may appear on bulletin boards or in the company newsletter inviting employees to submit their ideas to HR. A simple statement written in large, boldface letters is sufficient.

With *directed suggestion programs* (also called *attitude surveys*) employees are asked to comment on specific work-related issues. Management might want to solicit thoughts on switching over to flextime, for example, or be interested in how employees view the personal leave practices. This type of correspondence must be specifically worded yet easy for employees to comprehend. This may be accomplished by the use of headings and boldface type. For maximum effectiveness, address no more than three issues at a time. Clearly state how you want employees to respond (e.g., check off boxes or write in comments) and whether replies are anonymous. Indicate, too, the deadline and place where the forms are to be submitted, and when the results of their responses will be made known. Keep the form to one page; more employees are likely to respond.

Employee Assistance Programs

[Samples 10-1–10-3]

Employee assistance programs (EAPs) are best described in brochures that highlight services provided, location, phone number, hours, fees, and procedure for participation. Confidentiality should be stressed. The information should be printed in an easy-to-read type, with headings, preferably in color, to separate topics. Double spacing is recommended. Illustrations of typical problems might be included: drug or alcohol abuse, divorce, parenting issues, and relationship concerns, among others. A wallet-sized card with the name, location, phone number, and hours of the EAP will facilitate employee decisions to avail themselves of the service. One company offers a variation on this theme by distributing a magnet in the shape of a telephone with the essential information printed on it.

Dependent Care Programs

[Sections 10-4–10-6]

Increasingly employers nationwide are responding to the need for a greater balance between work and family by heeding the call for child and elder care programs. For working parents or employees who are also caretakers of their own elderly parents, the need for quality dependent care programs is undeniable.

When preparing a report for senior management on the merits of a company-sponsored dependent care program, present data in an easy-to-read format. Use graphs and tables to demonstrate the impact of dependent care on such factors as productivity and motivation in similar organizations. Charts are also helpful, enclosed in borders to set them apart from the text, as are photographs and illustrations of actual facilities.

Include statistics to support your recommendations, but do not place them all in one portion of the report. This can be taxing for readers who have to digest many numbers all at once. Sprinkle the figures throughout the document, linking them with specific suggestions.

In addition, since this is going to be a lengthy report, use headings and subheadings, double-space the text, indent for each new paragraph, and periodically summarize the information.

To enhance the report, include the following:

1. A cover page with a statement or quotation summarizing the gist of your report. Repeat or paraphrase the statement every few pages in the body of your report as a reminder of its significance.
2. A Contents page.
3. A list of photographs and illustrations.
4. A list of resources.
5. Common questions concerning dependent care programs.
6. A final summary.

Literature relating to a company-sponsored dependent care program can parallel an EAP brochure. Highlight eligibility, cost, scope of services, location, and procedures. Photos and illustrations will assist employees to visualize the services.

Company-Sponsored Activities and Programs

[Samples 10-7–10-10]

A brochure describing recreation and social programs is likely to become employees' favorite HR-generated document. In it they will read about health clubs and gyms, weight-loss programs, stop-smoking clinics, country club membership, holiday parties, special dinners, picnics, sports activities, travel services, credit unions, raffles, discount tickets for theater, sports, cultural and public events, and any other activity or service your company offers.

With a dozen or more potential programs, organizing the information in a pamphlet that is not overwhelming can be a challenge. Bear in mind that employees will want to know the basics of each offering: what it is, how much it costs, and who to see for more information. One option, then, is to take each topic, present it apart from the others—by enclosing it within a box or with plenty of white space—and provide three statements encompassing the essential categories. Each one can be distinguished by a different color (which can be costly) or a distinct typeface. Another possibility is to group the services according to type. For example, a heading that reads "wellness programs" might group together health clubs, stop-smoking clinics, and weight-loss programs. Yet another option is to have more than one brochure; certain major programs could be announced separately from other programs that would be described in a single pamphlet.

If your company offers many options, limit or eliminate the use of photos or illustrations in the brochure to avoid an overly busy or distracting appearance. But if your menu is limited, pictures will enhance the descriptions and promote employees' appreciation of each option. Quotations from employees, briefly describing how wonderful a particular program is, can further the "sales" effort.

Policies

[Samples 11-1–11-9]

Company policies come in two forms: employee handbooks, identifying employer expectations in addition to employee rights and obligations, and HR manuals, to assist managers and supervisors with managing day-to-day employer-employee relations.

For maximum effectiveness, these documents require the following organizational elements:

- *Title page.* This should include the name of the document, company logo, effective date, name of the employee who prepared the material, and the person to contact with questions.

- *Introduction.* The purpose of the document and how it is to be used should appear on a separate page.

- *Message from the chief executive officer.* This message sets the tone for the handbook or manual. The CEO message should welcome new employees. In addition, both the handbook and the manual should contain a statement regarding the company's commitment to policies and procedures contained in it. A statement concerning senior management's commitment to EEO should be included. Three distinct paragraphs will make an impressive beginning.

- *Table of contents.* Both employees and managers must be able to locate topics quickly. Depending on the size of your organization and the number of topics to be included, the table of contents is typically arranged in one of two ways: alphabetically for a limited number of topics or functionally, whereby topics are grouped under broader titles.

- *Page numbering system.* When choosing the best page numbering system, consider ease of use and updating. Companies using an alphabetical table of contents tend to prefer a consecutive numbering system. Those that rely on a functional approach use a decimal system tied in with each major section (e.g., 1.1, 1.2, 1.3, . . . , 2.1, 2.2, 2.3).

- *Index.* Cross-referencing topics will enable the user to locate easily all the information covering a given issue. For example, the topic "attendance" should also be indexed under "absences" and "tardiness."

- *Employment-at-will statement.* HR manuals and employee handbooks are increasingly viewed as legally binding contracts. Accordingly, companies are advised to develop at-will policies for inclusion at the end of these documents. Consider the following sample from an employee handbook:

> This handbook has been designed to serve as a general summary of our current policies, procedures, and benefits for general information purposes. It provides guidance with regard to what you may expect from us and what we expect

from you. We will make every effort to recognize the privileges described herein, unless doing so would impair the operation of business or expose the company to legal liability or financial loss. No provision of this handbook is to be construed as a guarantee of employment.

Note that this disclaimer may not be sufficient to provide legal protection against charges of unlawful termination. Consult with an attorney for the most appropriate at-will language tailored to your organization.

‣ *Acknowledgment.* Ask employees to acknowledge having read and understood the contents of the handbook; managers and supervisors should do the same with the HR manual. However, this acknowledgment is not a substitute for training in the proper use of these documents.

The contents of employee handbooks and HR manuals should be uniformly organized and written in clear, concise, complete, and consistent language.

- ‣ Choose headings that properly identify the subjects.
- ‣ Substitute efficient words for excessive phrases.
- ‣ Use the active voice.
- ‣ Avoid jargon.
- ‣ Make definite statements.
- ‣ Use specific language.
- ‣ Avoid opinions.
- ‣ Use transitions between ideas so readers can follow the logical progression of your thoughts.
- ‣ Use proper grammar, punctuation, spelling, and word usage.
- ‣ Convey a positive tone.

Counseling and Discipline

[Samples 9-9–9-12, 9-16]

Counseling may be defined as interaction between an employee and his or her manager focusing on a specific work-related issue. It may be preventive or corrective in nature. In either instance, the ultimate goal is for employees to function more effectively on the job.

Disciplinary action might be brought against an employee when counseling fails to produce agreed-on results. For most infractions, such as excessive tardiness or absenteeism, an established disciplinary procedure is implemented, beginning with a verbal warning, followed by two written warnings, then suspension, and, finally, termination.

The documentation of counseling and disciplinary sessions should be tightly structured, with the following twelve components:

1. Date.
2. Employee's name, title, and department or division.
3. Manager's name and title.
4. Reason for the documentation.
5. Reference to a specific work-related issue for counseling documentation or a particular infraction in the case of a disciplinary matter. With regard to the latter,

identify the specific section of the employee handbook that identifies unacceptable behavior.

6. Relative facts, including dates, times, and the names of anyone else involved,
   including witnesses. Use clear and precise language; do not express opinions or
   draw conclusions.
7. The next step.
8. The consequences of subsequent infractions.
9. Manager's signature and the date.
10. Employee's signature indicating understanding of the contents and the date.
11. Employee's comments.
12. Signature of witnesses, if any, and the date.

Since this is a formal document, the full-block format is recommended.

Newsletters

[Samples 10-11–10-12]

Interesting newsletters contain a mixture of business news, company-sponsored events,
introductions or new employees, and employee-related announcements. They generally
run from one to four pages in length and are published monthly.

There is no visual limit to the format for a newsletter. Variations in design, as well
as the use of graphics, will attract readers and enhance the contents. Use various colors,
fonts, type size, photos, illustrations, diagrams, tables, graphs, and charts. Alternate, too,
the kind of format selected for the text. In addition to full block and modified block, try
the hanging-indented format: The first line of each paragraph is flush with the left margin, all of the other lines are indented five spaces, and single spacing is used within the
paragraph—for example:

> This style, dramatic and unconventional, is not recommended for serious docu-
> ments; however, the hanging-indented format might work well in the less
> formal pages of a company newsletter.

Other format choices include lining up the text in two or more columns and encasing
selected passages, quotations, or announcements in boxes or other shapes.

Summary

It can take as few as 4 seconds for the person receiving your HR document to react to
what may have taken you hours, days, or longer to write. Accordingly, the way it is
presented—that is, its structure, format, and design—can make the difference between
acceptance and rejection.

Letters should be written in one of two formats: full block or semiblock. The structure should consist of the date, recipient's address, salutation, contents, complimentary
close, and signature block. Allow at least 1 inch of white space on all four sides to make
it easier for the recipient to read.

HR professionals generate a multitude of forms, among them job requisitions, employment applications, references, performance appraisals, and exit interviews. HR forms should be well designed and provide clear instructions for their completion.

Job descriptions are formalized documents describing the requirements and responsibilities of a given job. Although the exact contents of this multipurpose tool will be dictated by the specific needs of an organization, every job description should include a well-spaced listing of tasks, beginning with the one requiring the greatest amount of time or carrying the greatest responsibility. Each of these tasks should be identified as essential or nonessential.

Advertisements should stand out visually, through the use of boldface letters, varied type size, logos, borders, white space, and color. The language should be direct and straightforward.

Promotional booklets, orientation materials, and benefits packets highlight selected aspects about a company. The design of these brochures should be visually pleasing and the language easy to understand.

Organizations sponsor numerous programs, including suggestions programs, EAPs, dependent care programs, and various activities. The success of these programs depends in part on how effectively pertinent information is communicated.

Employee handbooks identify employer expectations and employee rights and obligations; HR manuals assist managers and supervisors with managing day-to-date employer-employee relations. Both of these documents require certain organizational elements, including a message from the chief executive officer, a table of contents, an easy-to-follow page numbering system, an index, an employment-at-will statement, and a statement of acknowledgment.

Counseling is interaction between an employee and his or her manager focusing on a specific work-related issue. Disciplinary action may be brought against an employee when counseling fails to produce agreed-on results. The documentation of counseling and disciplinary sessions should be tightly structured, including reference to a specific work-related issue or infraction, relative facts, and appropriate signatures. Since this is a formal document, the full-block format is recommended.

Newsletters reflect a combination of business news, company-sponsored events, introductions of new employees, and employee-related announcements. Variations in design, as well as the use of graphics and format selected for the text, will attract readers and enhance the contents.

Having familiarized yourself with the components of effective HR writing, examined the elements of style and tone, learned the seven stages of writing, identified writing pitfalls, and reviewed the appropriate structure, format, and design of various HR documents, it is time to turn to Section Two, a collection of more than one hundred writing samples.

Section Two
Samples of Human Resources Documents

Samples of Human Resources Documents

6

Recruiting

Organizations typically generate six types of HR documents as part of the recruiting process: requisitions, job descriptions, job posting notices, job posting applications, job advertisements, and letters to applicants as to whether they have been selected for interviews. Write each document by focusing on its overall objective and intended purpose. Consider, too, your likely audience. Then write in an appropriate style, tone, and format, and include the necessary topics or categories.

Job Requisition Forms

Objective: Communicates overall departmental needs and requirements for a given job in accordance with applicable EEO laws

Purpose: To inform

Readers: HR representatives responsible for recruitment

Style: Standard and familiar phrases, limited jargon

Tone: Descriptive, factual, clear

Format: Heads, boldface type, varying fonts and point sizes, white space, boxes, columns, borders

Contents: Job title, department, location, schedule, reporting relationship, unusual working conditions, responsibilities and educational or work experience requirements, and current status. (Categories of exemption status, grade, and salary range can be provided by HR.)

Sample 6-1

This job requisition form clearly communicates some of the basic information HR needs to begin the recruitment process. The use of boldface type for headings, ample white space, borders, and boxes for checking off relevant status creates an easy-to-read format.

Especially impressive is the wording that introduces the services that would not be performed without this position. Thereby, the reader can appreciate the importance of filling this position.

The form could be improved by allotting space for a description of the duties and position requirements.

Sample 6-1

REQUISITION FOR EMPLOYEE

Date Initiated _____   Date Needed _____

POSITION INFORMATION

STATUS

☐ Regular Full Time

☐ Regular Part Time

☐ Exempt

☐ Non-Exempt

☐ Budgeted Addition to Staff

☐ Unbudgeted Addition to Staff

Replacement of _____

No. of hours regularly scheduled/week _____

Work hours/days _____   FTE _____

CURRENT POSITION DATA	**CHANGE IN POSITION DATA**
Title _____	Title _____
Comp. # _____ Grade _____	Comp. # _____ Grade _____
Hiring Range _____	Hiring Range _____
Department _____	Department _____
Location _____	Location _____

Describe the service that would not be performed without this position.

_____

_____

_____

APPROVALS

Immediate Supervisor	Date
Manager with Budget Authority	Date
SMG Member	Date
President/CEO	Date
Human Resources	Date

FOR HUMAN RESOURCE DEPARTMENT USE ONLY: Posting Date: _____   End of Posting: _____

Filled by:	
Starting Date:	Salary: $
Recruiter:	

Revised 9301

Sample 6-2

This job requisition form is completed by managers seeking to hire temporary employees. It offers a great deal of information, providing HR with what is essential to fill the slot. Managers will appreciate the check-off format that minimizes the amount of additional writing.

The arrangement of information is well designed. Two important categories—essential skills and physical requirements—stand out by being especially well located in the center of the page and boxed in with double borders. The use of columns also facilitates a focus on key information.

Noting the percentage of time certain physical tasks will require is helpful, particularly when recruiting individuals with disabilities. Note, too, the company's statement at the bottom of the page with reference to providing reasonable accommodations for qualified individuals with disabilities.

Sample 6-2

TEMPORARY PERSONNEL REQUEST FORM

THE HUMAN RESOURCES DEPARTMENT IS THE ONLY GROUP AUTHORIZED TO FILL TEMPORARY ASSIGNMENTS AND TO NEGOTIATE ANY FEES FOR THE ASSIGNMENT.

Requesting Department _____	Charge to Dept. No. _____
Department Manager _____	Telephone Ext. _____
Temp Name _____	Replacement for _____
Temp Job Title _____	Temp Agency _____
Assignment Begins _____	Assignment Ends _____ Renewal _____

\# Hours
Needed/Day ___ Full time _____ Part time _____ Requested by _____

ESSENTIAL JOB FUNCTIONS (Briefly describe reason for this request and nature of work to be done.)

_____

_____

INDICATE ESSENTIAL SKILLS REQUIRED	Typing: words/minute	PC
Dictating Equipment	Word Processor	Telephone (# of lines)
Wizard Mail	Calculator/Adding Machine	Other

% of Time	PHYSICAL REQUIREMENTS		% of Time
	Use written (verbal visual) sources of information, e.g., read reports, procedural documentation, reference materials.	Stand	___
	Use non-verbal visual sources of information, e.g., reference graphs, tables.	Sit	___
		Reach	___
	Perform detailed work requiring visual acuity, e.g., repair electronic equipment.	Grasp	___
		Lift/Carry	___
	Use non-verbal auditory sources of information, e.g., alarms, beepers	Walk	___
		Climb	___
	Use oral communication to perform work, e.g., answer telephone, receive visitors.	Kneel	___
		Squat/Bend	___
	Digital dexterity, e.g., using computer keyboard.	Push/Pull	___

PLEASE CHECK AS APPROPRIATE Within budget ____ Over budget (____) Unbudgeted (____)

AUTHORIZATION SIGNATURES (to be obtained prior to submission of form to HR Department)

Supervisor _____ Date _____

Next Level _____ Date _____

SMG Member _____ Date _____

HUMAN RESOURCES DEPARTMENT USE ONLY   Job Code _____

COST CALCULATIONS

Total Temp Hours _____ X Hourly Rate $ _____ = Total Department Cost $ _____

VP Human Resources _____ Date_____

Director Human Resources _____ Date_____

Temp Coordinator _____ Date_____

will provide reasonable accommodations for qualified individuals with a disability.

Sample 6-3

This straightforward, easy-to-read job requisition form contains all the necessary categories for the manager to complete, thereby providing HR with the information needed to fill the opening.

Sample 6-3

Job Requisition Form

Job title: Exemption status:
Division/Department: Reason for opening:
Reporting relationship: Work schedule:
Location of job: Grade/Salary range:

Summary of primary duties and responsibilities:

Education, prior work experience, and specialized skills and knowledge:

Working conditions:

Equipment/Machinery used:

Other:

Signatures:

_____   _____
name (requesting manager)   title

_____   _____
name (department head)   title

_____   _____
name (human resources representative)   title

Job Descriptions

Objective: Identifies primary and secondary duties, responsibilities and requirements of a job

Purpose: To inform

Readers: HR representatives responsible for recruiting and interviewing, managers in charge of the available position, applicants applying for the opening

Style: Formal, jargon limited to common job-specific terms, active voice, consistent

Tone: Factual, descriptive, clear

Format: Heads, boldface type, white space, lists, columns, boxes, varying fonts and type sizes

Contents: Date, name of analyst, title, department, location, reporting relationship, exemption status, salary grade and range, work schedule, job summary, primary duties, requirements, other categories (e.g., working conditions, equipment used)

Sample 6-4

With the exception of failing to note the work schedule, this position description form is comprehensive, identifying all of the necessary categories. It is easy to read and well organized. The box format, with columns for physical and mental requirements, provides visual relief from the narrative required under the two preceding headings: "Purpose of the Position" and "Essential Functions."

The form contains additional categories that provide useful information, including percentage of time required of each task, measurement of performance, and internal and external relationships.

Sample 6-4

POSITION DESCRIPTION

POSITION TITLE		COMPLEMENT NO.	
DIVISION/DEPARTMENT		LOCATION	
JOB CODE	GRADE	EXEMPT	NON EXEMPT

PURPOSE OF THE POSITION:

ESSENTIAL FUNCTIONS

PHYSICAL AND MENTAL REQUIREMENTS (The following physical and mental requirements pertain only to the above "essential functions" of the position. Please indicate the approximate % of time spent on each function [will exceed 100%].)

% of Time	PHYSICAL REQUIREMENTS		% of Time
	Use written (verbal visual) sources of information, e.g., read reports, procedural documentation, reference materials.	Stand Sit	____ ____
	Use non-verbal visual sources of information, e.g., reference graphs, tables.	Reach Grasp Lift/Carry	____ ____ ____
	Perform detailed work requiring visual acuity, e.g., repair electronic equipment.	Walk Climb	____ ____
	Use non-verbal auditory sources of information, e.g., alarms, beepers	Kneel Squat/Bend	____ ____
	Use oral communication to perform work, e.g., answer telephone, receive visitors.	Push/Pull	____
	Digital dexterity, e.g., using computer keyboard.		

% of Time	MENTAL REQUIREMENTS
	Make minor decisions requiring limited judgment, e.g., task sequencing, filing, sorting mail.
	Make general decisions in the absence of specific directions, e.g., prioritizing.
	Perform activities requiring sustained concentration, e.g., designing, planning.

% of Time	OTHER PHYSICAL OR MENTAL REQUIREMENTS

ADDITIONAL FUNCTIONS

MEASUREMENT OF PERFORMANCE

RELATIONSHIPS

Internal:

External:

EQUIPMENT (e.g., PC, typewriter, calculator, copy machines, telephone, etc.)

QUALIFICATIONS (e.g., education, training, experience, licenses and skills)

PREPARED BY	DATE
APPROVED BY	DATE
HUMAN RESOURCES	DATE

posdescr

Sample 6-5

The following job description is designed to simplify matters. Unfortunately, in striving for simplicity, several critical categories—such as reporting relationship, work schedule, and summary of duties and responsibilities—have been omitted, rendering the job description incomplete.

Title: _____ Date: _____

Department: _____

Essential job duties:

_____

_____

_____

_____

_____

_____

_____

_____

_____

_____

Nonessential job duties:

_____

_____

_____

_____

Education/Experience Required:

Sample 6-6

Here is a completed job description for an assistant to the director of human resources. The categories on the form are all relevant and well placed. Especially effective is the request for essential and nonessential functions and percentage of time devoted to each task.

The summary statement is succinct and clearly written. Listing the primary duties and responsibilities facilitates reading and comprehension. In addition, each task begins with an action word that implies its levels, scope, and nature of responsibilities.

Education and prior work experience are defined in broad-based terms, as opposed to a specific number of years. This form allows the recruiter great latitude in selecting the best candidate.

Sample 6-6

Sample Job Description

Job Description

Job title: Assistant to the Director of Human Resources

Division/Department: Human Resources

Reporting relationship: Director of Human Resources

Location of job: Headquarters

Work schedule: 9:00 A.M. to 5:00 P.M., Monday through Friday; overtime as
required.

Exemption status: Exempt

Grade/Salary range: Grade 14; $38,500–$54,500 (midpoint: $46,500)

Summary of duties and responsibilities: Assists the Director of Human Resources in the HR-related matters concerning the organization's 1,000 employees. This includes the areas of recruitment, interviewing, hiring, benefits,
orientation, policies and procedures, job descriptions, compensation, performance reviews, records, EEO and affirmative action, and exit interviews.

Primary duties and responsibilities:
(E) = essential functions (N) = nonessential functions

*Percentage of time
devoted to each task*

20	1. (E) Recruits applicants for nonexempt positions.
20	2. (E) Interviews and screens applicants for nonexempt positions; refers qualified candidates to appropriate department managers.
8	3. (E) Assists manager with hiring decisions.
8	4. (E) Performs reference checks on potential employees, by telephone or in writing.

8	5. (E) Processes new employees for payroll and benefits; informs new employees of all pertinent information.
8	6. (E) Conveys all necessary insurance information to employees and assists them with questions, processing of claims, and other related areas.
5	7. (E) Helps Director of Human Resources plan and conduct each month's organizational orientation program.
5	8. (E) Assists in the implementation of policies and procedures; may be required to explain or interpret certain policies.
5	9. (E) Assists in the development and maintenance of up-to-date job descriptions for nonexempt positions throughout the company.
5	10. (E) Assists in the maintenance and administration of the organization's compensation program; monitors salary increase recommendations as they are received to ensure compliance with merit increase guidelines.
2	11. (E) Advises managers of schedules for employee performance appraisals; follows up on delinquent or inconsistent appraisals.
2	12. (N) Maintains orderly, systematic employee records and files.
2	13. (E) Maintains all necessary HR records and reports; this includes unemployment insurance reports, flow-log recording, EEO reports, and change notices.
1	14. (E) Assists EEO officer with advising managers on matters of EEO and affirmative action as they pertain to the interviewing and hiring process and employer-employee relations.
1	15. (E) Conducts exit interviews for terminating nonexempt employees.

Performs other related duties and assignments as required.

Education, prior work experience, and specialized skills and knowledge: Thorough general knowledge and understanding of the human resources function; prior human resources experience, preferably as a generalist or a nonexempt interviewer in an environment similar to this one; demonstrated ability to work effectively with all levels of management and employees; ability to deal effectively with applicants and referral sources.

Physical environment/working conditions: Private office in the Human Resources Department.

(continues)

Sample 6-6. Continued.

Equipment/machinery used: IBM personal computer

Other (e.g., customer contact or access to confidential information):   Access to all confidential information regarding employees.

Job analyst: Diane Arthur

Date: May 15, 1996

Job Posting Notices

Objective: Specifies grade level, overall responsibilities, salary range, and reporting relationship of an available job

Purpose: To inform

Readers: Employees interested in changing jobs within the company

Style: Standard and familiar phrases

Tone: Descriptive, clear, concise, factual

Format: Heads, boldface type, varying fonts and type sizes, white space, boxes, lists

Contents: Emphasize duties and responsibilities, grade, and salary range; provide clear instructions regarding posting procedures and eligibility

Sample 6-7

The heading "Job Opportunity" is inviting and projects a positive tone. All of the categories are relevant and easy to locate on the form. Instructions for the disposition of applications are clearly written; however, there is no mention of eligibility requirements. The statement near the bottom regarding relocation expenses could be replaced with a category for reimbursement, to be checked off if the available position qualifies. While not required, the EEO/AA claim at the end of the form projects an image of commitment to employment equality on the part of management.

Sample 6-7

JOB OPPORTUNITY

EMPLOYEES INTERESTED IN BEING CONSIDERED FOR THE POSITION DESCRIBED BELOW SHOULD MAKE IT KNOWN TO THE HUMAN RESOURCES DEPARTMENT WITHIN SEVEN WORKING DAYS OF THE DATE OF THIS ANNOUNCEMENT. APPLICATIONS MUST BE RECEIVED BY THE HUMAN RESOURCES DEPARTMENT BY 5:00 P.M. ON THE DAY OF EXPIRATION.

All internal candidates will be advised as to the disposition of their application.

Job Title_____ **Grade**____ **Exempt**___ **Nonexempt**___

Department_____ **Location**_____

ESSENTIAL JOB FUNCTIONS

QUALIFICATIONS

REPORTING RELATIONSHIP

DATE OF NOTICE_____ **DATE OF EXPIRATION**_____

EXEMPT POSITIONS ARE POSTED AT ALL   LOCATIONS. HOWEVER, ONLY SELECTED POSITIONS ARE ELIGIBLE FOR RELOCATION EXPENSES. QUALIFIED CANDIDATES WILL BE NOTIFIED WHETHER RELOCATION EXPENSES ARE AVAILABLE FOR THE POSITION FOR WHICH THEY ARE APPLYING.

WILL PROVIDE REASONABLE ACCOMMODATIONS FOR QUALIFIED INDIVIDUALS WITH A DISABILITY.
An EEO/AA Employer m/f/d/v -- ADA Compliance organization

Sample 6-8

This completed job posting notice is for two openings: an office services assistant and a tax department secretary. In each instance, the job requirements and necessary skills are provided.

Employees would benefit from additional information, such as grade levels, exemption status, salary ranges, and reporting relationships. Also, instructions for scheduling an interview are vague. Is there a job posting application? Are employees required to notify their current supervisors before contacting HR? A statement clarifying the procedure would be helpful.

JOB POSTINGS

Office Services Assistant

JOB REQUIREMENTS ARE: maintain daily schedules, process department invoices, handle purchase orders, publish internal directories, calculate department time cards, provide audio room backup, maintain numerous lists and databases, answer phones, provide switchboard and fax room coverage and provide clerical support.

SKILLS REQUIRED: good organizational skills, strong computer skills, ability to handle diverse jobs, ability to work well with others

DEADLINE FOR SCHEDULING AN INTERVIEW: WEDNESDAY MAY 17th

Tax Department Secretary

JOB REQUIREMENTS ARE: typing, filing tax returns, answering phones, photocopying, labeling and organizing folders, mailings

SKILLS REQUIRED: good organizational skills, hardworking individual, good phone skills

DEADLINE FOR SCHEDULING AN INTERVIEW: WEDNESDAY MAY 17th

If you are interested in applying for either of these positions, please notify your supervisor and then contact me at extension 288.

Sample 6-9

The design of this form enables employees to determine quickly if the posted position is of interest. In addition, the eligibility requirements and application procedure are clearly listed, providing employees with the information necessary to proceed.

Sample 6-9

Job-Posting Notice Form

Job-Posting Notice

Job title:

Division/Department:

Location:

Summary of primary duties and responsibilities:

Exemption status: Grade/Salary range:

Work schedule/Working conditions:

Qualifications/Requirements:

Closing date:

Job-Posting Eligibility Requirements:

1. You must be employed by XYZ, Inc., for at least 12 consecutive months.
2. You must be in your present position for a minimum of 6 months.
3. You must meet the qualifications/requirements listed above.
4. Your most recent evaluation must reflect your job performance as satisfactory or better.
5. You must notify your immediate supervisor/manager of your intent to submit a job-posting application.

Job-Posting Application Procedure:

1. Complete a job-posting application form, available in the Human Resources Department.
2. Return the completed form to the Human Resources Department and give a copy to your immediate supervisor/manager by the closing date noted above.
3. You will be contacted within three working days of receipt of your application.

Job Posting Applications

Objective: Permits employees to compare their qualifications with the requirements of a given job opening

Purpose: To inform

Readers—Blank Form: Employees interested in changing jobs within the company

Readers—Completed Form: HR representatives in charge of employee applications for promotions or transfers; managers with the available opening

Style: Standard and familiar phrases

Tone: Clear, factual, direct

Format: Boxes, columns, heads and subheads, boldface type, different fonts and type sizes, white space, lists

Contents: Employee name; position applied for; current job title, department, supervisor, grade, and salary. Optional: qualifications and career goals. A description of employee eligibility and required approval, similar to the one on the job posting notice, should appear as well.

Sample 6-10

An informative, easy-to-complete format, with comprehensive and relevant categories, characterizes this job posting application. Repeatedly using *your* and *you* personalizes the form. Offering to interview employees without the consent of their current supervisors exhibits sensitivity.

<u>Job Posting Application</u>

If you have been employed by us for a minimum of 18 consecutive months, have been in your current position for at least one year, and have received a satisfactory or above evaluation at the time of your most recent performance review, you are eligible to apply for posted positions.

Submit your completed job posting application to the Human Resources Department before the closing date noted on the accompanying job posting notice. Requests for interviews by HR without your supervisor's approval will be considered.

Name_____Date_____

Current Job Title_____Department_____

Supervisor_____Salary/Grade_____

Job Posting Position_____Department_____

Qualifications (education and experience within and outside this company)_____

_____

_____

_____

_____

_____

_____

_____

_____

_____

_____

_____

Employee's Signature_____Supervisor's Signature_____

Sample 6-11

The non-nonsense, authoritative tone of this form renders it most suitable for use in a regimented work environment. Note these examples of forceful words used in the job posting requirements: "Job transfer from posted openings will not be made unless transfer represents a promotion"; Job transfer . . . will not be made because of working conditions . . . or other similar factors"; an employee . . . will be ineligible for another transfer on a posted job for six months." Use of positive language would make the form more inviting and employee friendly.

The space for comments does not clearly communicate what the employees should write: Credentials? Experience? Reasons for wanting the job? Reasons for wanting to leave their current positions? Any of these constitutes a logical response.

Sample 6-11

APPLICATION FOR JOB POSTING

Name of Applicant _____ Date _____

Applied for Position _____

Division _____ Department _____

Present Div. _____ Present Section _____ Present Dept. _____

Telephone Ext. _____ Present Supervisor _____

Supervisor's Signature _____

Comments:

JOB POSTING REQUIREMENTS:

1. EMPLOYEE WILL MAKE WRITTEN APPLICATION IN PERSON TO THE INDUSTRIAL RELATIONS DEPARTMENT WITH A COPY TO THE IMMEDIATE SUPERVISOR.

2. JOB TRANSFER FROM POSTED OPENINGS WILL NOT BE MADE UNLESS TRANSFER REPRESENTS A PROMOTION FOR THE INDIVIDUAL.

3. JOB TRANSFER RESULTING FROM JOB POSTING WILL NOT BE MADE BECAUSE OF WORKING CONDITIONS, WORKING HOURS OR OTHER SUCH SIMILAR FACTORS.

4. AN EMPLOYEE WILL NOT BE ELIGIBLE TO APPLY FOR A POSTED JOB UNTIL SIX MONTHS OF CONTINUOUS EMPLOYMENT WITH THE CORPORATION IS COMPLETED.

5. AN EMPLOYEE WHO HAS TRANSFERRED ON A POSTED JOB WILL BE INELIGIBLE FOR ANOTHER TRANSFER ON A POSTED JOB FOR SIX MONTHS.

ORIGINAL COPY TO INDUSTRIAL RELATIONS DEPARTMENT
YELLOW COPY TO IMMEDIATE SUPERVISOR

2-0896-00

Sample 6-12

This posting application takes an employee by the hand and provides a gentle guide through the categories. Not only does the form tell the employee what information to provide, it specifies how to complete certain sections—for example, "in a narrative paragraph" and "List any courses." The section devoted to related work experience requires that the candidate provide dates, as well as duties performed.

The format and design of the application facilitate the identification of relevant factors by HR.

Adding the EEO-related statements at the bottom of the first page signifies management's commitment to equal employment.

Sample 6-12

INTERNAL JOB APPLICATION

Name	Ext.	Date

Present Job Title _____ Grade _____

Present Department _____

Date of Latest Merit Review   /   /   Reviewer

Posted Job Title _____ Grade _____

Department   Posting Date   /   /

What are your career goals?

_____
_____

In a narrative paragraph, discuss any other special skills or related work experience which qualify you for this position.

_____
_____
_____
_____
_____
_____
_____
_____

List any courses you have taken since you became an employee with Avedon.

_____
_____

List other relevant courses you have taken since you became an employee with Avedon.

_____
_____

Degrees Obtained	School	Date

Avedon will provide reasonable accommodations for qualified individuals with a disability.
AN EEO/AA EMPLOYER M/F/D/V - ADA COMPLIANCE ORGANIZATION

List related work experience which helps qualify you for the posted position.

From _____ To _____ Job Title _____

Duties Performed _____

_____

_____

_____

_____

From _____ To _____ Job Title _____

Duties Performed _____

_____

_____

_____

_____

From _____ To _____ Job Title _____

Duties Performed _____

_____

_____

_____

_____

From _____ To _____ Job Title _____

Duties Performed _____

_____

_____

_____

_____

Interviewed by: _____

Comments: _____

_____

Interviewed by: _____

Comments: _____

_____

Final Recommendation:

Job Advertisements

Objective: Attracts qualified candidates

Purpose: To inform and influence

Readers: Individuals currently unemployed, those currently employed but seeking a change in job, employees basically content in their work but curious about other possibilities

Style: Active voice, job-specific jargon

Tone: Descriptive, factual, friendly, positive, persuasive, intriguing, arousing curiosity

Format: Different type sizes and fonts, underlining, boldface type, italics, white space, logo, graphics, borders

Contents: Job title; identity or, if a blind ad, description of the organization; position description and qualifications (degree of detail depends on whether you are scouting for general talent or looking for someone with specific skills and knowledge); benefits

Sample 6-13

The format and design of this ad contradict the level of the available position. A company "seeking an individual to assume the key role of President and Chief Operating Officer" would make a more effective statement if the ad were more compatible with the status of the opening. This could be accomplished by making it larger, varying the size and boldness of print, using more white space, and adding graphics, such as a company logo.

Information as to the qualifications being sought and job specifications are clearly and concisely presented.

PRESIDENT

National administrative services company is seeking individual to assume the key role of President and Chief Operating Officer.

Successful candidate will have a minimum of ten years senior management experience and a strong financial and analytical background. The President and COO will be responsible for overseeing the development of the organization and must possess superior interpersonal and leadership abilities. Send resume with salary history to **Director of Human Resources, Keyboard Communications, Inc. One Old Country Road, Suite 200, Carle Place, NY 11514, Fax (516) 742-8777.**

Courtesy: Keyboard Communications, Inc.

Sample 6-14

This ad, which begins with a brief description of the hospital and rehabilitation center's philosophy, succeeds in conveying a dual message of patient commitment and growth.

The requirements of eligibility for both physical therapist and physical therapy assistant positions are concisely stated. Instructions for submitting resumés are clear.

The ad's text is effectively staggered toward the end, balanced by graphics and the name of the organization. The use of white ink on a black background for the job titles is eye-catching.

The spelling error of the word *strategically* detracts slightly from an otherwise effective ad.

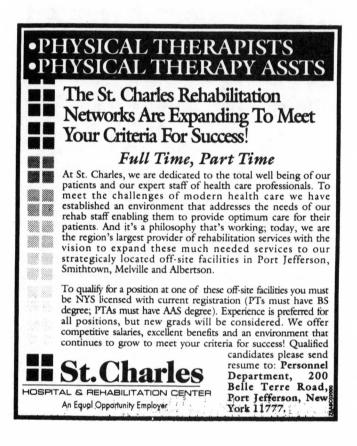

Courtesy: St. Charles Hospital & Rehabilitation Center.

Sample 6-15

This is a real eye-catcher! The graphic depictions of various nations combined with the question-answer, "Do you speak any of these languages? If so, can we talk?" is an effective way to capture the reader's attention.

Separating the text from the graphics signals the reader to stop looking and start reading. This delineation is effectively done in two ways: with columns and the reversal of white ink on a black background.

The description of the organization is interesting. Requirements for the job are identified in relation to the ideal candidate, and skills are noted as preferred. This approach invites a broad array of responses and gives the company great flexibility in selection of candidates.

Choices on how to (and not to) contact the company are clearly stated.

Sample 6-15

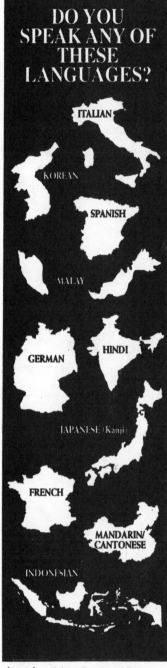

DO YOU SPEAK ANY OF THESE LANGUAGES?

ITALIAN

KOREAN

SPANISH

MALAY

GERMAN

HINDI

JAPANESE (Kanji)

FRENCH

MANDARIN/ CANTONESE

INDONESIAN

IF SO, CAN WE TALK?

Multi-Lingual Customer Service Representatives

Immediate opportunities exist for Japanese speaking professionals.

Fax International is a dynamic, high-tech telecommunications company. We're currently seeking people fluent in the listed languages to offer around the clock support to our customers. If you have multi-language skills, and/or you are available for off-shift schedules, you may be eligible for pay differentials.

Suburban Boston Opportunities

Openings exist for individuals to troubleshoot and resolve delivery problems of facsimile documents using a PC. The customer service department is a fast-paced and constantly changing environment. The positions require a strong service ethic, as well as excellent problem-solving and customer interaction skills. Ideal candidates will have language skills in two listed languages as well as English. The following skills preferred:

- Solid knowledge of computer applications in a Windows environment

- Experience in a service environment involving direct customer contact

- College degree

Relocation assistance is available.

Fax or mail your resume to:
Fax International, HRCF/DD,
67 S. Bedford St., Suite 100E,
Burlington, MA 01803
FAX: 617-564-6598
No phone calls please.
e-mail: carla.ferreira@faxint.com
An equal opportunity employer.

FAX INTERNATIONAL.

Courtesy: Bernard Hodes Advertising, Boston, Mass.

Sample 6-16

The ad starts out with an upbeat description of the company and includes colorful terms to describe the future incumbent. The listing of responsibilities, coupled with the prerequisites, support the title: Director, HR Development. The comment about a competitive base salary plus bonus is intriguing. Application instructions are clear, although "in *complete* confidence" is excessive terminology.

Since the ad appeared in a national journal and relocation is probable, it would have been more effective if details were provided describing a few of the key incentives in the "very attractive upper Midwest city."

The straight-text format of this ad is acceptable for a journal but would be more interesting with additional white space and graphics.

POSITION OPEN

....

Director, HR Development—Successful, rapidly growing, well-established telecommunications company seeking bright, enthusiastic HR professional for newly created position. We are located in a very attractive upper Midwest city. Responsibilities include training and development, staffing, succession planning, field HR programs, and employee communications. In addition to a business degree (MBA preferred), requirements include a minimum of 10 years HR experience with an emphasis on training and development, and staffing. Candidates must have exceptional interpersonal and communication skills. We offer a competitive base plus bonus, and relocation reimbursement. Please send resume, including salary history, in complete confidence to: *Kate Lambrecht, Wojdula & Associates, Ltd., 700 Rayovac Drive, Suite 204, Madison, WI 53711. Fax: 608/271-7475.*

Courtesy: Wojdula & Associates, Ltd.

Sample 6-17

The company's many areas of focus are listed in the opening statement, as a lead-in to its need for a publisher for the business book publishing division. By using terms such as "strong track record," "solid experience," and "working knowledge," the organization is inviting candidates with varied levels of expertise to apply, in spite of the requirement that the ideal candidate possess a specific number of years of relevant experience.

Its EEO statement goes beyond the minimum requirement of stating that it is an EEO employer. The addition of "M/F/D/V" and "minorities are encouraged to apply" sends a message of management commitment.

Because the information is separated into three paragraphs with white space in between, the ad is easy to read, even though the format is straight text.

The logo at the end of the ad balances the job title at the top.

Publisher

The **American Management Association** is an international membership organization and worldwide leader in the fields of training and development, business books, periodicals and audio tapes. AMACOM, our business book publishing division, is looking for a Publisher with the vision to lead our winning team toward continued growth.

The ideal candidate will have a minimum of 4 years' experience as Editor-In-Chief or Publisher and at least 3 years of solid experience in business book publishing. We are looking for someone who has a strong track record in publishing books to be sold via the retail/wholesale marketplace, as well as solid experience with the publication of database-direct-marketed professional books. Also required is a working knowledge of book production and multi-channel marketing, including the planning and analysis that these activities require.

We offer a competitive salary and an excellent benefits package. For immediate consideration, please submit your resume to: **American Management Association, Box WR, 1601 Broadway, New York, NY 10019.** We are an EEO/AA M/F/D/V Employer. Minorities are encouraged to apply.

AMERICAN MANAGEMENT ASSOCIATION

Courtesy: American Management Association.

Sample 6-18

This ad for positions within the art and product management departments of a party goods company is, not surprisingly, creative. The use of different fonts and designs subliminally signals readers as to the nature of the industry and prevailing atmosphere.

A brief statement about the company precedes more detailed descriptions for three openings that adequately define each job's requirements and responsibilities.

Courtesy: Amscan Inc.

Letters to Applicants

Objective: Invites applicants in for an interview or thanks them for their interest

Purpose: To inform

Readers: Candidates who may or may not be called in to discuss their qualifications

Style: Personal pronouns, active voice, varied pace, consistent

Tone: Factual, descriptive, clear, neutral

Format: Straight text

Contents: Date; address; salutation; identity of the job applied for; status of the person's application; instructions, if any, for how to proceed; complimentary close; signature block

Sample 6-19

This minimalist letter inviting a candidate for an interview sends a clear and complete message: It identifies the available opening and informs the recipient how to proceed.

October 12, 199X

Mr. Martin Augusto
898 Peninsula Blvd.
Hartwell, Maine 34321

Dear Mr. Augusto:

Thank you for applying for the position of Project Manager. Based on your qualifications we would like to invite you in for an interview.

Please call me at 555-6491 so we can set up an appointment.

I look forward to hearing from you.

Sincerely yours,

Jefferson Ackerman
Employment Manager

JA/bdt

Sample 6-20

This sample inappropriately suggests to the applicant that she stands a good chance of being selected before the interview has even taken place.

December 3, 199X

Ms. Margaret Kenny
56 Privy Court
Belmont, Idaho 30330

Dear Ms. Kenny:

I just read your resumé in response to our ad for an office manager and am very impressed with your background and credentials. You seem to possess all the qualifications we are looking for in an office manager.

Please give me a call right away so we can get together to discuss the opening in detail, and I can learn more about you.

I can be reached at 555-4773 during the day; if it's more convenient, call me at home during the evening at 555-9982.

I look forward to meeting you soon.

Very truly yours,

Susan J. Woods
HR Coordinator

SJW/aph

Sample 6-21

This "thank you for applying but we're not interested" letter is brief and direct, gives a reason for rejection, and ends on a positive note.

March 18, 199X

Christopher Dodderman
74 Hellman Way
Georgia, Kentucky 43456

Dear Mr. Dodderman:

Thank you for applying for the position of customer service representative with our organization. Although we were impressed with your resumé, the job requires someone with more experience than you currently have.

Best wishes on finding a suitable position soon.

Sincerely yours,

Richard Pentergast
HR Manager

RP/pag

Sample 6-22

This letter is written to an applicant who submitted an unsolicited resumé. It acknowledges receipt and explains that the company has no available openings that match his qualifications. It invites the candidate to apply again in the future and offers to keep the application on file.

The use of personal pronouns and the applicant's name personalizes the letter and projects a friendly tone. The likely result is that the recipient, while rejected, would feel comfortable in approaching this company again.

August 23, 199X

Lance Villers
45 Douglaston Avenue
Brackenridge, Washington 43456

Dear Mr. Villers:

Thank you for inquiring about employment opportunities at Avedon Industries. I appreciated the opportunity to review your qualifications in relation to our current job openings.

Avedon does not have any positions open that are compatible with your training and experience at this time. Since this is a growing company, however, that may change in the future. Therefore, I would like to keep your resumé in our active file so that I may consider you for any appropriate openings that arise in the next six months.

I wish you success, Mr. Villers, in your pursuit of an appropriate job.

Sincerely yours,

Robert S. Boyster
Director of Human Resources

RSB/tie

7
Employment Interviewing

The interviewing process requires numerous documents, among them employment application forms, interview evaluations, selection checklists, reference forms, and letters to selected and rejected candidates. As with recruiting documents, consider the objective, purpose, and targeted readers when preparing each document. Then select the most suitable style, tone, and format, and zero in on the appropriate topics or categories.

Employment Application Forms

Objective: Elicits pertinent job-related information about a candidate

Purpose: To inform

Readers: Blank application: applicants interested in applying for a job. Completed application: HR representatives responsible for interviewing, and supervisors, managers, and department heads with job openings

Style: standard and familiar phrases, words most applicants are likely to know

Tone: Clear, factual, direct

Format: Boxes, columns, questions, heads and subheads, boldface type, varying fonts and type sizes, white space, lists

Contents: EEO statement; date; applicant's name, address, and phone number; position applied for; available schedule; source of referral; former applicant or employee status; relatives or friends employed by the company; above minimum legal working age; U.S. citizenship or legal work status; record of convictions; ability to perform the essential functions of the job; U.S. military service record; job-related language skills; job-related professional organization affiliation; employment experience; education; additional qualifications; professional references; notices for veterans and individuals with disabilities; agreements; accuracy of contents; at-will employment (recommended)

Sample 7-1

This employment application covers all necessary categories (except for an at-will statement) and then some. It reflects an understanding of EEO laws by excluding non-job-related questions. In addition, the company is identified as an equal opportunity employer and emphasizes that its employment decisions are based strictly on an individual's qualifications.

Personal references are called for, but are unnecessary; they rarely have merit, since the candidate will list only those references likely to provide rave reviews.

The format is easy-to-read and complete. The use of heads, different point sizes, boldface type, columns, and boxes results in an effective design.

One minor suggestion: When this company revises its application, the word *disability* should replace *handicap*.

Sample 7-1

APPLICATION FOR EMPLOYMENT

PERSONAL DATA

Name in Full (Print) _____ Social Security No. _____ Today's Date _____

(Last)   (First)   (Middle)

Present Address _____ Telephone No. _____

(Street)

_____

(City)   (State)   (Zip)

Do You Have the Legal Right to Live and Work in the United States? _____

Have You Ever Been Convicted of a Crime (Misdemeanor or Felony) in the Past Five Years? _____ If Yes, Please Explain. _____

_____

(Note: A Conviction Will Not Necessarily Bar You From Employment.)

Are You 18 Years of Age or Older? ❑ Yes   ❑ No   If No, Specify Age _____ Years.

Individual to Notify in Case of Emergency _____

Telephone _____

JOB INTEREST

Position Applied For _____ Date Available _____ Salary Desired _____

Are You Available for Full-Time Work? _____ If Not, What Hours Can You Work? _____

Have You Worked for Us Before? _____ If Yes, When? _____

List Any Relatives Working for Us _____

How Did You Learn of This Opening? _____

MEDICAL DATA

Are You Willing to Take a Physical Exam and/or Drug Screening at Our Expense if the Nature of the Job Requires It? _____

(Note: No Medical Exam Will Be Required Prior to an Offer of Employment.)

EDUCATION AND TRAINING

Education	Name & Location of School	Courses Taken	No. of Years Completed	Did You Graduate?
High School				
College				
Business Trade, Technical				
Other				

SPECIAL SKILLS

Typing _____ WPM

Shorthand _____ WPM

Dictating Machine _____ Yrs. _____ Mos.

Adding Machine _____ Yrs. _____ Mos.

Calculator _____ Yrs. _____ Mos.

Switchboard _____ Yrs. _____ Mos.

(Type) _____

Cash Register _____ Yrs. _____ Mos.

(Type) _____

Telex Machine _____ Yrs. _____ Mos.

Communications Terminal _____ Yrs. _____ Mos.

Data Processing Equipment _____ Yrs. _____ Mos.

(Type) _____

TRAVEL

Are You Willing to Travel? _____ Yes _____ No   Are You Willing to Relocate? _____ Yes _____ No

AN EQUAL OPPORTUNITY EMPLOYER M/F/H/V

(continues)

Sample 7-1. Continued.

EMPLOYMENT EXPERIENCE

Please give an accurate, complete full-time and part-time employment record, beginning with your most recent employer. Include any U.S. military service.

Company Name & Address	Dates Employed	Last Salary	State Your Job Title & Describe Your Duties	Reason for Leaving
1.	Month/Yr. From: To:			
2.	Month/Yr. From: To:			
3.	Month/Yr. From: To:			
4.	Month/Yr. From: To:			

PERSONAL REFERENCES

(Give names of three persons to whom you are not related and by whom you have not been employed. These people should have known you personally for at least five years.)

Name	Address	Business	Years Known

READ BEFORE SIGNING

IT IS THE POLICY OF THIS COMPANY TO EMPLOY PERSONNEL STRICTLY ON THE BASIS OF AN INDIVIDUAL'S QUALIFICATIONS. SELECTIONS ARE MADE WITHOUT REGARD TO RACE, COLOR, SEX, RELIGION, NATIONAL ORIGIN, AGE, VIETNAM ERA VETERAN STATUS, OR PHYSICAL OR MENTAL HANDICAP.

I HEREBY CERTIFY THAT THE STATEMENTS CONTAINED HEREIN ARE TRUE AND UNDERSTAND MISREPRESENTATION OR OMISSION OF FACTS CALLED FOR HEREIN OR IN ANY ATTACHMENTS SUPPLIED IS CAUSE FOR REFUSAL OF EMPLOYMENT OR IMMEDIATE DISMISSAL OF EMPLOYMENT. I AGREE TO A THOROUGH INVESTIGATION OF MY BACKGROUND WHICH MAY BE MADE AND USED RELATIVE TO MY EMPLOYMENT STATUS. I HEREBY AUTHORIZE MY FORMER EMPLOYERS AND ANY OTHER PERSONS OR ORGANIZATIONS TO PROVIDE ANY INFORMATION THEY HAVE ABOUT MY EMPLOYMENT AND BACKGROUND, AND I RELEASE ALL CONCERNED FROM ANY LIABILITY IN CONNECTION THEREWITH. IF EMPLOYMENT IS OFFERED, I UNDERSTAND I MUST COMPLY WITH ALL RULES AND REGULATIONS SET FORTH AND COMMUNICATED TO EMPLOYEES BY THE COMPANY.

SIGNATURE_____ DATE _____

APPLICATION MUST BE COMPLETED AND SIGNED TO BE VALID

DO NOT WRITE BELOW THIS LINE

Interviewed By: _____ Date: _____   **REMARKS:**

_____ Date: _____

_____ Date: _____

Approved By: _____ Starting Date: _____

Dept.: _____ Job Title: _____

Rate of Pay: _____ Job Grade: _____

Special Instructions: _____

Sample 7-2

This sample represents a comprehensive, legal application form. Most of the first page is devoted to EEO-related statements, and all of the questions are in accordance with EEO laws.

The application uses a varying format: color (turquoise ink against a white background), double borders, columns, boxes, varying type sizes, boldface type, heads and subheads, uppercase letters, and questions. The form is designed to focus the applicant's attention on reading and completing all four pages.

The last page contains a number of statements requiring an applicant's signature. These statements, relating to compliance with the Immigration Reform and Control Act of 1986, conditions of employment, and testing and confidentiality, are written in terms that are readily comprehensible. The tone is direct yet not threatening.

Sample 7-2

APPLICATION FOR EMPLOYMENT

NAME (please print)   _____

SOCIAL SECURITY NO.   _____

POSITION APPLYING FOR   _____

DATE   _____

AVEDON IS AN EQUAL OPPORTUNITY/AFFIRMATIVE ACTION EMPLOYER. OUR POLICY IS TO ABIDE BY ALL FEDERAL, STATE, AND LOCAL LAWS PROHIBITING DISCRIMINATION IN EMPLOYMENT BECAUSE OF RACE, COLOR, SEX, RELIGION, NATIONAL ORIGIN, AGE, DISABILITY (WHERE THE PERSON IS ABLE TO PERFORM THE ESSENTIAL FUNCTIONS OF THE POSITION), VETERAN STATUS, CITIZENSHIP STATUS, OR OTHER PROHIBITED REASONS.

AVEDON WILL PROVIDE REASONABLE ACCOMMODATIONS FOR QUALIFIED INDIVIDUALS WITH KNOWN DISABILITIES. ADDITIONALLY, AN APPLICANT WITH A DISABILITY WHO NEEDS AN ACCOMMODATION DURING THE APPLICATION OR INTERVIEWING PROCESS SHOULD REQUEST SUCH AN ACCOMMODATION FROM THE HUMAN RESOURCES DEPARTMENT, OR ANY OTHER REPRESENTATIVE.

This application for employment addresses items your resumé may not; therefore all individuals should take the time to complete it thoroughly and accurately.

Falsification, misstatement, or misrepresentation of data shall be considered sufficient cause for termination of consideration for employment or, if employed, termination of employment.

PERSONAL INFORMATION (please print)

PRESENT ADDRESS: STREET/CITY/STATE/ZIP	HOME ADDRESS IF DIFFERENT: STREET/CITY/STATE/ZIP

PRESENT TELEPHONE NUMBER: ( )	HOME TELEPHONE NUMBER: ( )

TYPE OF EMPLOYMENT FULL TIME ☐ PART TIME ☐ TEMPORARY ☐ INTERNSHIP ☐	LOCATION PREFERENCE, IF ANY

REFERRAL SOURCE:
☐ STATE EMPLOYMENT AGENCY   ☐ ADVERTISEMENT   ☐ COLLEGE/UNIVERSITY
☐ SOCIAL SERVICES   ☐ EMPLOYEE REFERRAL   ☐ BUSINESS SCHOOL
☐ WALK-IN   ☐ PRIVATE EMPLOYMENT AGENCY   ☐ HIGH SCHOOL
   ☐ OTHER _____

ARE YOU AVAILABLE TO WORK THE NORMAL BUSINESS HOURS REQUIRED FOR THE
POSITION FOR WHICH YOU HAVE APPLIED?   YES ☐ NO ☐

ARE YOU AVAILABLE TO WORK DURING SEASONAL PERIODS AS WORK DICTATES?   YES ☐ NO ☐

ARE YOU AVAILABLE TO WORK OVERTIME IF REQUIRED?   YES ☐ NO ☐

HAVE YOU PREVIOUSLY APPLIED FOR EMPLOYMENT HERE?   YES ☐ NO ☐

HAVE YOU PREVIOUSLY BEEN EMPLOYED HERE?   YES ☐ NO ☐
     IF YES, FROM _____ TO _____

FOR AVEDON ONLY: DO YOU HAVE ANY RELATIVES WHO NOW WORK FOR AVEDON? **(THE PURPOSE OF
THIS QUESTION IS TO ENSURE COMPLIANCE WITH AN ANTI-NEPOTISM POLICY AND A RULE OR
PRACTICE PROHIBITING AN EMPLOYEE FROM SUPERVISING A RELATIVE.)**   YES ☐ NO ☐
IF YES, PLEASE EXPLAIN. _____

HAVE YOU EVER BEEN CONVICTED OF A FELONY OR A MISDEMEANOR OTHER
THAN FOR TRAFFIC VIOLATIONS?   YES ☐ NO ☐
IF YES, PLEASE EXPLAIN _____

THE EXISTENCE OF A CRIMINAL RECORD IS NOT AN AUTOMATIC BAR TO EMPLOYMENT; AVEDON WILL CONSIDER THE OFFENSE FOR WHICH THE PERSON
WAS CONVICTED, THE RECENCY OF THE CONVICTION, AND THE JOB FOR WHICH THE PERSON HAS APPLIED IN DETERMINING THE EXTENT TO WHICH
SUCH INFORMATION WILL BE CONSIDERED.

EDUCATION

	NAME	LOCATION	GRADUATED YES NO	MAJOR/MINOR	IF NO DEGREE INDICATE NO OF CREDITS RECEIVED TOWARD DEGREE
HIGH SCHOOL					
COLLEGE					
GRADUATE					
BUSINESS					
OTHER					

HONORS AND EXTRACURRICULAR ACTIVITIES

SKILLS	APPROXIMATE TYPING SPEED

PLEASE LIST ALL BUSINESS MACHINES YOU CAN OPERATE AND COMPUTER SOFTWARE WITH WHICH YOU ARE FAMILIAR:

PLEASE LIST ANY PROFESSIONAL LICENSES HELD (e.g., CPA, CLU, NOTARY PUBLIC, MASTER PLUMBER, ETC.):

PLEASE LIST ANY ADDITIONAL SKILLS WHICH CAN ENHANCE YOUR ABILITY TO PERFORM THE JOB:

PLEASE LIST ANY PROFESSIONAL OR TRADE ORGANIZATION MEMBERSHIPS RELEVANT TO THE JOB FOR WHICH YOU ARE
APPLYING:

(continues)

Sample 7-2. Continued.

EMPLOYMENT HISTORY: *Please list positions you have held. If lapses occurred between periods of employment, please specify in the space provided at the bottom of this page. List the most recent employment first.**

EMPLOYER _____	STARTING POSITION _____
ADDRESS _____	FINAL POSITION _____
TELEPHONE _____	EMPLOYED FROM ___ / ___ / ___ TO ___ / ___ / ___
SUPERVISOR _____	STARTING SALARY _____ ENDING SALARY _____
SUPERVISOR'S TITLE _____	AMOUNT OF LAST INCREASE _____ DATE OF LAST INCREASE ___ / ___ / ___
DEPARTMENT _____	FULL-TIME ☐ PART-TIME ☐ TEMP ☐ INTERN ☐
PRIMARY DUTIES _____	REASON FOR LEAVING _____
	MAY WE CONTACT?** YES ☐ NO ☐

EMPLOYER _____	STARTING POSITION _____
ADDRESS _____	FINAL POSITION _____
TELEPHONE _____	EMPLOYED FROM ___ / ___ / ___ TO ___ / ___ / ___
SUPERVISOR _____	STARTING SALARY _____ ENDING SALARY _____
SUPERVISOR'S TITLE _____	FULL-TIME ☐ PART-TIME ☐ TEMP ☐ INTERN ☐
DEPARTMENT _____	REASON FOR LEAVING _____
PRIMARY DUTIES _____	MAY WE CONTACT?** YES ☐ NO ☐

EMPLOYER _____	STARTING POSITION _____
ADDRESS _____	FINAL POSITION _____
TELEPHONE _____	EMPLOYED FROM ___ / ___ / ___ TO ___ / ___ / ___
SUPERVISOR _____	STARTING SALARY _____ ENDING SALARY _____
SUPERVISOR'S TITLE _____	FULL-TIME ☐ PART-TIME ☐ TEMP ☐ INTERN ☐
DEPARTMENT _____	REASON FOR LEAVING _____
PRIMARY DUTIES _____	MAY WE CONTACT?** YES ☐ NO ☐

EMPLOYER _____	STARTING POSITION _____
ADDRESS _____	FINAL POSITION _____
TELEPHONE _____	EMPLOYED FROM ___ / ___ / ___ TO ___ / ___ / ___
SUPERVISOR _____	STARTING SALARY _____ ENDING SALARY _____
SUPERVISOR'S TITLE _____	FULL-TIME ☐ PART-TIME ☐ TEMP ☐ INTERN ☐
DEPARTMENT _____	REASON FOR LEAVING _____
PRIMARY DUTIES _____	MAY WE CONTACT?** YES ☐ NO ☐

*   Reason for gaps in employment: _____
**   If you are extended a conditional offer of employment, Avedon will verify previous academic and business references.

ADDITIONAL INFORMATION: Please list the name, address and telephone numbers of three business/academic references, other than relatives.

NAME	ADDRESS	TELEPHONE NUMBER
1.		( )
2.		( )
3.		( )

PLEASE READ THE FOLLOWING PARAGRAPHS CAREFULLY BEFORE SIGNING THIS APPLICATION.

I understand that in order to comply with the Immigration Reform and Control Act of 1986, I must produce the required documentation to establish my identity and eligibility to work. Such requirements are:

- United States passport
- Certificate of United States Citizenship
- Certificate of Naturalization
- Unexpired foreign passport with attached Employment Authorization
- Resident Alien Card with a photograph

OR

Two (2) documents, one for identification such as a driver's license or state issued card with photograph and one document which established eligibility to work, such as United States birth certificate or Social Security card

Any employment by Avedon is contingent upon my producing the required documentation, or evidence of having made application for it at the time of or within three (3) calendar days after my hire.

CONDITIONS OF EMPLOYMENT: I understand that falsification, omission, or misstatement of data shall be considered sufficient cause for denying employment or termination or my employment. I understand that my employment and compensation can be terminated at any time without cause, and with or without notice at any time, at the option of Avedon or myself. I understand that no one has authority to promise permanent employment or employment for a definite period of time. My employment may be based on receipt of satisfactory information from former employers, schools, and other references. I authorize Avedon and its representatives to investigate, without liability, any information supplied by me including occupational, police, and governmental records. I also authorize listed employers, schools, and references, as well as other reference sources, to make full response to any inquiry by Avedon and its representatives without liability.

TESTING: Except as limited by law, Avedon reserves the right to test applicants and employees prior to or during employment for usage of controlled substances which may impair ability to perform at expected levels and for the use of illegal drugs or substance abuse.

CONFIDENTIALITY: Avedon's future depends on our development of innovative programs and materials. Therefore, I agree to use the greatest discretion in discussing financial information, member names, council deliberations or new program ideas, including data contained in the Management Information System, and any other confidential information related to our business activities. I understand that release of such information is grounds for immediate termination. I agree not to disclose any trade secrets or any other confidential or proprietary information of Avedon either during or after the termination of employment.

I certify that all information contained in this application is true and complete.

Applicant's Signature: _____   Date: _____

THIS SECTION FOR HUMAN RESOURCES USE ONLY.

INTERVIEWER	DATE
1.	
2.	
3.	
4.	

FINAL DISPOSITION	POSITION
DIVISION/DEPARTMENT	SUPERVISOR
STARTING DATE	STARTING SALARY
DATE REFERENCES MAILED	FIRST DAY ORIENTATION: DATE / /
/ / INITIALS	TIME: A.M. P.M. INITIALS

EMPLOYMENT/EDUCATION REFERENCES CHECKED   YES ☐   NO ☐   IF YES, BY:

Sample 7-3

This sample does not offer as much visual interest as the preceding application, but it is no less comprehensive. It also complies fully with applicable EEO laws.

Sample 7-3

Avedon Industries
An Equal Opportunity Employer M/F/V/D

Application for Employment

Avedon Industries considers applicants for all positions without regard to race, color, religion, sex, national origin, age, veteran status, non-job-related disabilities, or any other legally protected status.

(Please Print)

Name_____**Date**_____

Address_____

Phone No._____ **Social Security No.**_____

Position Applied For_____

Available To Work: ( ) Full Time ( ) Days   ( ) Temporary
                  ( ) Part Time ( ) Evenings   ( ) Telecommuting

Referral Source_____

Have you ever filed an application at Avedon Industries before? ( ) yes ( ) no
                                    Dates_____
Have you ever been employed by Avedon Industries before? ( ) yes ( ) no
                                    Dates_____

Do you have any relatives, other than a spouse, currently employed by Avedon Industries? ( ) yes ( ) no If yes, please list their names_____

_____

Are you above the minimum working age of _____? ( ) yes ( ) no
If you are under the age of _____ **can you furnish a work permit?** ( ) yes ( ) no

Are you legally permitted to work in this country? ( ) yes ( ) no
If yes, will you be prepared to produce proof at the time of hire, in accordance with the Immigration Reform and Control Act of 1986? ( ) yes ( ) no

Have you ever convicted of a felony? A positive response will not necessarily affect your eligibility to be hired ( ) yes ( ) no
If yes, please explain_____

_____

Are you able to perform the essential functions of the job applied for either without accommodation or with a reasonable amount of accommodation?
( ) yes ( ) no

(continues)

Sample 7-3. Continued.

As related to the position applied for, what language do you speak, read, and/or write? What is your degree of fluency?

_____

_____

What professional organizations or business activities are you involved with, relative to your ability to perform the position applied for?

_____

_____

Employment Experience

Please list present or most recent employer first. Include military service, if any.

Employer_____**Phone No.**_____

Address_____

Position(s)_____

Manager_____**Starting Salary**_____**Final Salary**_____

Dates Employed_____

Reason for Leaving _____

Primary Responsibilities_____

_____

_____

Employer_____**Phone No.**_____

Address_____

Position(s)_____

Manager_____**Starting Salary**_____**Final Salary**_____

Dates Employed_____

Reason for Leaving_____

Primary Responsibilities_____

_____

_____

Employer_____Phone No._____

Address_____

Position(s)_____

Manager_____Starting Salary_____Final Salary_____

Dates Employed_____

Reason for Leaving_____

Primary Responsibilities_____

_____

_____

Education and Training

List all schools attended, including trade, business, or technical institutions, beginning with the most recent.

Name/Location	No. of Years Completed	Diploma/Degree

_____

_____

_____

_____

Please describe any additional academic achievements or extracurricular activities relative to the position applied for_____

_____

Please identify any additional knowledge, skills, qualifications, publications, or awards which will be helpful to us in considering your application for employment.

_____

_____

_____

Please provide the name, title, address, and phone number of three business references, other than present or former employers, who are not related to you.

1._____

2._____

3._____

(continues)

Sample 7-3. Continued.

Special notice to disabled veterans, Vietnam Era veterans, and individuals with disabilities

Government contractors are subject to Section 402 of the Vietnam Era Veterans Readjustment Act of 1974, which requires that they take affirmative action to employ and advance in employment qualified disabled veterans and veterans of the Vietnam Era; and Section 503 of the Rehabilitation Act of 1973, as amended, which requires that they take affirmative action to employ and advance in employment qualified individuals with disabilities.

If you consider yourself to be covered by one or both of these Acts, and wish to be identified for the purposes of proper placement and appropriate accommodation, please sign below. Submission of this information is voluntary and failure to provide it will not jeopardize employment opportunities at Avedon Industries. This information will be kept confidential.

( ) Disabled   ( ) Disabled Veteran   ( ) Vietnam Era Veteran

Agreement

I certify that the statements made in this application are correct and complete to the best of my knowledge.

I understand that false or misleading information may result in termination of employment.

I authorize Avedon Industries to conduct a reference check so that a hiring decision may be made. In the event that Avedon Industries is unable to verify any reference stated on this application, it is my responsibility to furnish the necessary documentation.

( ) you may ( ) you may not contact my present employer
( ) you may ( ) you may not contact the schools I have attended for the release of my educational records

If accepted for employment with Avedon Industries, I agree to abide by all of its policies and procedures. If employed, I understand that I may terminate my employment at any time without notice or cause, and that Avedon Industries may terminate or modify the employment relationship at any time without prior notice or cause. In consideration of my employment, I agree to conform to the rules and regulations of Avedon Industries and I understand that no representative of Avedon Industries, other than the President or a designated Human Resources Office, has any authority to enter into any agreement, oral or written, for employment for any specified period or time or to make any agreement or assurances contrary to this policy. If employed, I understand that my employment is for no definite period of time, and if terminated, Avedon Industries is liable only for wages earned as of the date of termination. I also agree to have my photograph taken for identification purposes if hired.

Signed_____

Date_____

Interviewer_____Date_____
Interviewer_____Date_____
Interviewer_____Date_____
Employed ( ) yes ( ) no
If employed: Title_____
                    Department_____
                    Starting Date_____
                    Starting Salary_____

Interview Evaluations

Objective: Records interviewer's assessment of a candidate's job suitability

Purpose: To inform

Readers: Managers and HR representatives when making a hiring decision, HR representatives when reconsidering a rejected candidate at a later date

Style: Job-related phrases and categories

Tone: Clear, descriptive, distinct, factual

Format: Checklists, some text, boxes, quotations

Contents: Candidate's name, date, position, department, summary of experience and education, relationship between position requirements and applicant's qualifications, overall evaluation, interviewer's name

Sample 7-4

This candidate evaluation form begins with an important notation: that all comments must be job related. The format used is a combination of checking off an appropriate rating, ranging from poor to excellent, and supporting that choice with remarks. This backup information is important, since ratings should always be accompanied by job-related notations.

The form also calls for an evaluation of both tangible and intangible factors, which is fine, as long as all factors are relevant.

Sample 7-4

Candidate Evaluation Form

NAME OF CANDIDATE _____ DATE OF INTERVIEW _____

POSITION CONSIDERED FOR _____ EXEMPT ____ NON-EXEMPT ____

Note: All comments must be job-related.

EDUCATIONAL QUALIFICATIONS

Does this candidate have the necessary educational qualifications for this position?

Yes _____ No _____

Level of education attained, schools attended, degrees, special training, and further

education. _____

_____

_____

PERSONAL QUALIFICATIONS AND EXPERIENCE

Consider personal qualifications necessary for this position including: speaking ability (diction, grammar, articulation), poise, personal appearance, and interview behavior.

Poor __ __ __ __ __ Excellent
      1 2 3 4 5

Remarks _____

_____

_____

TECHNICAL QUALIFICATIONS AND EXPERIENCE

Consider experience with skills necessary for this position (example: systems, direct mail, platform, writing, editing, typing, clerical, and supervisory skills and/or adequate years of relevant experience).

Poor __ __ __ __ __ Excellent
      1 2 3 4 5

Remarks _____

_____

_____

_____

_____

(continues)

Sample 7-4. Continued.

CANDIDATE AWARENESS AND INTEREST

Consider knowledge, understanding and interest in field, position, and Avedon; personal goals; goals and objectives; motivation; potential for growth.

Poor __ __ __ __ __ Excellent
        1 2 3 4 5

Remarks _____

_____

_____

_____

TESTS TAKEN/SCORE:

          Test   Score

_____   _____

_____   _____

_____   _____

_____   _____

OVERALL RECOMMENDATION

Not Recommended __ __ __ __ __ Recommended
                   1 2 3 4 5

Remarks/Additional Comments (consider advancement history, reasons for leaving jobs, stability). _____

_____

_____

_____

_____

_____

_____

_____

_____

Interviewer _____ Date _____

Sample 7-5

This sample requires interviewers to evaluate candidates on the basis of three categories: technical skills, education, and experience. No comments are called for: just a check mark under the heading of exceptional, above average, average, or marginal. These terms are subjective and cannot stand alone without supporting job-related data. Note that the page also leaves room for comments, but this does not tie in directly with the evaluation portion. In addition, at the end, interviewers are asked to support their recommendation.

The form asks interviewers to compare candidates with employees possessing comparable experience. This may not be feasible, since on-the-job experience can contribute substantially to a person's skill level.

Sample 7-5

INTERVIEW EVALUATION REPORT

Name of Applicant _____ Date _____

Position Interviewed for _____

Interviewer _____ Department & Section No. _____

I. Indicate your evaluation of the Application: (All indicated qualities should relate directly to the position)

	Exceptional	Above Average	Average	Marginal
Technical Ability/Skill Level				
Education (as related to job)				
Experience				

	Directly	Mostly	Partly	Not at all
To what extent is applicant's background applicable to position?				

II. Where would applicant's technical ability and skill level rank him/her in relation to others in your group with comparable experience?

Upper Third _____   Middle Third _____   Lower Third _____

III. Other Comments:

IV. What was applicant told concerning prospect of employment?

Recommendation:
_____ No offer be made _____
                        Reason must be given
_____ Applicant should be considered for another position.
        Specify _____

_____ An offer be made

        Rate _____ Position Title _____

In order to support your recommendation, please note the specific reasons for your rating of this applicant.

_____

Sample 7-6

This evaluation form calls for the assessment of objective, tangible categories, such as technical skills. Relevant intangibles can be described under "other job-related information."

The form is distinguished by its reliance on the relationship between position requirements and an applicant's qualifications. Interviewers can take each item in a job description and compare it with some aspect of the applicant's background. This approach is completely objective (assuming the job description is well written) and lends itself to one of two logical conclusions: the candidate meets or fails to meet the job requirements.

Sample 7-6

Interview Evaluation Form

Applicant Evaluation

Applicant: _____ Date: _____

Position: _____

Department/Division: _____

Summary of experience: _____

_____

_____

Summary of education/academic achievements: _____

_____

_____

Relationship between position requirements and applicant's background, skills, and qualifications:

Position Requirements	*Applicant's Qualifications*
_____	_____
_____	_____
_____	_____
_____	_____
_____	_____
_____	_____
_____	_____
_____	_____

Interview Evaluation Form

Applicant: _____

Position: _____

Additional factors, as relevant:

    Clerical skills: _____

    _____

    Verbal communication skills: _____

    _____

    Writing skills: _____

    _____

    Technical skills: _____

    _____

    Numerical skills: _____

    _____

    Language skills: _____

    _____

Other job-related information: _____

_____

Overall evaluation:
    (   ) Meets job requirements
    (   ) Fails to meet job requirements

Additional comments: _____

_____

                   Interviewer: _____

Selection Checklists

Objective: Identifies key skills, abilities, traits, and characteristics relative to a specified job

Purpose: To inform

Readers: Managers and HR representatives making a hiring decision

Style: Job-related phrases and categories

Tone: Descriptive, factual

Format: Charts, lists, comparisons

Contents: Work history, education, job-related intangibles, reactions to key questions, salary requirements, reasons for leaving previous employers, appropriate job match

| Sample 7-7 |

This sample requires too much text, thereby negating the overall purpose of a selection checklist: to sum up a candidate's job suitability.

Sample 7-7

Selection Checklist

Candidate's name_____Date_____

Position applied for_____Dept._____

Experience_____

_____

Education_____

_____

Independent worker v. team player_____

Best traits_____

_____

Areas requiring improvement_____

_____

_____

Salary History_____

_____

Potential_____

_____

Other_____

_____

Completed by_____Date_____

Sample 7-8

This selection checklist is easy for interviewers and managers to complete and review. To preclude reducing candidates to mere numbers, support for each rating is required, but not on the checklist page.

A suggested variation of this form would assess several candidates on the same checklist in order to compare them at a glance.

Selection Checklist

Candidate *Kerri Paddington*   Position *Marketing Representative*   Date *6/14/9X*

Instructions for use:

Apply the following rating scale to each of the factors evaluated:

1 = exceeds the requirement or trait sought

2 = meets the requirement or trait sought

3 = fails to meet the requirement or trait sought

4 = offers an alternative quality that may satisfactorily substitute for the requirement or trait sought

5 = offers an alternative quality that does not satisfactorily substitute for the requirements or trait sought

Be prepared to support each rating with job-related information and examples (attached copy of interview evaluation is acceptable).

Requirement or Trait	Rating
Work experience	*1*
Education	*3/4*
Job-related intangibles (refer to job description)	*2*
Reactions to key questions	*1*
Salary requirements	*2*
Reasons for leaving previous employers	*2*
Appropriate job match	*2*

Prepared by_____Date_____

References

Objective: Confirms information acquired during the interview, acquires additional job-related information to assist interviewer in making a hiring decision

Purpose: To inform

Readers: Written reference forms: former employers. Telephone reference forms: HR representative conducting the reference call

Style: Direct

Tone: Distinct, clear, concise, factual

Format: Asks questions, heads and subheads, boxes, some straight text

Contents: Applicant's name; position applied for; name, title, and company of the person contacted; former position; responsibilities; reason for leaving; strengths; areas requiring improvement; other specific job-related factors (e.g., attendance and punctuality for nonexempt positions and decision making and time management abilities for exempt positions); overall evaluation; eligibility for rehiring.

Sample 7-9

This one-page, well-designed, easy-to-read reference form begins with a release from the applicant. Typically a release appears on the employment application, but adding it to the reference form clearly indicates to the former employer that the candidate has given permission for the inquiry.

The lead-in statement implies that very little time is required to complete the form, encouraging the former employer to do so.

The next box requests verification of five straightforward facts to be provided by the former employer. Attendance and punctuality are the only other areas requiring feedback, facilitated by the use of checkoff boxes.

This reference form is appropriate for nonexempt-level employees.

Sample 7-9

EMPLOYMENT REFERENCE FORM

TO: _____

_____

I, _____, authorize the release of all information as requested by Avedon Industries in consideration of my application for employment.

Signature _____

Date _____ Social Security Number _____

Please Print Name (first/last) _____

Name at Time of Employment

_____ is currently being considered for a position with Avedon Industries. His/her records indicate that he/she was formerly employed by you. We would appreciate your verification of the stated facts and your frank comments on other points.

_____, **Human Resources Representative**

Employed with you from _____ to _____   ☐ Yes   ☐ No
(If dates are incorrect, please state correct dates.)

Position _____   ☐ Yes   ☐ No

Salary _____   ☐ Yes   ☐ No

Reason for leaving _____

Eligible for rehire (If no, please explain.) _____   ☐ Yes   ☐ No

Attendance: Excellent ☐ Good ☐ Fair ☐ Poor ☐ (If poor, please explain.)

Punctuality: Excellent ☐ Good ☐ Fair ☐ Poor ☐ (If poor, please explain.)

Signature _____

Title _____

Date _____

Sample 7-10

This telephone reference check serves as a guide for the HR representative making the call. The questions focus on verification of information supplied by the candidate. Any additional information volunteered by the person supplying the information is to be noted under "Remarks."

    Since telephone references generally yield more information than written references, more space for notes should be allowed.

TELEPHONE REFERENCE CHECK

Person conducting investigation: *Please advise party this reference check will be held confidential.*

Name				
Former Employer _____				
Address _____ _____				
Telephone				
Former Supervisor	Peer	Direct Report	Vendor/Supplier	Other
Name of Person Supplying Information				
Title of Position(s) Held				
Employed from to Salary Verified as $ /				
Responsibilities				
Reason for Leaving Eligible for Rehire ☐ Yes ☐ No				
Remarks _____ _____ _____ _____ _____				
Strength Areas				
Development Areas				
Reference Conducted by Date / /				

Sample 7-11

This sample represents a detailed employment reference form for exempt positions. It may be submitted as a written request or conducted as a telephone reference. Although it is improbable that all questions will result in answers, the form targets a sufficient number of categories relevant to a professional-level position so that even if only half are answered, the prospective employer is likely to gain valuable insight into the candidate's qualifications.

Sample 7-11

Employment Reference Form for Exempt Positions

Exempt Employment Reference Check

Date:

- -

Applicant's name: ＿＿＿＿＿＿＿＿ Position: ＿＿＿＿＿＿＿＿＿＿

Person contacted: ＿＿＿＿＿＿＿ Title: ＿＿＿＿＿＿＿＿＿＿＿＿

Company: ＿＿＿＿＿＿＿＿＿＿ Telephone no.: (＿＿) ＿＿＿＿＿

Address: ＿＿＿＿＿＿＿＿＿＿＿＿＿＿＿＿＿＿＿＿＿＿＿＿＿＿＿

- -

The above named individual has applied to Avedon Industries for employment. He/She has listed you as a former employer, and has authorized us to conduct a reference check. We need your assistance in verifying and providing certain information regarding his/her work performance.

1. ＿＿＿＿＿＿＿＿＿＿ worked in the ＿＿＿＿＿＿＿＿＿＿＿
   department as a(n) ＿＿＿＿＿＿＿＿＿＿＿＿＿＿＿＿＿＿＿
   from ＿＿＿＿＿＿ to ＿＿＿＿＿＿.
   (　) correct (　) incorrect
   If incorrect, please explain.

2. His/Her primary responsibilities included: ＿＿＿＿＿＿＿
   ＿＿＿＿＿＿＿＿＿＿＿＿＿＿＿＿＿＿＿＿＿＿＿＿＿＿＿
   ＿＿＿＿＿＿＿＿＿＿＿＿＿＿＿＿＿＿＿＿＿＿＿＿＿＿＿
   ＿＿＿＿＿＿＿＿＿＿＿＿＿＿＿＿＿＿＿＿＿＿＿＿＿＿＿
   (　) correct (　) incorrect
   If incorrect, please explain.

(continues)

Sample 7-11. Continued.

Employment Reference Form for Exempt Positions

Applicant's name: _____   Position: _____

Person contacted: _____   Company: _____

- -

3. He/She stated that his/her reason for terminating employment with your company was: _____

   _____

   (   ) correct (   ) incorrect
   If incorrect, please explain.

4. How would you evaluate his/her overall work performance?

5. What were his/her greatest strengths?

6. What were the areas in which he/she required improvement and/or additional training?

7. What made him/her an effective supervisor/manager?

Applicant's name: _____   Position: _____

Person contacted: _____   Company: _____

8. How did he/she handle job-related situations involving pressure? Involving difficult tasks?

9. How would you describe his/her management style? Decision-making style?

10. Please provide an example of the type of decision he/she would commonly have to make on the job, and the ramifications of this decision.

11. How effectively did he/she handle meeting deadlines?

12. How did he/she generally respond to repetitious tasks? To new assignments?

(continues)

Sample 7-11. Continued.

Employment Reference Form for Exempt Positions

Applicant's name: _____   Position: _____

Person contacted: _____   Company: _____
- -

13. Please describe any work-related travel required, in terms of location, duration, and frequency.

14. This job calls for the ability to: _____
    What experience did he/she have in doing this?
    (Note: This question can be expanded to encompass several different factors. Use your job description as a guide.)

15. How effectively did he/she interact with peers? Senior management? Employees?

16. Would you rehire him/her?
    (   ) yes (   ) no
    If no, why not?

17. Is there anything else we should know about his/her work performance?

Reference conducted by: _____

_____

Sample 7-12

This reference format for nonexempt employees can be mailed or conducted by phone. Beyond the first question, seeking verification of information provided by the candidate, the form poses numerous open-ended questions. If the person conducting the reference check is fortunate enough to encounter a former employer willing to take the time to answer these questions, the results will undoubtedly prove significant in making a hiring decision.

Sample 7-12

Employment Reference Form for Nonexempt Positions

Nonexempt Employment Reference Check

Date:

- -

Applicant's name: _____ Position: _____

Person contacted: _____ Title: _____

Company: _____ Telephone no.: ( ) _____

Address: _____

- -

The above named individual has applied to Avedon Industries for employment. He/She has listed you as a former employer, and has authorized us to conduct a reference check. We need your assistance in verifying and providing certain information regarding his/her work performance.

1. _____ worked in the _____ department as a(n) _____ from _____ to _____ .

   ( ) correct ( ) incorrect
   If incorrect, please explain.

2. His/her primary responsibilities included: _____
   _____
   _____
   _____

   ( ) correct ( ) incorrect
   If incorrect, please explain.

Employment Reference Form for Nonexempt Positions

Applicant's name: _____   Position: _____

Person contacted: _____   Company: _____

- -

3. He/She stated that his/her reason for terminating employment
   with your company was: _____
   _____

   (   ) correct (   ) incorrect
   If incorrect, please explain.

4. How would you describe his/her attendance record? Punctuality
   record?

5. How would you evaluate his/her overall work performance?

6. What tasks did he/she perform particularly well?

7. What were the areas in which he/she required improvement
   and/or additional training?

(continues)

Sample 7-12. Continued.

Applicant's name: ⸻   Position: ⸻

Person contacted: ⸻   Company: ⸻

⸺⸺⸺⸺⸺⸺⸺⸺⸺⸺⸺⸺⸺⸺⸺⸺⸺⸺

8. How closely did you need to supervise his/her work?

9. How did he/she respond to requests to work overtime? To be on call?

10. How did he/she respond to repetitious tasks? To new assignments?

11. How effectively did he/she interact with co-workers? With management?

12. This job calls for the ability to: ⸻.
     What experience did he/she have in doing this?
     (Note: This question can be expanded to encompass several different factors. Use your job description as a guide.)

Employment Reference Form for Nonexempt Positions

Applicant's name: _____   Position: _____

Person contacted: _____   Company: _____

- -

13. Would you rehire him/her?
    (   ) yes (   ) no
    If no, why not?

14. Is there anything else we should know about his/her work performance?

Reference conducted by: _____

Sample 7-13

This reference form requires authorization to release the candidate's educational records. The college is asked for verification of basic facts and additional comments, if desired.

The tone of the form is clear, the style is concise, and the two-box format facilitates reading and completion.

Schools may charge a fee for providing educational references.

Sample 7-13

EDUCATION REFERENCE FORM

TO: _____

_____

I, _____, authorize the release of all information as requested by the Avedon Industries in consideration of my application for employment.

Signature _____

Date _____ Social Security No. _____ Date of Birth _____

Please Print Name (first/last) _____

Name at Time of Graduation

_____ is currently being considered for a position with the Avedon Industries and has informed us that he/she has attended your college and received a degree. We would appreciate your verification of the stated facts and your frank comments on other points.

_____   **Human Resources Representative**

ATTENDANCE From _____ to _____ (include graduate work even if not completed)

Has applicant completed all courses? If no, please explain. ☐ Yes ☐ No

_____

Has degree been granted? If no, please explain. ☐ Yes ☐ No

_____

Comments: _____

_____

Authorized Signature _____

Title _____   Date _____

Sample 7-14

This sample, written entirely in text, is unique. Perhaps the sender feels that former employers react negatively to formal reference requests and are more likely to respond to a more relaxed approach.

This technique is likely to backfire, however, since the recipient must compose a lengthy response from scratch. At the very least, a letter of this type should be preceded by a phone call.

July 29, 199X

Martha Sandstone
Director of Human Resources
Valdart, Ltd.
419 Main Street
Windsor, Texas 09876

Dear Ms. Sandstone:

Jonah Braverman has applied to Avedon Industries for the position of Quality Control Supervisor. He listed your company as his most recent employer.

We need to verify Mr. Braverman's employment at Valdart. Could you please provide me with the dates he worked there, as well as his title and salary at the time he terminated? I am also interested in his reason for leaving, as well as gaining some insight into his performance.

Of course, all of the information you provide will be kept confidential.

I would appreciate your response by August 12, 199X. If you have any questions, call me at 555-7741.

Thank you.

Sincerely,

Mary Evans
HR Coordinator

ME/cs

Letters to Rejected Applicants

Objective: Thanks candidates for their time and interest, welcomes future applications

Purpose: To inform

Readers: Applicants not selected for a job

Style: Personal pronouns, active voice, varied pace, consistent

Tone: Clear, concise, direct, neutral, positive

Format: Straight text

Contents: Date, address, salutation, appreciation for the applicant's time, statement regarding the rejection of the application, encouragement for future application, complimentary close, signature block

Sample 7-15

Written in a full-block format, this rejection letter is concise in its message. It is also clearly written, except for the statement, "Your resumé will be retained for a reasonable length of time." How long is a reasonable length of time? That paragraph would be better rewritten as, "We will retain your resumé for six months and contact you if our employment needs change during that time."

The letter effectively begins and ends with a positive tone, sandwiching the bad news in between.

The mixture of a passive and active voice makes the letter a bit formal.

February 9, 199X

John Doe
123 Apple Blossom Lane
Cherry Hill, PA 19608

Dear Mr. Doe:

Thank you for the interest you have expressed in employment opportunities within Avedon Industries.

Your qualifications have been carefully reviewed. However, at the present time no position is available that would utilize your skills and experience.

Your resumé will be retained for a reasonable length of time, and you will be contacted in the event our employment needs should change.

We appreciate your interest in our company and wish you success in your search for a suitable career position.

Sincerely,

Evelyn J. Waxman
Human Resource Representative

EJW/dia

Sample 7-16

This rejection letter starts and ends positively. Rather than advising the candidate of rejection, the middle paragraph refers to the selection of another applicant, thereby softening the impact.

February 21, 199X

Beth White
121 Salamander Circle
Forksville, PA 54321

Dear Ms. White:

Thank you for the time you spent with us discussing the position of benefits department secretary.

After carefully reviewing your qualifications, we have chosen another candidate who more closely matches our current requirements.

Although we cannot offer further encouragement at this time, your expressed interest in Avedon Industries is appreciated. Should any positions become available within the corporation for which you might qualify, we will contact you. Good luck in your future endeavors.

Sincerely,

Michael C. Robertson
Human Resource Representative

MCR/pde

Sample 7-17

This letter, written in a semiblock format, is an example of how too positive a tone at the outset can have a detrimental effect. The first paragraph offers the applicant false hope: How can anyone described as outstanding and impressive be rejected? Yet in the following paragraph, which repeats how impressive his qualifications were, that is exactly what is communicated. The applicant is effectively rejected again when he reads on and learns that, as good as he was, someone else was apparently better.

Adding the sentence about contacting him if the number one choice fails to accept is inappropriate.

Some of the tired expressions should be replaced ("feel free to try us again in the future"), and several of the sentences should be reworked to avoid overusing the word *we*.

June 23, 199X

Mr. Josh Struckman
411 Hillbrow Avenue
New Britain, Connecticut 32345

Dear Mr. Struckman:

We thank you for your application and interest in the position of production manager. We think you have an outstanding background and impressive credentials.

As impressed as we were with your qualifications, however, we regret to say that we cannot offer you the position. Someone else, also with excellent qualities, better suits our needs at this time. If for any reason that person cannot accept our offer, we will contact you since you are our second choice.

We hope you won't be discouraged and will feel free to try us again in the future.

Very truly yours,

Heather M. Sondheim
Assistant HR Director

HMS/jsr

Letters to Selected Applicants

Objective: Advises applicants that they have been selected for a given job

Purpose: To inform

Readers: Person being offered a job

Style: Personal pronouns, active voice, varied pace, consistent

Tone: Distinct, clear, direct, complete, factual, friendly, descriptive

Format: Straight text

Contents: Date, address, salutation, reference to the job applied for, congratulations on being selected, salary, starting date, information concerning what to do next, complimentary close, signature block. Note that salary should always be stated as a monthly figure; annual salaries imply that the person is guaranteed the job for a year.

Sample 7-18

This is a straightforward job offer letter. The HR director congratulates the candidate on having been selected for the job, confirms the agreed-on starting salary and starting date, and tells her what to do prior to her first day of work.

May 15, 199X

Ms. Sandra Wilshire
16 Quaker Lane
Pottsdam, West Virginia 23234

Dear Ms. Wilshire:

On behalf of Avedon Industries, I am delighted to offer you the position of assistant controller. As discussed, your starting monthly salary will be $5,166. Since you indicated during our last interview that you would want to give your current employer four weeks' notice, we are hoping you will be able to start with us on June 24.

When you receive this letter, please call me to confirm your acceptance and starting date. I will then go over your benefits and schedule your preemployment orientation.

I look forward to hearing from you.

Sincerely yours,

James MacIntyre
Senior HR Representative

Sample 7-19

This job offer takes too long to get to the point. The applicant has to wade through excess verbiage before learning that he is being offered the position.

July 17, 199X

Mr. Vincent Scaramach
459 Grully Place
Bethany, North Carolina 23215

Dear Mr. Scaramach:

I must say that I thoroughly enjoyed our meeting two weeks ago when you came in to discuss our opening for a communications supervisor. In fact, of the 25 interviews I conducted, I found my meeting with you to be the most enlightening. In addition to learning a great deal about your qualifications, I was impressed with your avocation of parachute jumping—you certainly have a great deal of courage; I could never imagine jumping out of a plane!

I hope we'll be able to continue our conversation about parachute jumping after you have begun working here. You see, I wasn't the only one impressed with your qualifications; the director of communications and I both agree that you should get the job.

We hope you will accept and be able to start right about Labor Day. We are prepared to offer you a monthly salary of $3,958.

Please call me to say yes as soon as you get this letter. I will then send you our benefits booklet.

I'm sure you'll be happy here. I look forward to your call.

Sincerely,

Tabitha K. Jacadiah
Employment Coordinator

TKJ/lma

Sample 7-20

The contents of this letter are direct, clear, descriptive, concise, and complete. The tone is positive. One problem is that the applicant's salary is stated as an annual figure. Moreover, the writer welcomes the person to the "family," implying a long-term relationship.

April 21, 199X

Ms. Laura Brinker
1794 Youngblood Avenue
Denver, Colorado 80017

Dear Ms. Brinker:

We are pleased to confirm our verbal offer to you of employment as a benefits analyst in our HR department at an annual salary of $34,000. Your starting date will be June 1, 199X; your hours are 8:30 A.M.–4:30 A.M., Monday through Friday. After three months, you will be eligible for flextime.

We feel your abilities and experience will be an asset to our department and hope that you will take advantage of the growth opportunities and numerous benefits offered by this company.

When you report to work on June 1, please see Mr. Steven Bryan, Benefits Manager. He will direct you to your work station and provide you with the orientation schedule that will take up most of your first day.

We hope you are as pleased to be joining our family as we are to have you. Call me at 555-1548 if you have any questions.

Sincerely,

Patrick D. Delawado
Human Resources Manager

PDD/vlh

8

New Employees

Paul reported for work on his first day thirty minutes early. He was anxious to make a good impression and was a little nervous. It was, after all, his first "real" job after graduating from college. Paul was not sure where to go or who to see. Since receiving a written job offer four weeks earlier, there had been no additional communication. He decided to go to the Human Resources Department and approached the receptionist. When advised of his name, she stared and replied, "Do you have an appointment?" Paul was startled by this response: Wasn't he expected? He informed the receptionist that he was reporting for work. She told him to take a seat. Paul sat and waited. Fifteen minutes later, a woman approached him and introduced herself as Cynthia, one of his coworkers. Their mutual manager expected to be tied up all day in meetings, and she was to get him started. That translated into Paul's being shown his work station and left alone to sift through a tower of reports and manuals. So much for Paul's first day on the job. As a result of that experience, Paul never felt a part of the company; within eighteen months he left the organization.

Contrast Paul's all-too-common scenario with Peggy's experience. On the first day of work, Peggy was greeted by her department manager, who spent an hour going over various aspects of her job. A schedule outlining her activities for the day was also provided. Included on the agenda was the first of three orientation sessions, during which time Peggy would learn about her benefits. At the end of the day she received her first piece of interoffice mail: a copy of the company newsletter, containing a section entitled, "Welcome Aboard!" Included was Peggy's name and a blurb about her prior experience as well as a description of her new duties. Peggy went home feeling she had made a wise employment decision.

Peggy's positive first-day experience resulted from a minimal amount of effort on the part of her employer: a packet of orientation materials, a description of the benefits policies, and a new employee announcement. These three items contributed to the beginning of a solid employer-employee relationship.

Organizational Orientation Materials

Objective: Identifies and describes the organization's philosophy, structure, benefits, policies, and expectations of its employees

Purpose: To inform and influence

Readers: New employees

Style: Standard and familiar phrases, personal pronouns, active voice

Tone: Descriptive, clear, complete, factual, friendly

Format: Questions and answers, illustrations to break up text, heads and subheads, lists

Contents: History, function, philosophy, position on EEO, current status and future goals of the company; unique organizational features; an overview of what it means to be employed by the company; organizational chart; overview of various departmental functions; map of the premises; information on the phone system; general industry information and special terminology (Note: Benefits, employee handbooks, and policies and procedures manuals will be treated separately in subsequent chapters.)

Sample 8-1

This sample offers a history of the company, its products, and its philosophy.

The forty-year company is sufficiently described within three paragraphs in succinct terms without dwelling on any one fact. Naming major customers is effective and may impress new employees.

The company philosophy is clearly stated. The list of personnel policies established to support the goals identified as part of the philosophy statement makes that statement more credible. One suggestion is that item 2, regarding job security, should be followed by a modified at-will statement to preclude any misinterpretation.

(continues)

Sample 8-1

HISTORY, PRODUCTS, AND PHILOSOPHY

The Roban Company was founded in Riverhead in February, 1957, in a portion of the two-story stone mill which presently constitutes our Compression Press Department.

Roban was formed to be a producer of a precision molded rubber parts of the highest quality. By mid-1958, demand had grown sufficiently to warrant an increase in personnel from two to six, and in 1959 Roban expanded its production operations to the entire building. Additions were subsequently made in 1960, 1961, 1962, 1964, and 1966.

Roban's continued growth, necessitated by an ever increasing demand for its precision products, prompted the Company to erect a large manufacturing facility in the area in 1968 and added to it in 1972 and 1974. In 1979 a large warehouse facility was added to the existing buildings here. Built on a large tract of land, the electronic equipment segment of Roban's operation offers an ideal location for future growth. Today, Roban is a company that is still growing rapidly. There are presently approximately 350 employees.

Roban's highly skilled team works smoothly to sell its products all over the world, to many widely known companies. Besides being one of the world's largest producers of rubber molded ball bearing seals, Roban also produces parts for the following industries: Power Tools, Cosmetics, Textiles, Sporting Goods, Small Appliances, and Agriculture. Major customers include such well known companies as American Standard, Fafnir Bearing Company, Federal Mogul Corporation, General Motors, Hoover N.S.K. Bearing Company, Marlin-Rockwell Corporation, Rockwell Manufacturing Company, The Singer Company, SKF Industries, Inc., Revlon, Stanley, Amtrol, Link Belt Company, Split Ball Bearing, and Torrington Company.

The Company's steady growth and expansion, the satisfaction of its customers, and its reputation all attest to the soundness of its policies and the excellence of their execution.

COMPANY PHILOSOPHY

The continuing goal of the Roban Company is to provide its customers with high-quality products at lowest possible prices; to meet its responsibilities to its stockholders, customers, employees, and the community; to achieve a return on investment and expansion; to continue to expand employment opportunities and growth within the Company.

To attain this goal, the following basic personnel policies have been established by the Company:

1. Select employees on the basis of their ability and capacity to do the job.
2. Provide job security to the fullest extent of our ability.
3. Provide dependable leadership and competent on-the-job training.
4. Pay wages commensurate with each employee's contribution and to equal or exceed wages for comparable work in area industries.
5. Give employees the opportunity for advancement by filling vacancies by promotion from within the Company whenever qualified individuals are available.
6. Provide adequate vacation and holiday time, retirement income, and other benefits based upon service.
7. Provide a safe and pleasant place to work.
8. Keep employees fully informed on matters of mutual interest and concern.
9. Provide reasonable opportunity for employees to be heard on any problem pertaining to their employment.

Sample 8-2

New hires are introduced to the company by this brief statement describing the company's products. It is factual and interesting, leaving the reader curious to know more.

Greetings to Avedon's hires!

Avedon Industries is a subsidiary of Eldridge, Inc., which is known all over the world for its high-quality electric resistance alloys, fasteners, and chain products.

Much of the raw material required for our products is purchased from the parent company in Norway in the form of heavy rod and wire, which is processed by us to the sizes required by our customers. Certain alloys are made from domestic raw material in our melting shop.

Some of the applications for our alloys are as heating elements in ceramic kilns; industrial furnaces for heat treating; appliances such as toasters, hot plates, and flatirons; cigarette lighters for automobiles; and electric resistors in electronic equipment, such as radar and computers.

You should also know about our newest product, which is used for heating elements in industrial electric furnaces up to 3,100 degrees F, temperatures much higher than attained with any previously known metallic element material.

Ours is a quality industry. Our customers will accept only products of the highest quality. In order to maintain and expand our business, each one of us has to be quality minded. At all times, we must do our utmost to satisfy our customers' high demands for quality and manufacture a product that will enhance the reputation of our organization. We hope that you will contribute to our good standing with customers and thus welcome you to Avedon Industries.

Sample 8-3

This company clearly conveys its commitment to equal employment opportunity by virtue of this statement distributed to all new hires. The tone is serious and factual, the style straightforward and direct. Portions read like a legal document; in that regard, it is a bit heavy-handed. It does, however, drive home the importance of EEO to this organization.

It has always been the established policy of our company to select the best-qualified person for every job. The term *qualified* applies to educational background, previous experience, proven skills, relevant characteristics, and growth potential.

No one will be discriminated against in any aspect of employment on the basis of race, color, religion, gender, age, national origin, veteran status, disability, or any other characteristic protected by federal, state, and local law. "Any aspect of employment" pertains to recruiting, interviewing, selecting, promotions, lateral moves, demotions, compensation, benefits, training, educational opportunities, termination, and all other privileges, terms, and conditions of employment.

All company facilities and company-sponsored activities shall be available to all employees on a nonsegregated, nondiscriminatory basis. This includes but is not limited to health and country club memberships and sports activities.

Sample 8-4

Here is a table of organization for the Human Resources Department of a U.S.-based, midsized financial institution with branches overseas. The chart is easy to read and understand. New hires can determine at a glance what the Human Resources Department consists of and know where to go with questions or concerns.

Backup sheets, not shown here, provide job descriptions for each position.

Sample 8-4

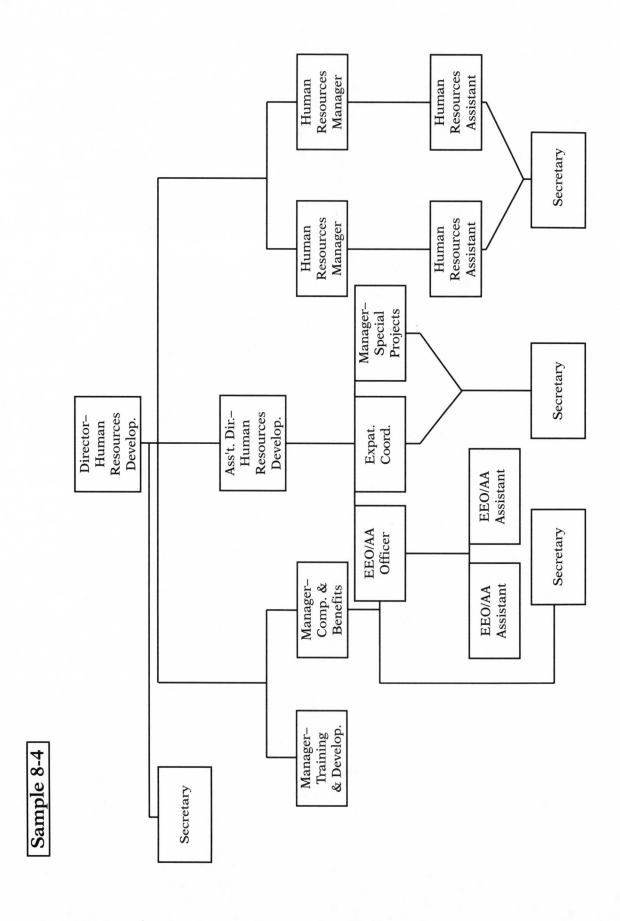

Sample 8-5

The company that generated the table of organization for the Human Resources Department in Sample 8-4 provides each department's new hires with a detailed chart of the functions within that unit. Following is a sample of the compensation and benefits segment.

The same easy-to-read format prevails, providing employees with a clear sense of the distribution and levels of responsibility.

Sample 8-5

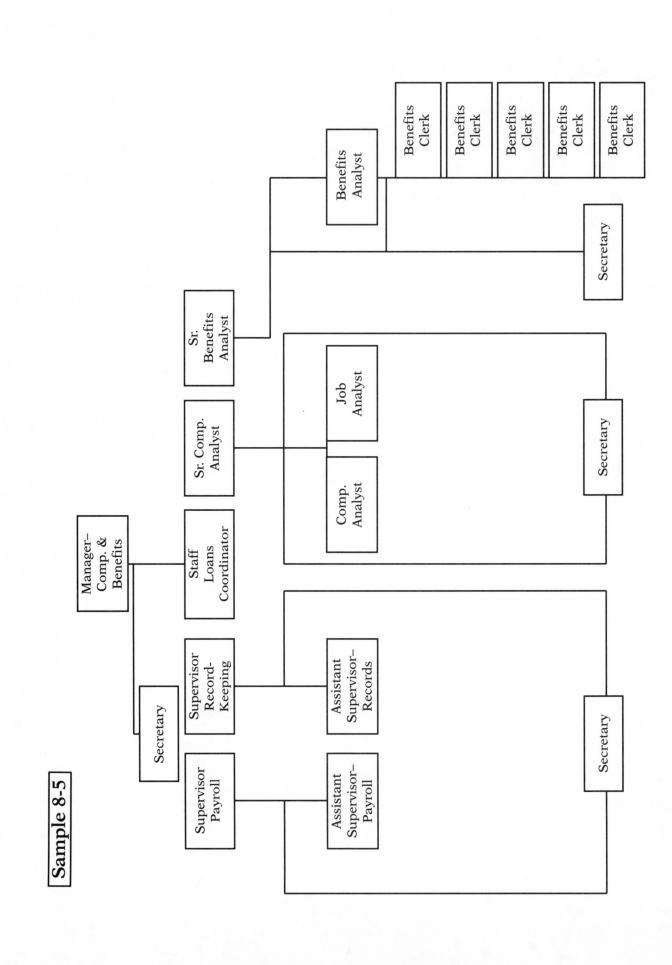

Sample 8-6

Any industry that uses a language of its own should provide new hires with a glossary of terms and definitions.

This sample shows a page from a booklet designed to assist financial institution employees to become familiar with the terms they will use in their daily routine. A portion of the introduction states, "Familiarity with financial and data processing terminology will produce better-informed and more efficient employees."

The booklet consists of nearly fifty pages of expressions and special terms commonly used in financial work. For easy access, the words are arranged alphabetically. The terms stand out in capital letters and boldface type; definitions follow.

Two problems are that the booklet uses sexist language (e.g., referring to bookkeepers as "she"), and some of the definitions contain the very word being defined.

Sample 8-6

BAD DEBTS. Commercially speaking, bad debts are the amounts due on open account that have been proved to be uncollectible. Financial institutions, as well as commercial enterprises, charge current operations with an amount (usually a given percent of the total outstanding) which past experience indicates to be the amount (or percentage) of the accounts or loans outstanding that will be uncollectible. The amount charged to current operations is credited to an account termed "Reserve for Bad Debts."

BALANCE AS A WHOLE. A form of proof method employed in banks, usually in the bookkeeping department. A control total is established for several books or ledgers. Each bookkeeper processes her work by posting to her accounts. At the end of the posting run, several bookkeepers will add their combined totals, and will "balance as a whole" to the control total for their group of ledgers.

BALANCE SHEET. An itemized statement which lists the total assets and the total liabilities of a given business to portray its net worth at a given moment of time. When statements of this nature are prepared by financial institutions, they are termed a "Statement of Condition." See also definition of that term.

BANK EXAMINATION. An examination made by representatives of a federal or a state bank supervisory agency. Its purpose is to make certain that a bank is solvent and is operating in conformity with banking laws, and to correct any errors in management or operations that may be found to exist.

BANKING BUSINESS. Primarily the business of receiving funds on deposit and making loans.

BANKRUPTCY. A state of conditions in which the financial position of an individual, corporation, or other legal entity is such as to cause it to be actually or legally bankrupt. Such condition is commonly referred to as a condition of insolvency.

BANK STATEMENT. A statement of a customer's account which the bank sends periodically, usually monthly, for the customer's information. It shows all deposits made and all checks paid during the period and balance, and is accompanied by the customer's canceled checks.

BEQUEST. A gift of personal property made by a decedent in his or her will. The party receiving the gift is called a legatee. See also "Legacy."

BILL OF SALE. A formal legal document which conveys title to, or right or interest in, specific personal property from the seller to the buyer.

BLUE SKY LAW. A name given to certain laws enacted by the various states which regulate the sale and issuance of securities, in an attempt to prevent fraud in their sale and disposition.

Benefits Policies

Objective: Outlines all insurance-related information, including medical, disability, pension plans, vacation days, and other days off

Purpose: To inform and influence

Readers: Primarily new hires but also prospective employees and current staff

Style: Straightforward, familiar language, explanations of any specific terms

Tone: Clear, distinct, descriptive, concise, direct, complete, factual

Format: Varied format as much as possible—use lists, questions and answers, comparisons, illustrations, columns, and boxes to break up the text

Contents: Medical, dental, life, accidental death and dismemberment, and travel accident insurance plans; long- and short-term disability; wellness plans; pension plans; savings and investment plans; annuity programs; vision care; prescription drug coverage; employee assistance programs; dependent care programs; educational assistance programs; direct deposit plans; credit unions; relocation; holidays; vacation days; sick days; bonus days; club memberships; exercise facilities. Where applicable, topics should include information regarding eligibility, deductibles, coinsurance, copayments, and limits.

Sample 8-7

This organization's two-page employee benefits summary highlights its main offerings. For more in-depth information, new hires are directed to four accessible sources. This approach prevents information overload, leaving the individual to seek out additional data as needed.

The summary begins with a clear statement concerning eligibility. The information that follows is arranged by category, set off in boldface type, with concise descriptions, making the information quite easy to absorb.

A disclaimer alerts employees to the possibility that the benefits not only are subject to change but that the offerings do not constitute any obligation on the part of the organization. This is, in effect, an at-will statement.

Sample 8-7

EMPLOYEE BENEFITS SUMMARY

ELIGIBILITY: All regular salaried employees who work at least 20 hours per week are eligible.

INSURANCE PLANS

MEDICAL: CIGNA POS (Point of Service)

—Unlimited lifetime maximum benefit, no deductible for in-network benefits.
—Hospital stay: 100%, pre-certification required.
—$10 copay for doctor visits at participating primary care physicians.
—$10 copay for eye examination by participating doctor; 40 to 60% discounts at participating Eye Care Plan of America for glasses/contacts.
—$10 brand/$7.50 generic copay for drugs prescribed by participating physicians and dispensed at participating pharmacies.
—No claim forms for in-network medical care.
—No exclusions on pre-existing conditions.
—Out-of-network coverage 80% of reasonable and customary charges on all eligible medical expenses after calendar year deductible.

DENTAL: Covers diagnostic, restorative, periodontic and orthodontic services

LIFE: Provides to you at no cost Life Insurance and Accidental Death and Dismemberment insurances each equal to one times your annual salary, in addition to Business Travel Accident coverage equal to three times your annual salary.

Optional coverage is available at low group rates. Dependent Life Insurance is provided by Avedon for those who insure dependents under any of our medical insurance plans and for those not insuring dependents, but who pay for the Dependent Life Insurance.

ADDITIONAL BENEFITS

Employee Assistance Program (EAP): Provides a limited number of counseling sessions paid for by Avedon to help staff members to overcome personal problems

Disability: Pays 60% of salary up to a maximum of $1,960 per week for short-term disability and up to $8,500 per month for long-term disability at no cost to you.

Pension Plan: Eligibility—one year from date of employment provided you are age 21 or older

—Entire cost paid by Avedon.
—Avedon provides a spouse's benefit feature for continuation of income to your surviving spouse if you die after retirement.
—Avedon provides a pre-retirement spouse's benefit of income to your surviving spouse if you die before retirement age provided you are vested.
—Vesting credit begins at age 18; 100% vesting after 5 years of service.
—You may elect early retirement any time after attaining age 55 and prior to 65. Normal retirement may be elected at age 65, delayed retirement after age 65.

(continues)

Sample 8-7. Continued.

Savings and Investment Plan

—Once you have completed 6 months of employment and are over age 20½, you may join the SIP on the first of any January or July.
—Generally, Avedon matches 50% of your contributions (up to 6% of your annual salary). You may defer up to a legally prescribed percentage of your untaxed salary into SIP.
—Immediate 100% vested on Avedon and employee contributions.

Tax Deferred Annuity Program

—You may participate, at any time, in a tax-deferred investment program for supplemental retirement annuities.
—You may defer up to a legally prescribed percentage of your untaxed salary into investments managed by the Teachers Insurance Annuity Association/College Retirement Equity Fund (TIAA/CREF).
—Withdrawals are permitted but subject to restrictions and penalties imposed by IRS.

Educational Assistance: Eligibility—employed by Avedon for 6 months. Avedon refunds tuition and registration fees up to a fixed maximum amount provided you meet grade requirements.

Sick Pay: After 6 months of employment, you receive 5 sick days. On your anniversary date and every anniversary date thereafter, you will receive 10 sick days up to a maximum of 90 days.

Vacation Pay

—If grade level is up to and including 16 and hire date is January–May, then after 6 months you are entitled to 5 days' vacation. If hire date is June–December, you are entitled to 10 days after 6 months and after December 31.
—If grade level is 17 or above, and hire day is January–May, then after 6 months you are entitled to 10 days' vacation. If hire date is June–December, you are entitled to 15 days after 6 months and after December 31.

Holidays: Generally there are 9 scheduled days per year and 2 optional holidays if hired by December 1 of that year.

Direct Deposit Plan: Paychecks can be directly deposited into your checking account or savings account.

SPECIAL PROGRAMS

—Avedon Scholarship Program
—Influenza inoculations and hypertension screening

The above information is a brief summary of your employee benefits. For a more detailed description, see your supervisor for the Policies Manual, your Summary Plan Description, or call/visit the Human Resources Department or the Employee Benefits Rep at your location.

DISCLAIMER: *The benefits and policies set forth above are those currently in existence at Avedon. Avedon may change these benefits at its discretion. Nothing contained herein shall be deemed to create an obligation on the part of Avedon to offer these benefits to employees in the future.*

Sample 8-8

The employee benefits summary for this Fortune 500 apparel company begins with a simple statement of eligibility. It then proceeds to describe, in list fashion, its twenty-three primary benefits.

A comparison format is effectively used to identify the four health plan options. Similarly, the company's dental plan is described using columns for three types of services. The result is a clear delineation of the plan's offerings.

Each of the remaining twenty-one benefits is numbered and underlined, followed by two to five succinct statements.

I have two suggestions. First, since there are twenty-three categories for employees to thumb through, a cover page listing the contents would guide employees to the pages that are of interest to them. Second, employees should be provided with a cross-reference for additional information. For example, item 13, "Holidays," states that there are nine paid holidays per year but does not specify what they are.

Sample 8-8

EMPLOYEE BENEFITS SUMMARY

NOTE: A minimum of 32 hours per week required to be eligible for Company insurance benefits.

BENEFITS:

1.   Health Care
         -Exempts - no waiting period
         -Non-Exempts - 3 month waiting period
         -Effective date - 1st of calendar month based on above eligibility
         -All health care premiums are paid with pre-tax dollars

PLAN COMPARISON

	ABC Health Plan In Network*	ABC Health Plan Out of Network	Health Plan X* (H.M.O)	Health Plan Y* (H.M.O.)
Benefit Max.	$1,000,000	$1,000,000	Unlimited	
Office Visits	100% after $15 Copayment per visit (includes periodic exams and well baby care)	70% (periodic exams & well baby care are not covered)	$3 Copayment per visit	$5 Copayment per visit
Surgery				
Inpatient	Paid 90%	Paid 70%	Paid 100%	Paid 100%
Outpatient	Paid 90%	Paid 70%	Paid 100%	Paid 100%
Hospital				
Inpatient	90%	70%	100% Semi-Private	100% Semi-Private
Outpatient	90%	70%	100%	100%
Emergency	90%	70%	$25 Copay per visit	$25 Copay per visit
Maternity Care	90% Doctors' Charges 90% Hospital Charges	70% 70%	100% Doctors' Charges 100% Hospital Charges	100% Doctors' Charges 100% Hospital Charges
Well Baby Care	100% after $15 Copayment subject to schedule	Not Covered	$3 Copay per visit includes immunizations	$5 Copay per visit includes immunizations
Prescriptions	80%	70%	$3 Copay Generic $8 Copay Name Brand	$8 Copay per prescription
Annual Deductible	none	$400 individual $800 family	none	none
Cost to Employee	(monthly)			
Employee Only	$ 15.50	$ 15.50	$ 15.00	$ 15.50
Employee & Spouse	$117.50	$117.50	$123.00	$143.50
Employee & Children	$117.50	$117.50	$ 98.00	$143.50
Employee & Family	$180.50	$180.50	$181.00	$171.50

*Requires use of Participating Providers

2.   <u>Dental Plan</u> - Dental Benefit Plan, Inc.
        - Eligibility - same as health care
        - Premiums are paid with pre-tax dollars

        <u>Plan summary</u>
        Benefit Maximum - $1,000 per person, per calendar year

Services	*Insured Percent*	*Services Included*
Type I Services	- 100% of allowable charges	• routine oral exam once every 12 months • dental cleanings - once every 12 months • treatments for children - fluoride, sealants, space maintainers, harmful habit appliance (restrictions apply for all) • x-rays, bitewing - once every 12 months
Type II Services	- 80% after deductible of allowable charges	• x-rays - full-mouth - once every 60 months • simple extractions, removal of exposed roots, incision and drainage • new fillings and replacement fillings • certain lab tests, pain treatment, therapeutic drug injections
Type III Services	- 50% after deductible of allowable charges - waiting periods apply for Type III services	• root canal • complex oral surgery • gum disease treatment • initial placement, replacement and maintenance of inlays, crowns, bridges, and dentures

Deductible - $75.00 per person per calendar year

Cost to Employee (monthly):

Employee	$11.90
Employee & Spouse/child	$22.92
Employee & Children	$27.50
Employee & Family	$37.00

(continues)

Sample 8-8. Continued.

<u>NOTE</u>: Total life insurance cannot exceed 3-1/2 times total compensation up to maximum of $1,000,000.

3.   <u>Life Insurance</u>, basic
       -face value 1-1/2 times annual salary
       -basic coverage: Company paid up to maximum of $50,000 coverage
       -for basic coverage in excess of $50,000 cost is 16¢/month per $1,000
       -exempt - coverage begins first day of month following employment
       -non-exempt - 3 month waiting period

4.   <u>Life Insurance</u>, supplemental - optional (one times base salary)
       -employee pays according to age level
              Example: age 45 to 49 is 26¢/month per $1,000
       -deducted from 2nd check of the month

5.   <u>Life Insurance</u>, additional supplemental (step rate)
       -one times base salary
       -employee pays according to age level
              Example: age 45 to 49 is 26¢/month per $1,000

6.   <u>Dependent Life Coverage</u>

       OPTION 1: $4.50/Month   -   Spouse $10,000
                                           Dependent Children $5,000
                                           14 Days - 6 Months $500
       OPTION 2: $2.25/Month   -   Spouse $5,000
                                           Dependent Children $2,500
                                           14 Days - 6 Months $250

7.   <u>AD&D Coverage</u> - optional
       -covers 24 hours a day
       -employee pays 36¢/month per $10,000 Individual Plan,
              54¢/month per $10,000 Family Plan
       -deducted from 2nd check of the month

8.   <u>LTD Insurance</u> - optional
       -employee pays
       -payment of benefit begins 180 days after accident or illness; 60% of monthly
              salary up to $16,666.67 for maximum benefit up to $10,000 monthly
       -premium is 48¢/month per $100 monthly covered earnings.
       -deducted from 1st check of the month

9.   <u>Business Travel Accident Insurance</u>
       -Company paid
       -$200,000 maximum benefit, for exempt employees
       -$750,000 Officers and Board of Directors

10.   <u>Tax Advantaged Savings Plan (401K)/Employee Stock Ownership Plan (ESOP)</u>
       -one year service is required
       -withhold 2% to 10% in pre-tax earnings
       -company matching contribution is entirely in Corporation stock,
        "ESOP Convertible Preferred", beginning April 1, 1990
       -50¢ on the dollar on employee contributions of 2% to 6%
       -no Company matching at 7% to 10% maximum; % of salary includes base pay,
              overtime, incentive bonus
       -vesting in Company contributions takes 60 months

11. Pension Plan (Defined Benefit) - Company Paid
-exempt receive booklets - date of hire
-All others receive when become participants. Eligibility: reaches age 21 and has completed one year of service

12. Vacation
-1 week after 6 months (when hired before June 30)
-2 weeks after 1 year of employment
-3 weeks after 10 years of employment
-4 weeks after 20 years of employment

13. Holidays - 9 paid holidays per year

14. Normal Hours - 8:00 AM - 5:00 PM (40 Hours)
1 Hour Lunch

15. Pay
-every 2nd Friday
-deductions: 1st check - LTD, 1st Half Premium for Health Insurance
2nd check - AD&D, Supp. Life Insurance, 2nd Half Premium for Health Insurance

-Taxes: State   2.8%
County   1.0%
Occupational $9.80 fixed, per person, per year

16. Exercise Facilities (Reading only - employees in Corporate office only *)

17. Community Blood Bank (Reading only)
-Annual fee paid by Company

18. Sick Pay
-5 days per calendar year paid
-STD - Short Term Disability - length of payment will depend on years of service with Company, up to maximum of 26 weeks of pay. Must have Doctor's authorization on Company form.

19. Travel Expense Policy for Management Personnel
-auto mileage 30 ¢ per mile
-never charge any travel expense to Company. Employee must pay and be reimbursed.
Exception: Employees holding Company authorized credit cards.

20. Educational Assistance
-Company pays 100% of tuition, lab fees and registration.
-Grade of C or better is required for reimbursement.
-One year service required before reimbursement is received by employee.

21. Matching Grants to Colleges, Universities, and Public Television Stations
-Company matches dollar for dollar up to $10,000 maximum.
-One year service required.

22. Federal Credit Union (CTCE)
-New employees eligible upon enrollment.

23. Direct Deposit available
-Form to be completed and void check to be attached. Will start with the second paycheck.

*For exceptions, check with VP Human Resources & Administration

New Employee Announcements

See Chapter 1 for additional samples of new employee announcements.

Objective: Describes new hire's background and responsibilities to existing staff

Purpose: To inform

Readers: All employees and members of management

Style: Conversational, use of personal pronouns

Tone: Friendly, descriptive

Format: Straight text, questions and answers, quotations, photographs

Contents: Background, starting date, responsibilities, other interesting information

Sample 8-9

This announcement comes across as friendly and informative. Acknowledging a sampling of the employee's accomplishments gives existing staff some insight into her abilities. Her photograph, not included here, accompanies the announcement.

We are pleased to announce the hiring of Dana Stockwell to the position of manager, benefits administration. Dana joined us on March 13 after working for three years in a similar capacity at Yift Industries. While she was at Yift, Dana developed and implemented the company's Managed Health Care Plan, resulting in improved health care coverage and significant savings to the organization. She looks forward to developing a similar plan for us.

Please join in welcoming Dana to our staff!

Sample 8-10

This sample puts too much pressure on the new hire. By announcing the company's expectations in a memo distributed to the entire staff, the employer is compelling the new employee to meet certain goals. Although he may work toward these objectives, it is inappropriate to announce them publicly. The lecturing tone of the language also puts pressure on the existing staff of the controller's office.

The announcement is ill timed. Announcements are appropriate after a person has started so that existing staff can connect the person with the description and the new employee feels welcome.

Finally, the announcement uses vague terms, such as "extensive experience and knowledge." Readers would appreciate specifics as to how many years and where this experience and knowledge were acquired.

We are all anxiously awaiting the arrival of John Mercy on July 19 so he can begin to tackle the mountain of work that has accumulated in the controller's office. He has a background that consists of extensive experience and knowledge that will enable him to do this.

John will be counting on the staff in the controller's office for help in getting started. Please be there for him and give him all the support he needs.

Sample 8-11

This announcement requires readers to wade through a sea of verbiage to determine the identity of their new coworker. It begins inappropriately, with a testimony to the incumbent, and then rambles on about irrelevant issues. The clichés make reading tiresome. This effort is virtually worthless, since it provides little pertinent information.

Just when we thought we would never find someone to replace Joanie, our one-of-a-kind employee relations manager, who is retiring after fifteen years of outstanding service, we struck it rich! Of course, it didn't happen overnight, as many of you in the Human Resources Department know. We ran a newspaper ad three weeks in a row, did a spot on the radio for two weeks running, and listed the opening with an agency. Finally, after what seemed like forever, in walked Christopher Forbes. (Actually, he was referred to us by a friend, Jocelyn, over in Benefits.)

Although Joanie is a tough act to follow, Christopher promises to be every bit as effective in the job. He's got a couple of years of really solid experience and some interesting ideas. I'd say Chris was worth waiting for!

9

Performance Management

I once worked for a vice president assigned the responsibility of revamping the organization's compensation structure. To do this he first had to account for the salaries and job functions of over three thousand employees. "I'm perfectly willing to tackle the task," he said, "as long as human resources suspends documenting performance management until I'm finished!" I asked him what this meant.

"Don't you see?" he continued. "Employees keep doing things that HR insists on writing about: anniversary dates generate written performance appraisals; outstanding accomplishments lead to letters of commendation; problems on and off the job result in written-up counseling sessions and disciplinary notices; and when employees terminate, HR sends out letters and writes up the exit interviews. How am I supposed to evaluate our existing compensation structure when human resources people keep writing about things that result in changes? I just wish that for one week HR would stop writing. Hell, I'd even settle for a day!"

He would have a better chance at winning the lottery than persuading HR to stop generating performance management documents.

While employee performance undeniably results in a great deal of paperwork, it need not be a major drain of time and energy. Keep your objectives and purpose clear, remember who your readers are, and adhere to a concise, consistent style, tone, and format. Make certain, too, that the contents are job related and appropriate for your environment.

Performance Appraisals

Objective: Identifies how an employee's performance has measured up against previously agreed-on objectives, pinpoints areas requiring improvement, identifies an action plan with a new set of objectives

Purpose: To inform and influence

Readers: Employee being evaluated; HR representatives for purposes of compensation, job posting, and training; managers who are considering an employee for transfer or with regard to counseling and disciplinary matters

Style: Moderate to formal, limited jargon, no clichés

Tone: Direct, factual, positive

Format: Forms: heads and subheads, different type sizes, boldface type, white space, lists, columns, boxes, instructions for use, explanation of rating terms. Contents: straight text, partial sentences acceptable.

Contents: In addition to noting the employee's name, department, job title, appraisal period, and date of the appraisal meeting, generic categories include areas of responsibility, knowledge of the job, demonstrated skill level, communication, quality of work, and quantity of work. Additional exempt categories may include problem solving and decision making, leadership, time management, and business development. Forms for nonexempt employees may call for attendance and punctuality and the ability to work independently. There should be room for mutually agreed-on steps for improving performance and for comments by the evaluator and the employee.

Sample 9-1

This nonexempt performance appraisal starts out with a clear set of instructions and rating term definitions. The space allotted for areas of responsibility encourages evaluators to write a great deal here (referring to the employee's job description is an effective way of doing this). The topics listed under "Aspects of Performance" are relevant to most nonexempt jobs. Item 10, "Other" could be expanded to allow for additional topics.

Placing the overall rating at the end of the evaluation of specific topics is effective. Reversing this order often results in a forced effort to make specific comments fit in with the overall appraisal.

More space should be allotted for the mutually agreed-on steps to improve performance. Including target dates for marked improvement is important.

Identifying the employee's goals and interests accomplishes two objectives: (1) it tells employees that the evaluator is interested in what matters to them, and (2) it pinpoints appropriate training or education.

Allowing as much room for the employee's signature as the manager's communicates a message of interest and concern to the employee. So, too, does the qualifier that the employee's signature indicates understanding, not agreement.

This form is easy to read. The heads are in boldface type, there are some columns, and the use of white space is sufficient to break up the categories.

Sample 9-1

Nonexempt Performance Appraisal Form

Employee Performance Appraisal (Nonexempt)

Name:_____

Dept./Div.:_____

Job title:_____

Appraisal period:_____to_____

Date of appraisal meeting:_____

Instructions

1. The manager and employee should jointly define specific performance objectives to be achieved during the specified appraisal period.
2. During the appraisal period, progress will be measured against the performance plan developed in Item 1 above.
3. At the end of the appraisal period, the manager will measure the employee's performance against the plan, using the following ratings:

   (1) *Outstanding*   Far exceeds expectations in all aspects of the job
   (2) *Above Average*   Consistently exceeds expectations in many aspects of the job
   (3) *Average*   Consistently meets expectations in all job areas
   (4) *Below Average*   Fails to meet expectations consistently in several aspects of the job
   (5) *Unsatisfactory* Fails to meet expectations in most or all aspects of the job

4. During the appraisal meeting, the manager and employee will develop a plan addressing the areas requiring improvement and the employee's goals and interests.
5. Following the appraisal meeting, the form will be signed and dated by both the manager and the employee and forwarded to the next level of management or human resources, as required. The employee should be given a copy of the completed and signed form.

(continues)

Sample 9-1. Continued.

A. ***Areas of Responsibility***

Responsibility	Results Achieved	Rating

B. *Aspects of Performance* (Circle the appropriate rating and support your selection under "Comments.")

1. Knowledge of the job, department/division, and organization
   (1)   (2)   (3)   (4)   (5)

   Comments:

2. Demonstrated skill level
   (1)   (2)   (3)   (4)   (5)

   Comments:

3. Communication
   (1)   (2)   (3)   (4)   (5)

   Comments:

4. Ability to work with others
   (1)   (2)   (3)   (4)   (5)

   Comments:

5. Customer relations
   (1)   (2)   (3)   (4)   (5)

   Comments:

6. Ability to work independently
   (1)   (2)   (3)   (4)   (5)

   Comments:

(continues)

Sample 9-1. Continued.

7. Quality of work
   (1)   (2)   (3)   (4)   (5)

   Comments:

8. Quantity of work
   (1)   (2)   (3)   (4)   (5)

   Comments:

9. Attendance/Punctuality
   (1)   (2)   (3)   (4)   (5)

   Comments:

10. Other (Describe)
    (1)   (2)   (3)   (4)   (5)

    Comments:

C. *Overall Rating*   (Circle the rating that best describes the employee's over-
                       all performance during the appraisal period.)

   (1)   (2)   (3)   (4)   (5)

D. *Mutually Agreed-On Steps to Improve Performance*

Step	Target Date

E. **Employee's Goals and Interests**

F. **Comments**
Manager's Comments:

Employee's Comments:

G. **Signatures** (Note: Employee's signature indicates understanding of contents, not necessarily agreement.)

_____		_____
(Appraising manager)		(Date)

_____
(Appraising manager)   (Date)

_____
(Employee)   (Date)

_____
(Next level of management)   (Date)

_____
(Human resources representative) (Date)

Sample 9-2

This exempt performance appraisal follows the style and format of the preceding nonexempt form. Several of the same generic categories appear, such as areas of responsibility and some aspects of performance. Additional topics relevant to professional jobs are also listed.

Sample 9-2

Exempt Performance Appraisal Form

Employee Performance Appraisal (Exempt)

Name:_____ Appraisal period:_____to_____

Dept./Div.:_____ Date of appraisal meeting:_____

Job title
(functional and official):_____

Instructions

1. The manager and employee should jointly define specific performance objectives to be achieved during the specified appraisal period.
2. During the appraisal period, progress will be measured against the performance plan developed in Item 1 above.
3. At the end of the appraisal period, the manager will measure the employee's performance against the plan, using the following ratings:

   (1) *Outstanding*   Far exceeds expectations in all aspects of the job
   (2) *Above Average* Consistently exceeds expectations in many aspects of the job
   (3) *Average*   Consistently meets expectations in all job areas
   (4) *Below Average* Fails to meet expectations consistently in several aspects of the job
   (5) *Unsatisfactory* Fails to meet expectations in most or all aspects of the job

4. During the appraisal meeting, the manager and employee will develop a plan addressing the areas requiring improvement and the employee's goals and interests.
5. Following the appraisal meeting, the form will be signed and dated by both the manager and the employee and forwarded to the next level of management or human resources, as required. The employee should be given a copy of the completed and signed form.

(continues)

Sample 9-2. Continued.

A. *Areas of Responsibility*

Responsibility	Results Achieved	Rating

B. *Aspects of Performance*   (Circle the appropriate rating and support your selection under "Comments.")

1. Knowledge of the job, field, department/division, and organization
   (1)   (2)   (3)   (4)   (5)

   Comments:

2. Demonstrated skill level
   (1)   (2)   (3)   (4)   (5)

   Comments:

3. Problem solving and decision making
   (1)   (2)   (3)   (4)   (5)

   Comments:

4. Communication
   (1)   (2)   (3)   (4)   (5)

   Comments:

5. Responsiveness to department/organization needs
   (1)   (2)   (3)   (4)   (5)

   Comments:

6. Leadership
   (1)   (2)   (3)   (4)   (5)

   Comments:

(continues)

Sample 9-2. Continued.

7. Business development
   (1)   (2)   (3)   (4)   (5)

   Comments:

8. Time management
   (1)   (2)   (3)   (4)   (5)

   Comments:

9. Resource administration (staff, budget, and materials)
   (1)   (2)   (3)   (4)   (5)

   Comments:

10. Quality of work
    (1)   (2)   (3)   (4)   (5)

    Comments:

11. Productivity
    (1)   (2)   (3)   (4)   (5)

    Comments:

12. Other (Describe)
    (1)   (2)   (3)   (4)   (5)

    Comments:

(continues)

C. *Overall Rating* (Circle the rating that best describes the employee's over-all performance during the appraisal period.)

(1)   (2)   (3)   (4)   (5)

D. *Mutually Agreed-On Steps to Improve Performance*

Step	Target Date

E. *Employee's Goals and Interests*

(continues)

Sample 9-2. Continued.

F. *Comments*
   Manager's Comments:

   Employee's Comments:

G. *Signatures*   (Note: Employee's signature indicates understanding of contents, not necessarily agreement.)

_____   _____
(Appraising manager)   (Date)

_____   _____
(Employee)   (Date)

_____   _____
(Next level of management)   (Date)

_____   _____
(Human resources representative)   (Date)

Sample 9-3

The instructions for completing this nonexempt performance appraisal form are detailed and clear. Key responsibilities are tied in directly with results and are individually rated. Each item listed under "Performance Qualities" provides definitions for the numbered ratings. While somewhat wordy, this approach saves evaluators time otherwise wasted in flipping back to the first page to review what the ratings 1 through 5 mean. It also precludes misinterpretation of the qualities. Requiring an explanation to support the rating mitigates against arbitrary selections.

The "Development Plans" section reflects communication between the manager and the employee. Ample room exists for comments from both.

The form is well presented, using boldface type, columns, boxes, and bold lines to separate subtopics.

Sample 9-3

Non-Exempt
Performance Appraisal Form

Name _____

Department _____

Job Title _____

Division _____

Department Number _____

Appraisal Period _____ To _____
Beginning Date   Ending Date

Date Original Responsibilities Set _____

Dates of _____
Periodic
Feedback _____
Sessions _____

Date of Appraisal Discussion _____

Instructions for Completing this Form:

■ At the beginning of the appraisal period, the manager and employee jointly define specific performance objectives or key job responsibilities, and performance qualities to be achieved during the next 12 months.

■ During the appraisal period, progress is monitored against the performance plan. Both manager and employee should conduct periodic feedback sessions to ensure that performance is "on track." Be sure to note (a) when such sessions occur (at the appropriate point on the front of the form) and (b) any comments about progress to date or modifications to the plan (in the applicable section of the form).

■ At the end of the appraisal period, the manager will measure the employee's performance against the plan. Managers will review objectives or key job responsibilities and assign one of the ratings below to each:

1 Clearly Outstanding
Results produced in all areas of the job far exceed expectations

2 Consistently Exceeds Expectations
Performance consistently exceeds expectations in many job areas

3 Consistently Meets Expectations
Results produced in all job areas consistently meet expectations. This rating applies to a solid performer making a tangible contribution to the Bank

4 Somewhat Less Than Satisfactory
Results fall short of consistently meeting expectations in some job areas

5 Unacceptable
Results fall seriously short of meeting expectations.

■ Prior to the annual appraisal session, the employee will review the year's achievements against the performance plan and conduct a self-appraisal. The manager and employee will compare the self-appraisal and the manager's ratings during the appraisal session.

■ The manager, after reviewing ratings selected for objectives or responsibilities, performance qualities, and the employee's self-appraisal, will assign an overall rating. Using the scale above, this rating will reflect the definition that best describes the employee's overall performance during the appraisal period.

■ During the annual appraisal session, the manager and employee will formulate a development plan that addresses the employee's career interests and goals as well as areas in which improvement is needed.

■ At the end of the annual appraisal discussion, the form will be signed and dated by the employee and the manager, and then sent on for review and signature by the next upper level manager.

I. Key Job Responsibilities

List and number the mutually agreed upon key job responsibilities. At the end of the appraisal period, describe the results achieved as specifically as possible.

Responsibilities	Results Achieved and Comments	Rating

Responsibilities Added or Revised During Review Period	Results Achieved and Comments	Rating

(continues)

Sample 9-3. Continued.

II. Performance Qualities

Mutually agree upon which performance qualities relate to the employee's job. At the end of the appraisal period, assess the employee's performance for each applicable quality and then indicate which rating and description is the best fit. Check the appropriate box and explain why you chose that performance rating in the space provided.

1. Knowledge/Skill

Understanding and knowledge of policies, procedures and facts relevant to job. Demonstration of technical expertise and skill required (e.g., typing skill, credit skill, numbers skill, etc.)

1 ☐
Far exceeds knowledge required for job and is always thoroughly informed. Demonstrates excellent technical skill. Expertise is widely acknowledged and sought after. Instructs peers in area of expertise.

2 ☐
Exceeds required level of knowledge in many instances. Demonstrates skill that is often above what is expected in job.

3 ☐
Has a fully satisfactory understanding of the job and the knowledge needed. Fully demonstrates skill required.

4 ☐
Fair knowledge of job duties and procedures. Requires some improvement in skill level. Regularly requires assistance and instruction. (Possibly new to job and in learning stage.)

5 ☐
Lacks knowledge of job. Does not meet skill requirements.

Explanation _____

2. Problem Solving/Decision Making

Ability to resolve work problems and make appropriate decisions. Application of prior experience to new situations.

1 ☐
Exceptional ability to anticipate and solve problems. Often helps others in resolving problems. Makes innovative, highly effective decisions.

2 ☐
Often anticipates problems and is able to resolve them independently. Makes highly effective, often innovative decisions or suggestions.

3 ☐
Successfully identifies and resolves problems independently. Decisions are based upon a thorough analysis of the problem. Makes good, effective decisions.

4 ☐
Usually able to resolve problems. Needs some assistance in analyzing situations to make effective decisions.

5 ☐
Unable to resolve problems. Makes ineffective decisions.

Explanation _____

3. Communication

Degree to which one communicates all matters of importance. Skill in transmitting and receiving information orally and in writing, with individuals or groups.

1 ☐
Exceptional skill in communicating with others. Far exceeds requirements of job in every aspect of communication. Always communicates appropriate information in a timely manner to the right people. Always checks for comprehension.

2 ☐
Exceeds communication requirements of job in many instances. Presents thoughts that are well prepared, precise and thorough in both oral and written form.

3 ☐
Shares information and knowledge appropriately. Is fully effective in communicating with others, and meeting communication requirements. Seeks additional information/explanation for clarification.

4 ☐
Usually shares appropriate information and knowledge. Requires some improvement in ability to give and receive information effectively.

5 ☐
Ineffective in communicating with others. Does not meet communication requirements of job. Does not share information in a timely way or to appropriate individuals.

Explanation _____

4. Internal Relations

Degree to which one works effectively and cooperatively with other workers and other departments in achieving organization goals. Degree of responsiveness to organization needs. Demonstration of teamwork in the facilitation of work flow.

1 ☐
Shows exceptional level of cooperation in working with others. Takes initiative in responding to organization needs and providing high level of teamwork.

2 ☐
Often takes initiative in responding to organization needs and offering high level of cooperation. Shows high level of teamwork. Anticipates and confronts obstacles.

3 ☐
Cooperates fully with others and is responsive to organization needs. Provides appropriate level of teamwork.

4 ☐
Needs some improvement in level of cooperation and responsiveness. Takes little initiative in providing teamwork. Is late in responding to requests.

5 ☐
Shows little cooperation or teamwork. Not responsive to organization needs.

Explanation _____

(continues)

5. Customer Relations

Degree to which one represents the Bank with courtesy, tact and efficiency in dealing with customers, and effectively counsels customers about Bank services.

1
☐
Exceptional level of tact, courtesy and efficiency. Skill in counseling customers is widely acknowledged and sought after.

2
☐
Often shows exceptional level of tact and courtesy. Is excellent in representing the Bank's services to customers.

3
☐
Fully represents the Bank's products and services, and shows appropriate level of courtesy and efficiency.

4
☐
Needs some improvement in representing the Bank with customers. Requires assistance to counsel customers effectively.

5
☐
Lacks courtesy and tact, and fails to effectively counsel customers about Bank services

Explanation

6. Leadership

Ability to guide others to the successful accomplishment of a task and to counsel, train and develop others.

1
☐
Skill in delegating and guiding others is widely acknowledged and sought after. Is exceptional in helping others to improve and develop, and in establishing a highly motivating climate.

2
☐
Often obtains exceptional results in guiding others and helping them to improve and develop. Able to establish a highly motivating climate.

3
☐
Fully effective in delegating work and overseeing its successful completion. Demonstrates skill in establishing a highly motivating climate and assisting others to improve and develop.

4
☐
Inconsistent results obtained when delegating work to others. Needs some improvement in helping employees to learn and develop, and in establishing a spirit of cooperation.

5
☐
Ineffective in overseeing workflow. Does little to assist employees in improving and developing.

Explanation

7. Self-Management

Degree to which one plans and organizes own work, uses time effectively and sets appropriate priorities. Amount of supervision required.

1
☐
Highly skilled in independently planning and organizing work to meet job requirements. Requires little supervision.

2
☐
Usually able to independently plan and organize work. Makes good use of time. Requires minimal supervision.

3
☐
Requires minimal assistance in planning and organizing work, and setting appropriate priorities. Needs reasonable amount of supervision. Very reliable.

4
☐
Requires assistance in establishing priorities, organizing work and making best use of time. Needs some improvement.

5
☐
Unable to organize own work or use time effectively. Requires excessive supervision.

Explanation

8. Quality of Work

Degree of accuracy, neatness, thoroughness, and/or cost effectiveness in work produced.

1
☐
Does work of highest level. Work is very complete and almost errorless.

2
☐
Work exceeds department standards with minimum errors. Shows complete attention to detail.

3
☐
Fully meets department's quality standards with reasonable errors.

4
☐
Occasionally work does not meet standards, some rework is required. Rate of errors needs some improvement.

5
☐
Work does not meet department standards. Error rate is unacceptable.

Explanation

(continues)

Sample 9-3. Continued.

9. Quantity of Work

Degree to which one produces the required amount of work within the required time frame.

1	**2**	**3**	**4**	**5**
☐	☐	☐	☐	☐
A top producer. Far exceeds required level of output. Finishes far ahead of deadlines.	Exceeds required level of output and finishes ahead of deadlines. Often does more than own share.	Fully meets required level of output within deadlines.	Usually produces required amount of work. Meets most deadlines. Some improvement is needed.	Insufficient output. Usually does not meet deadlines.

Explanation _____
_____

10. Attendance/Punctuality

Punctuality with regard to absence or tardiness.

1	**2**	**3**	**4**	**5**
☐	☐	☐	☐	☐
Never late or absent.	Rarely late or absent.	Attendance/punctuality record good.	Has received a written warning within the last 12 months.	Has been placed on formal probation for attendance punctuality within the last 12 months.

Explanation _____
_____

11. Other

Describe _____
_____

1	**2**	**3**	**4**	**5**
☐	☐	☐	☐	☐
_____	_____	_____	_____	_____
_____	_____	_____	_____	_____

Explanation _____
_____
_____
_____
_____

III. Overall Rating

Considering all factors, check the definition which best describes this employee's overall performance during the past period.

☐ **Clearly Outstanding**	☐ **Consistently Exceeds Expectations**	☐ **Consistently Meets Expectations**	☐ **Somewhat Less than Satisfactory**	☐ **Unacceptable**

IV. Development Plans

List mutually agreed upon steps to improve present performance or prepare for future assignments.	Note employee career interests and comments.

V. Comments

Supervisor's Comments

_____
_____
_____
_____
_____

Employee's Comments

_____
_____
_____
_____
_____

VI. Signatures

Employee (Acknowledging Receipt of This Appraisal)   Date

Immediate Supervisor   Reviewer (Next Upper Level Manager)

Date   Date

Note: Employee Must be Given Copy of This Appraisal   Effective Salary Date

Sample 9-4

This sample of an exempt performance appraisal form follows the same format and style as the preceding nonexempt form. Several of the "Performance Qualities" topics are different.

Sample 9-4

Exempt
Performance Appraisal Form

Name	Appraisal Period	To
	Beginning Date	Ending Date

Functional Title

Date Original Objectives Set

Officer Title

Dates of
Periodic
Feedback
Sessions

Department

Division

Date of Appraisal Discussion

Instructions for Completing this Form:

■ At the beginning of the appraisal period, the manager and employee jointly define specific performance objectives or key job responsibilities, and performance qualities to be achieved during the next 12 months.

■ During the appraisal period, progress is monitored against the performance plan. Both manager and employee should conduct periodic feedback sessions to ensure that performance is "on track." Be sure to note (a) when such sessions occur (at the appropriate point on the front of the form) and (b) any comments about progress to date or modifications to the plan (in the applicable section of the form).

■ At the end of the appraisal period, the manager will measure the employee's performance against the plan. Managers will review objectives or key job responsibilities and assign one of the ratings below to each:

1 Clearly Outstanding
Results produced in all areas of the job far exceed expectations.

2 Consistently Exceeds Expectations
Performance consistently exceeds expectations in many job areas.

3 Consistently Meets Expectations
Results produced in all job areas consistently meet expectations. This rating applies to a solid performer making a tangible contribution to the Bank.

4 Somewhat Less Than Satisfactory
Results fall short of consistently meeting expectations in some job areas.

5 Unacceptable
Results fall seriously short of meeting expectations.

■ Prior to the annual appraisal session, the employee will review the year's achievements against the performance plan and conduct a self-appraisal. The manager and employee will compare the self-appraisal and the manager's ratings during the appraisal session.

■ The manager, after reviewing ratings selected for objectives or responsibilities, performance qualities, and the employee's self-appraisal, will assign an overall rating. Using the scale above, this rating will reflect the definition that best describes the employee's overall performance during the appraisal period.

■ During the annual appraisal session, the manager and employee will formulate a development plan that addresses the employee's career interests and goals as well as areas in which improvement is needed.

■ At the end of the annual appraisal discussion, the form will be signed and dated by the employee and the manager, and then sent on for review and signature by the next upper level manager.

(continues)

Sample 9-4. Continued.

I. Objectives

List and number the mutually agreed upon objectives. At the end of the appraisal period, describe the results achieved as specifically as possible.

Objectives	Results Achieved and Comments	Rating

Objectives Added or Revised During Review Period	Results Achieved and Comments	Rating

II. Performance Qualities

Mutually agree upon which performance qualities relate to the employees job. At the end of the appraisal period, assess the employee's performance for each applicable quality and then indicate which rating and description is the best fit. Check the appropriate box and explain why you chose that performance rating in the space provided.

1. Knowledge/Skill

The comprehension of the job and knowledge of relevant theory, facts, processes Demonstrates technical expertise and skill (e.g., negotiations, sales, credit, marketing etc.) on the job.

1
☐
Expertise is widely acknowledged and sought after. Often instructs and consults to others in areas of expertise.

2
☐
Exceeds required level of knowledge in many instances. Very rarely needs technical help. Demonstrates skill that is often above what is expected in job. Expertise is acknowledged and useful to others.

3
☐
Demonstrates fully competent understanding of the job and the knowledge and skill needed to execute responsibilities. Seldom needs help.

4
☐
Has fair knowledge of job duties and procedures. Regularly requires assistance and instruction. (Possibly new to job and in learning stage.)

5
☐
Lacks knowledge of job. Requires close supervision. Fails to demonstrate or lacks appropriate skills.

Explanation

2. Problem Solving/Decision Making

The ability to analyze problems, evaluate alternatives, anticipate consequences and eliminate obstacles to successful completion of objectives or responsibilities.

1
☐
Exceptional ability to anticipate and solve problems. Can size up a situation with expert speed and analytical skill. Decisions reflect thorough appreciation of risks. Is sought out by others for counsel and advice.

2
☐
Excels in many aspects of problem solving and decision making. Almost always anticipates potential problems and resolves them. Often assists others in problem solving. Makes decisions on own initiative within limits of authority.

3
☐
Successfully identifies cause of problems and effectively resolves them. Makes routine decisions which are logically thought out, consistent with business strategy and Bank policy.

4
☐
Needs assistance in analyzing situations and/or making effective decisions. May over-analyze a problem or unnecessarily delay its resolution.

5
☐
Lacks ability to assess and solve problems. Makes decisions that are inconsistent, untimely or short-sighted.

Explanation

3. Communication

The degree to which one communicates all matters of importance, upward and downward, transmits directions and information orally and in writing, conducts and participates in meetings.

1
☐
Demonstrates outstanding communication abilities in oral and written form. Communicates all matters of importance in a clear and timely manner to manager, peers and/or subordinates. Gives and receives information using all modes of communication and always checks for comprehension.

2
☐
Demonstrates very good communication skills. Presents thoughts in both oral and written form that are well prepared, precise and thorough. Communicates appropriate information in a timely manner to the right people. Anticipates needs for communication.

3
☐
Shares knowledge and information clearly and appropriately. Conducts purposeful meetings and participates effectively. Seeks additional information/explanation for clarification.

4
☐
Usually shares knowledge and information appropriately. Needs improvement in written and/or oral communication skills. Is reluctant to ask for necessary additional information.

5
☐
Communicates in a manner which is unclear or verbose. Inattentive to detail, tone or implications of written/oral communication. Does not share information in a timely way or to appropriate individuals.

Explanation

4. Responsiveness

Ability to work collaboratively with users and other internal departments, to represent the department's services and products accurately, and to understand and respond to organization needs.

1
☐
Always far exceeds expectations in working with other internal departments. Always understands and uses the proper approach to get the best results.

2
☐
Excels in many aspects of collaboration and consultation. Often helps achieve more than expected. Anticipates and confronts objections/obstacles.

3
☐
Is fully responsive to user needs and collaboratively achieves results. Interfaces professionally and efficiently. Represents department services and products accurately.

4
☐
Exhibits difficulty in understanding and responding to user needs. Is late in responding to requests.

5
☐
Lacks skill to successfully interface with other department users to achieve results. Or over commits, promising products/services that can't be delivered within quality or timing parameters.

Explanation

(continues)

Sample 9-4. Continued.

5. Business Development

The ability to develop and maintain new and existing business, sell and cross-sell products and services, counsel customers about Bank services, participate in community and business affairs.

1 ☐
Demonstrates superior skill in every aspect of business development and ensures optimal bottom-line impact.

2 ☐
Excels in several business development functions. Demonstrates enthusiasm in putting best effort toward enhancing customer relations and profits.

3 ☐
Has thorough knowledge of Bank products and services. Effectively sells and counsels customers. Participates actively in community and business affairs.

4 ☐
Shows fair ability to develop business. Needs to strengthen sales skills and knowledge of products.

5 ☐
Shows marginal interest and skill in business development functions.

Explanation

6. Leadership

The ability to guide others to the accomplishment of objectives/responsibilities, develop teamwork, evaluate and develop people, and resolve conflict.

1 ☐
Demonstrates exceptional ability to inspire confidence, motivate and get results. Highly respected by associates. Is an excellent role model.

2 ☐
Leads very capably and consistently gets very good results. Has unusual ability to get commitment of others and resolve conflict.

3 ☐
Promotes teamwork. A good motivator and developer. Establishes personal, peer and/or staff accountabilities which are clear and specific to achieve results. Reorders priorities and/or reallocates resources to meet unexpected demands. Manages and resolves conflicts among staff members.

4 ☐
Has difficulty clarifying goals, delegating responsibilities and achieving results. Has fair degree of respect. Has some difficulty resolving conflicts.

5 ☐
Gets limited cooperation of staff. Lacks full control. Does not delegate sufficiently or to proper individuals.

Explanation

7. Self-Management

Works with minimal supervision, manages own time effectively, maintains control on all current projects/responsibilities and ensures proper follow-up.

1 ☐
Exceptional self-management. Demonstrates creativity in managing time and control over multiple projects and responsibilities.

2 ☐
Successfully works independently and with minimal supervision. Usually excels in managing own time and maintaining project control and priorities.

3 ☐
Works effectively with minimal supervision. Plans and schedules time efficiently in order to complete work on time. Ensures proper control and follow-up.

4 ☐
Usually works with minimal supervision. Needs some direction in maintaining proper control and follow-up.

5 ☐
Lacks self-management skills. Needs too much supervision. Does not complete work on time. Fails to follow up.

Explanation

8. Resources Administration

Identifies need for and allocates staff, budget and materials to ensure effective operating procedures and cost containment.

1 ☐
Balances changing priorities and resource allocations while maintaining high level of products and services. Budget preparation reflects a thorough analysis of current operating costs and contingencies for optimizing existing resources.

2 ☐
Analyzes resource allocations and variances to identify cost reduction opportunities. Budgets prepared anticipate business changes, are well documented and within guidelines.

3 ☐
Achieves individual/unit goals by utilizing appropriate level/type of resource for assigned responsibilities. Budgets submitted are complete, within prescribed guidelines, on time and reflect the unit's business plan. Monitors budget throughout the year.

4 ☐
Unit goals are not being met due to inappropriate utilization of available resources or failure to identify alternative resources. Budgets are not completely documented, within guidelines, on time or reflective of anticipated changes in unit goals. Fails to follow up on budget variances throughout the year.

5 ☐
Available resources are inappropriately allocated or utilized. Does not anticipate and assess impact of business changes and resources, does not control costs or explain budget variances.

Explanation

9. Concern for Quality

Demonstrates continuous concern about product/service design and delivery quality and, if a manager, instills in all employees the concept that the customer or internal department is a prime consideration in creating and delivering Bank services

1
☐
Far exceeds expectations in improving the outgoing quality of the product/service produced or managed. Has made significant improvements in design or customer information to increase the value of the product/service to the customer or internal receiving department. Has substantially reduced costs related to poor product/service quality.

2
☐
Has improved the outgoing quality level of the product/service produced or managed. Has made improvements to the product/service which have increased the product/service's value to the customer or internal receiving department. Has reduced costs related to poor product/service quality.

3
☐
Meets the goals for outgoing quality level of the product/service produced or managed. Ensures that the product/service value to the customer has not deteriorated. Holds costs of quality to established levels.

4
☐
Quality level or value of product/service produced or managed has deteriorated. Costs of poor product/service quality have increased.

5
☐
Quality level or value of product/service produced or managed has substantially deteriorated. Product/service value to the customer has substantially lessened. Costs of poor product/service quality have increased greatly

Explanation _____

10. Productivity

The degree of quantity of work produced.

1
☐
Far exceeds the required quantity of work. Outstanding output

2
☐
Exceeds the required quantity of work.

3
☐
Meets the required quantity of work.

4
☐
Needs to improve the quantity of work.

5
☐
Unsatisfactory quantity of work

Explanation _____

11. Other

Describe _____

1
☐

2
☐

3
☐

4
☐

5
☐

_____

Explanation _____

III. Overall Rating

Considering all factors, check the definition which best describes this employee's overall performance during the past period.

☐ **Clearly Outstanding**   ☐ **Consistently Exceeds Expectations**   ☐ **Consistently Meets Expectations**   ☐ **Somewhat Less Than Satisfactory**   ☐ **Unacceptable**

(continues)

Sample 9-4. Continued.

IV. Development Plans

List mutually agreed upon steps to improve present performance or prepare for future assignments.	Note employee career interests and comments.

V. Comments

Supervisor's Comments
_____
_____
_____
_____
_____

Employee's Comments
_____
_____
_____
_____
_____

VI. Signatures

Employee (Acknowledging Receipt of This Appraisal)   Date
_____

Immediate Supervisor   Reviewer (Next Upper
_____   Level Manager)
                                                      _____

Date   Date
_____   _____

Note: Employee Must be Given Copy of This Appraisal   Effective Salary Date
                                                      _____

Commendation Memos

Objective: Praises an employee for performing a task particularly well or accomplishing a difficult task

Purpose: To inform and influence

Readers: Employee being praised, HR representatives and managers who review the employee's file

Style: Moderate to conversational

Tone: Positive, friendly, descriptive

Format: Straight text

Contents: Any job-related task

Sample 9-5

This short memo is succinct and gushing with praise. The recipient is likely to feel pleased upon receiving it. Commenting that a copy of the memo will go to the employee's supervisor, as well as his HR file, is a nice touch.

November 19, 199X

To: Jed Bruckner
           Sales Representative

From: Mary Parker
           Director of Human Resources

What an incredible sales representative you are! After just 18 months on the job, you have broken our previously held record, set in 1994, for bringing in new clients.

Please accept my congratulations on an outstanding job; we are all proud to have you on our team.

A copy of this memo will be sent to your supervisor and will be placed in your HR file.

Sample 9-6

This positive and uplifting memo acknowledges the employee's contribution in specific terms and describes the result: a certificate and a luncheon. It concludes by effectively telling the employee that she is a valuable member of the company.

Using the employee's name in the body of the memo personalizes the message.

May 4, 199X

To: Lisa Flemengo
           Supervisor, Accounts Payable

From: Justin Brown
           Sr. HR Representative

Thank you for helping your department meet an incredibly difficult deadline by staying late each day for the past two weeks and giving up one weekend as well.

To express our appreciation for your dedication, we would like to present you with a certificate. Please accept our invitation to a 1:00 P.M. luncheon on Thursday, May 15, at which time the president and your manager will thank you personally.

Lisa, you are the kind of employee Avedon Industries can count on.

Sample 9-7

This memo contains the right information, but it is stiff and formal, lacking a positive tone.

April 4, 199X

To: Heather Cunningham
From: Malcolm Jacoby
Re: Division Report

Ms. Cunningham, you are to be acknowledged for your contributions to the annual division report at a ceremony being held on April 12, 199X, at 5:15 p.m. Nonalcoholic beverages and finger foods will be served until 6:00 p.m. Then the president will personally thank you and the other contributors.

Please let my office know no later than April 8 if you will be attending.

Thank you.

Sample 9-8

The last paragraph of this positive, friendly, and descriptive memo could be construed as a commitment to a promotion.

December 1, 199X

TO: Cecilia Murdock
FROM: Douglas Hunt

Dear Cecilia:

   Congratulations on your sales record in the last quarter. Not only did you succeed in selling a record number of training videos, but you generated an unprecedented interest in our new service, satellite training.

   I would not be the least bit surprised if you became the department's next vice president!

Counseling Sessions

Objectives: Addresses a specific problem that is interfering with effective job performance

Purpose: To inform and influence

Readers: Employee with the problem, HR representatives and managers who have occasion to review the employee's HR file

Style: Formal and structured

Tone: Descriptive, clear, concise, direct, complete, factual

Format: Straight text, full block

Contents: Date, employee's name, title, and department; reason for the counseling; related facts; consequences; signatures of the manager, employee, and witnesses, if any

Sample 9-9

This memo, documenting a counseling session, sets forth the facts without interjecting opinions or drawing conclusions. It identifies and discusses the particulars of the problem, describes the steps to be taken, and refers to the consequences of repeated offenses. It also stipulates when the manager and employee will meet again.

The tone is serious but not threatening or stern.

July 19, 199X

To: Jeffrey Sileck
                Customer Relations Assistant

From: Richard Jones
                Manager, Customer Relations

Re: Customer Complaints

This memo summarizes our meeting of July 18, 199X, at which time we discussed three recent complaints about your dealings with customers. Specifically, we talked about:

An incident on June 23, when a customer complained that you had made her wait for over 20 minutes before tending to her needs;

An incident on June 29, when a customer complained that you referred her to another line, even though you were not assisting another customer;

An incident on July 14, when you allegedly told a customer to go shop somewhere else if he didn't like the way he was being treated.

We went over each incident in detail. You acknowledged making the customer in the first complaint wait for 20 minutes, but explained that it was because you were taking care of important paperwork. You explained that the reason you referred a customer to another line was because you were on your break, and you denied telling a customer to shop elsewhere if he didn't like the way he was being treated in our store, adding that he had been verbally abusive toward you.

You agreed to be more attentive to customers in general, complete paperwork and take breaks when customers were not around, and talk to your supervisor if you feel that you need assistance with a difficult customer. You stated that you understood that further customer complaints would lead to appropriate disciplinary action.

We agreed to meet on August 18 to see if matters have improved.

Signature of Richard Jones _____ Date _____

Signature of Jeffrey Sileck _____ Date _____

Sample 9-10

The tone of this sample is negative, condescending, and accusatory; the style is inappropriately casual. The document is written in subjective terms (e.g., "I have not been happy with your work"). The supervisor does not offer any suggestions for correcting the problem or a specific date for reevaluation. Nor is space provided for the employee to sign an acknowledgment of any kind.

February 8, 199X

TO: William Terraine
            Auditor

FROM: Sylvester Putterman
            Auditing Supervisor

RE: Problems with your work

As you know, I have not been happy with your work over the past three months. Four of the last six reports you submitted to me were late. Also, there were a number of errors. I asked you if you were having problems at home, and you said there was nothing unusual going on.

Well, it's evident that something is going on. You used to be a great worker, Bill, but lately your work has been going downhill. Try to get back on track, O.K.? I'm sure you can do it!

Let's get together again in a few weeks and talk some more.

_____
Sylvester Putterman

Disciplinary Notices

Objective: Identifies the violation of a specific rule or policy and outlines the steps to be taken

Purpose: To inform and influence

Readers: Employee being disciplined, HR representatives and managers who have occasion to review the employee's file

Style: Formal and structured

Tone: Descriptive, clear, concise, direct, complete, factual

Format: Straight text, full block

Contents: Date; employee's name, title, and department; manager's name and title; nature of the infraction; specific rule or policy violated; relative facts; consequences of subsequent infractions; signatures of the manager, employee, and witnesses, if any

Sample 9-11

This sample represents the first written warning in a company's formal disciplinary process (the first step is a verbal warning). It is a statement of the problem, the rationale for disciplinary action, and the repercussions of continued violation. The employee is given room for comments and is asked to sign, acknowledging an understanding of the contents.

The tone is appropriately direct, objective, and serious.

Sample First Written Warning

TO: Kim Sanders/clerk-typist   June 23, 199X

FROM: Joyce Appleton/office manager

RE: Excessive Tardiness

In accordance with Section 8 of your Employee Handbook, of which you have a copy, all employees are expected to report to work before or at their regularly scheduled starting time. As you are aware, your regularly scheduled starting time is 9:00 A.M. On June 5, 1995, we discussed the matter of your excessive tardiness. Specifically, I pointed out six separate occasions during the preceding six-week period when you reported to work late. They were:

Tuesday, April 18	15 minutes late
Thursday, April 27	20 minutes late
Tuesday, May 2	30 minutes late
Thursday, May 11	25 minutes late
Monday, May 15	25 minutes late
Friday, June 2	20 minutes late

During the above-mentioned verbal warning, you acknowledged these occurrences and stated that you were sometimes having trouble making a certain train connection, which caused you to arrive at work late. You further stated that you planned on making different travel plans to avoid future tardiness.

Since our discussion three weeks ago you have been late on two occasions:

Friday, June 9	25 minutes
Monday, June 12	20 minutes

Failure to correct this behavior may result in a second written warning.

A copy of this first written warning will be placed in your HR file. If no additional instances of tardiness occur over the next 12 months, the warning notice will be removed.

_____   _____
(Manager's signature)   (Date)

_____   _____
(Employee's signature indicating   (Date)
   understanding of contents)

Employee's comments:

© 1997 by Arthur Associates Management Consultants, Ltd., Northport, N.Y.

Sample 9-12

This sample represents a second written warning for continued infraction. Reference is made to all proceedings prior to this step in the disciplinary process and what is likely to occur if the tardiness continues. The tone is sharper than the first written warning but still objective. The employee is given the opportunity to make comments and is asked to sign, indicating an understanding of the contents.

Sample Second Written Warning

TO: Kim Sanders/clerk-typist

FROM: Joyce Appleton/office manager

RE: Continued Excessive Tardiness

In accordance with our meeting and the verbal warning issued on June 5, 199X, and our meeting and the written warning issued on June 23, 199X (see attached), this constitutes a second written warning.

Over the past six weeks, you have been tardy four times:

Monday, June 26	10 minutes late
Wednesday, July 5	15 minutes late
Thursday, July 20	25 minutes late
Monday, July 31	20 minutes late

Failure to correct this behavior may result in suspension for one to three days without pay.

A copy of this second written warning will be placed in your HR file. If no additional instances of tardiness occur over the next 12 months, the warning notice will be removed.

_____   _____
(Manager's signature)   (Date)

_____   _____
(Employee's signature indicating   (Date)
   understanding of contents)

Employee's comments:

Exit Interviews

Objective: Determines what aspects of the job or company led to an employee's termination

Purpose: To inform

Readers: HR representatives interested in tracking patterns of termination and responsible for providing references

Style: Moderate

Tone: Friendly, positive, clear, descriptive

Format: Lists, boxes, columns, questions and answers

Contents: Varied, including: areas of work enjoyed most and least, compensation and benefits, areas employee would have changed, work environment, employer-employee relations, reason for leaving

Sample 9-13

This organization's exit interview form allows departing workers to evaluate employment in a number of ways: by selecting a relevant code, checking off boxes, and answering questions. Some of the questions may be difficult to answer (e.g., "How would you describe the internal management of your department?"). There is room for comments. Employees are assured that their answers will be kept confidential.

The form uses a varied format; it is easy to read and complete.

Sample 9-13

EXIT INTERVIEW FORM

Human Resources Department to Complete		
Name		Position
Location	Department	Supervisor
Original Date of Hire	Rehire Date	Last Day Worked
Total Experience	Grade	Last Performance Appraisal Rating
Years Months	Complement No.	Last Salary

Primary Reason for Resignation or Release

Resignations = C		Discharged for Cause = D	Retirement = F
20 Excessive Overtime	28 Attractive Offer	40 Absenteeism	50 Normal
21 Excessive Travel	29 Return to School	41 Tardiness	51 Early
22 Dissatisfied with Salary	30 Military	42 Insubordination	
23 Dissatisfied with Work	31 Maternity	43 Poor Job Performance	**Reduction in Force = I**
24 Dissatisfied with Supervisor	32 Mutual Agreement	44 Dishonesty	
25 Health Related	33 Start Own Business	45 Infraction of Company Rule	**Other Reason for**
26 Marriage	34 Change of Career	46 Misrepresentation of Data	**Leaving = K**
27 Relocation	35 Family Reasons		

Staff Member's New Affiliation

Company _____ Title _____

City/State _____ Phone _____ Base Salary $ _____

Property Returned

☐ Card key/ID Card
☐ Other keys
☐ Policies Manual
☐ Telephone credit card
☐ Uniforms
☐ Proprietary Information

Reminder of Policies

☐ Security of Data Base including hard copies and diskettes
☐ Non-compete agreement
☐ Other property (e.g., computer equipment, tools, etc.)

_____

Please Complete Reverse Side of Form

Your comments may be helpful in improving our personnel practices, thereby making Avedon a better place in which to work. Your answers will be kept confidential.

How would you rate the following within your department?

	Excellent	Above Average	Average	Below Average	Poor
A. Management skills of your immediate supervisor	___	___	___	___	___
B. Technical competence of your immediate supervisor	___	___	___	___	___
C. Adequacy of job-specific training	___	___	___	___	___
D. Adequacy of career development opportunities	___	___	___	___	___
E. Cooperation among those in your department	___	___	___	___	___
F. Cooperation among those outside your department	___	___	___	___	___
G. Equipment provided	___	___	___	___	___
H. Physical working conditions	___	___	___	___	___
I. Computer hardware/software	___	___	___	___	___

Additional Comments _____

_____

What did you like most about your job? _____

_____

What did you like least? _____

_____

What prompted you to search outside? _____

_____

Did you consider advancement from within by bidding on internal positions? _____

_____

How challenging did you find your job? _____

_____

How integral was your department with the rest of Avedon? _____

_____

How would you describe the internal management of your department? _____

_____

Would you return to Avedon?   Yes _____ No _____   Why? _____

Would you refer someone to Avedon? Yes _____ No _____ Why? _____

What one thing would you like to see changed at Avedon? _____

Please note that all tuition aid and scholarship compensation end upon your termination from Avedon.

Employee Signature _____   Date _____

Interviewer Signature _____   Date _____

Sample 9-14

The organization using the exit interview form in Sample 9-14 goes one step beyond eliciting reactions of terminating employees. It tracks former staff members to determine if their thoughts about the company have changed since termination.

This one-page questionnaire asks former employees to fill in some blanks, check off a few boxes, rate several work-related factors, and answer questions. Easy to read and complete, the entire form takes a maximum of 10 minutes.

Not many companies do this. More should.

Sample 9-14

POST-EXIT INTERVIEW FORM

Please complete this post-exit interview form, which is a follow-up procedure with former staff members to see how or if their thoughts about Avedon have changed since they left the organization. The information will help us in maintaining standards that are in accordance with the principles of superior management.

Name (please print) _____

Position held at Avedon _____

Name of supervisor _____

Last date employed at Avedon _____

Reason for leaving _____

1. Have you been employed since you left Avedon?　　　　　☐ Yes　☐ No

    If YES, answer questions 1a, 1b, 1c.

    1a Have you found that your training and experience at Avedon was
    helpful to you in acquiring your new position?　　　　☐ Yes　☐ No

    1b How does your new salary compare with what you earned at Avedon?

    _____

    1c How do the training programs at your new job compare with those at Avedon?

    _____

    1d How does your relationship with your new supervisor compare with your relationship with
    the supervisor you had at Avedon?

    _____

    _____

2. In regard to the work you did with Avedon, please rate the following on a scale of 1–5, with 5
    being the highest:

    Your own work performance _____　Your co-workers _____　Job satisfaction _____
    Work environment _____　Your supervisor _____　Benefits _____
    Compensation _____

3. In retrospect, is there anything you would have changed about your position
    at Avedon?　　　　　　　　　　　　　　　　　　　　☐ Yes　☐ No

4. Would you work for Avedon again?　　　　　　　　　　☐ Yes　☐ No

    Please offer any other comments you may have that could help to make Avedon a better
    place to work.

    _____

    _____

    Signature _____ Date _____

Sample 9-15

This form requires HR representatives to record the verbal responses provided by terminating employees. Instructions for use are clearly listed. The interview is limited to ten open-ended, generic questions. Employees are asked to review their comments as recorded by the interviewer, and then sign the form.

Instructions to HR representative conducting the exit interview:

1. Complete the boxed section.
2. Inform employees of the purpose for the meeting: to help Avedon Industries continue to improve employer/employee relations.
3. Assure them that all responses will be kept confidential.
4. Allow employees to read what you have written before having them sign the form.
5. Thank them for their cooperation and wish them well in their future endeavors.

Name_____Title_____ Department_____
Date of Hire_____Date of Termination_____
Starting Salary_____Salary at Termination_____

1. Why are you leaving Avedon Industries?_____
_____

2. Was your job accurately represented and described at the time of hire?_____
If not, please explain._____
_____

3. What did you enjoy most about working for Avedon Industries?_____
_____

4. What would you have changed about your employment if you could have?_____
_____

5. Do you feel the benefits you received were comprehensive?_____
Please explain._____

6. Do you feel that you were fairly compensated for the work you did?_____
Please explain._____

7. How would you describe the people with whom you worked?_____
_____

8. How would you describe the working conditions?_____
_____

9. What, if anything, could have been done to dissuade you from terminating your employment with Avedon Industries?_____
_____

10. Is there anything else we should know concerning your reason for leaving Avedon or about your employment with us?_____
_____

_____Date_____
HR representative's signature
The above information accurately reflects my verbal comments.

_____Date_____
Employee's signature

Letters of Termination

Objective: Advises an employee of the reason(s) for and effective date of termination

Purpose: To inform

Readers: Terminating employee

Style: Formal, structured

Tone: Clear, concise, direct, factual

Format: Straight text

Contents: Reason for termination, effective date, necessary papers to complete, items to return, reference to termination of benefits

Letters of termination should be sent by registered or certified mail, return receipt requested, to provide proof that the letter was mailed and received.

Sample 9-16

This letter of termination clearly states the reason for termination, as well as the effective date. To leave no room for confusion, copies of relevant letters and policies are attached.

One area is not clear: In the last sentence, the HR manager refers to outstanding monies due. Is that money the employee owes Avedon or vice versa?

April 2, 199X

Ms. Ethel Morningside
1212 Grand Avenue
Stalkin, Pennsylvania 45601

Dear Ms. Morningside:

Your employment with Avedon Industries has been terminated effective today, April 2, 199X, due to your failure to comply with our policy concerning attendance, and your failure to respond to repeated attempts to reach you by phone and mail. Copies of our written correspondence are attached. Also attached is a copy of Avedon's attendance policy, taken from the employee handbook, which you received and signed for at the time of hire.

Contact my office to discuss the return of your ID card, keys, and uniform. These items are the property of Avedon Industries. At that time we can also discuss our insurance company's policy concerning the continuation of certain benefits and any outstanding monies due.

Sincerely,

Sylvia H. Durham
HR Manager

SHD/ra
Encl.

Sample 9-17

Not everyone is terminated for poor performance or the violation of a company policy. The employee in this sample was the victim of a corporate takeover and downsizing. Certainly it is understandable that the HR director feels bad about this person's being terminated, but expressing these feelings in a formal letter is inappropriate.

October 9, 199X

Mr. Joseph Mare
8 Redding Drive
Post Village, Maryland 54557

Dear Joe:

I guess we both knew this day was coming when Megatron took over Avedon. It threatened to downsize and replace many of our employees with a handful of its own, and that's just what it did.

It pains me to tell you this, but you and about fifty other fine Avedon employees are being terminated, effective January 1, 199X. I want you to know this has nothing to do with your performance, and I will gladly sign reference letters to that effect.

Joe, come in to see me over the next few weeks so we can complete all the necessary paperwork. I can also refer you to outplacement and other recruitment sources.

I'm so sorry this has happened. You're a fine worker and a real asset to Avedon. Your termination is Megatron's loss.

Sincerely,

Virginia Russell
HR Director

10
Employee Services

As organizations compete to attract and retain qualified employees, the services offered beyond standard wages and benefits continue to expand into programs, such as employee assistance, dependent care, and recreation. Companies also share information through newsletters and solicit ideas from employees through a suggestion system. In addition, human resources departments generate numerous letters to employees on a number of occasions, including the birth of a child, illness, the death of a loved one, and retirement.

Employee Assistance Programs

Objective: Directs employees to help with personal matters that are affecting work performance

Purpose: To inform and influence

Readers: Staff members needing help with personal problems

Style: Active voice, standard and familiar phrases, personal pronouns

Tone: Clear, concise, complete, and consistent; empathetic; persuasive; positive; friendly

Format: Straight text, lists, comparisons, questions and answers, quotations, color, illustrations, photographs and other graphics

Contents: Services offered, including help with drug and alcohol addiction, divorce, parenting issues, and relationship concerns; location; phone number; hours; fee; procedure for participation, policy concerning confidentiality

Sample 10-1

This EAP brochure immediately personalizes the service via its title: "Our EAP." The text begins by validating personal problems as a normal part of living. It goes on to list twelve problems that exemplify the reasons employees avail themselves of EAP services. Following is a description of the EAP program, including the company's policy on confidentiality and the fact that there is no cost to employees and eligible family members. Additional details are provided regarding the program's approach and therapists and how to use the EAP.

All of this is accomplished in a brochure that consists of eight pages that fold into a 9- by 4-inch format.

In addition to adhering to the four C's (clear, concise, complete, and consistent), the tone is supportive and encouraging. The design incorporates muted shades of aqua and maroon for both the graphics and type to set it clearly apart from other literature the employee may receive.

Sample 10-1

Your Employee Assistance Program

Living in today's complex world is challenging. As we strive to balance the demands of work, family and our own personal needs, there may be times when we feel our ability to cope is being stretched. When a personal problem makes life difficult, it affects all aspects of our lives—at home and at work.

Personal problems are a normal part of living. For this reason your organization offers an Employee Assistance Program (EAP) to help deal with life's rough spots—whether they occur on or off the job. When you are helped with a personal problem, your home life improves, work improves and everyone benefits.

YOUR EAP CAN HELP WITH:

- ◆ *Emotional and personal conflicts*
- ◆ *Depression*
- ◆ *Family and relationship concerns*
- ◆ *Questions about drug/alcohol use*
- ◆ *Managing stress and change*
- ◆ *Budgeting*
- ◆ *Career concerns*
- ◆ *Divorce or separation*
- ◆ *Grief*
- ◆ *Work performance issues*
- ◆ *Parenting*
- ◆ *Care for elderly parents*

WHAT IS YOUR EAP?

Your EAP is a confidential program designed to help resolve personal problems. Information, consultation and brief, solution-oriented therapy are provided by professionals at XYZ Counseling Services, an independent firm.

The program encourages early use—when you first notice a problem and your own efforts to resolve it have not been satisfactory.

◆ **All EAP fees for employees and eligible family members are paid by your employer.**

◆ **Services are confidential.**

◆ **Use of your EAP is voluntary.**

WHAT IS SOLUTION ORIENTED THERAPY?

SOLUTION ORIENTED THERAPY OCCURS IN FOUR STEPS:

◆ **Clarifying the problem:** Discussing the situation to help you determine what steps to take.

◆ **Identifying options:** Exploring alternatives for resolving the problem.

◆ **Developing a plan of action:** Deciding on a course of action and implementing your plan.

◆ **Working together:** Achieving your goals.

You will be given a pre-addressed, postage-paid reply form asking for your evaluation of the program. This is completely anonymous and mailed by you. It provides your organization some helpful information about your satisfaction with the EAP.

(continues)

Sample 10-1. Continued.

WHO ARE THE EAP THERAPISTS?

They are experienced clinical professionals employed by XYZ, a firm specializing in providing and managing employee assistance programs for organizations of all types and sizes throughout the U.S., Canada, and Puerto Rico. Therapists have master's degrees in the fields of social work, counseling and psychology and hold appropriate licensure or certifications.

MUST I GO TO THE EAP IF MY EMPLOYER REFERS ME?

No. Participation in your EAP is voluntary. When a supervisor suggests using the program, he or she is offering a helpful resource to resolve any personal problem that may be affecting job performance.

IS THE EAP REALLY CONFIDENTIAL?

Your confidentiality is protected with private waiting rooms and clinical offices. Information shared in your EAP is always treated as confidential. Information about individual employees who use the program is not shared with your employer. Most individuals make their own appointments. When an employee is referred to the EAP as a result of performance concerns, information related to employee participation may be required by the workplace. There is no discussion of what occurred in the sessions—personal information remains **confidential.**

Employees who wish to disclose information about their consultation with the EAP must sign a release of information form. This permits specific information to be shared with designated individuals. There may be certain instances when the law requires disclosure. These exceptions will be discussed with you before your first session begins by reviewing XYZ's Statement of Understanding. This document describes your EAP and the confidentiality of the program.

ARE THERE ANY COST FOR EAP SERVICES?

All EAP services have been prepaid by your organization. Should you decide to use additional resources outside the EAP, you will be responsible for any fees associated with using these resources. Your medical benefits plan may cover some of the costs associated with these services. Every problem and every budget is different. Your EAP therapist will help you find an affordable solution. The decision to use outside resources is always left up to you.

HOW DO I CONTACT THE EAP?

You can call your EAP directly between 8:30 a.m. and 5:15 p.m. Monday through Friday. Appointments will be arranged for your convenience during the day, evening, or on Saturday. In crisis situations, professional therapists are available on a 24-hour basis by calling the toll-free telephone number that appears on the reverse side of this brochure.

Sample 10-2

This piece begins with a touch of history and includes a description of the organization's services, benefits, cost, questions to consider when searching for an on-site program, and a number to call for additional information. It is a good starting point for those curious about EAPs in general.

Sample 10-2

Employee Assistance Programs

Employee assistance programs (EAPs) originally focused on alcohol and drug issues, patterned after the concept of occupational alcoholism programs developed in the 1940s. They increased in popularity following enactment of the Drug Free Workplace Act of 1988, with many companies providing EAPs in an attempt to comply with the act's requirement that federal employees and employees of firms under government contract must have access to EAP services. Today EAPs are available to employees needing help with a wide range of concerns: family and work problems, legal and financial difficulties, mental health issues, and substance abuse. When properly managed, EAPs may prevent an increase in absenteeism, tardiness, sick leave abuse, health insurance claims, disability payments, employee theft, litigation, and turnover.

The cost of an EAP depends on a number of variables, such as size and scope of services, but most run about two to three dollars per month per employee for an off-site program (most small and mid-sized companies opt for an off-site program, while large corporations usually retain EAP personnel on staff). According to EAP experts, a well-run EAP will minimally return three dollars for every dollar spent on the program.

In searching for the most appropriate off-site program, or EAP vendor, Employee Assistance Professionals Association (703/522–6272) recommends that the following questions be asked:

- What is the vendor's reputation among its clients and among EAP professionals?
- Does the vendor have offices in all or most of the locations in which your company needs services?
- What kinds of employee problems can the vendor service?
- What services are offered?
- Is access by telephone, face to face, or both?
- What hours are services available?
- How are the counselors trained and supervised?
- Is the vendor's EAP compatible with your company's health care benefits?
- How does the vendor deal with confidentiality?
- What is the cost of the program?

It is also advisable to select an EAP that covers employee dependents, since often the dependent is the person having the problem or is the source of the employee's problem.

Employers are advised to ensure that EAP policies and procedures clearly comply with all relevant state and federal laws and regulations, such as those concerning confidentiality of client records. In addition, all program personnel should be covered by professional liability insurance.

From Diane Arthur, *Managing Human Resources in Small and Mid-Sized Companies*
(New York: AMACOM, 1995).

Sample 10-3

This sample was prepared by Terry, the human resources manager of a small company, in response to a hand-written note received from the company president. He wrote, "Terry, I went to a meeting the other night and heard a number of people talking about EAPs. What are they, and should we have one?"

After reading Terry's response, the president called her to his office and posed numerous questions that her memo prompted. Terry's analysis had failed to provide supporting examples and statistics—for example, how much is lost annually because of employees with drug, alcohol, mental health, and other problems; what percentage of workers are affected enough by these problems so that productivity decreases; how many companies currently have or work with EAPs; and what the characteristics are of on- and off-site programs.

March 23, 199X

To: S. Preston Wilmington
         President

From: Terry Antioch
         Human Resources Manager

Re: Employee Assistance Programs

It has long been recognized that employees' personal problems can impair job performance. Alcoholism, drug addiction, divorce, and the death of a loved one are just some of the issues that prevent employees from doing their best work.

Sometimes a leave of absence gives employees the time needed to "recover" from a problem and get back on track. All too often, however, the underlying issue prevails, and employees return, not only with the original problem but with resentment over being placed on leave as well. These employees clearly need professional help—help that cannot be provided by their managers or someone in human resources.

The solution for many companies is on- or off-site counseling, or a consortium model, where several companies pool their resources to develop a collaborative program. These employee assistance programs (EAPs) can help restore employees to full productivity status.

Making EAPs available to employees is both a humanitarian gesture and a cost-effective solution to excessive absenteeism and productivity problems.

Dependent Care Programs

Objective: Provides on-site services or referrals to off-site programs that offer child or elder care, or both, for employee family members

Purpose: To inform and influence

Readers: Employees needing child or elder care assistance

Style: Active voice, standard and familiar phrases, personal pronouns

Tone: Clear, concise, complete, and consistent; empathetic; persuasive; positive; friendly

Format: Straight text, lists, comparisons, questions and answers, color, illustrations, photographs and other graphics

Contents: Services offered, eligibility, location, phone and fax numbers, hours, fee, procedure for participation

Sample 10-4

This down-home, folksy memo from the CEO of a mid-sized company to his employees is more like a casual after-dinner chat among friends than a formal business document. This conversational style works, however, given the CEO's personality and what the employees are accustomed to receiving from him.

His message is clear and concise: This company has always cared about its employees and continues to demonstrate its commitment through a new dependent care program.

The CEO offers just enough information to arouse readers' curiosity. Interested employees know who to call for details.

November 11, 199X

To: All Avedon Industries employees

From: N.K. Avedon, CEO

Many of you have been with us since we started out over 10 years ago. At that time we were a family-run operation with fewer than 50 employees. We didn't have anything that we formally referred to as dependent care; if your child or parent needed help, we all pitched in.

Well, we're much bigger now and more structured. But we care about our workers just as much as we did back then. And we try to show it in many ways. One of those ways is through our new, on-site Avedon for All Ages dependent care program. We're bringing in a team of professionals devoted exclusively to child and elder care. They will tend to the intellectual, emotional, social, and physical needs of your loved ones while you work just a few steps away. You will have peace of mind; they will have care and attention.

Interested? We thought so. Call Nancy in HR on extension 421. She will give you literature on the program, describing its benefits in detail, as well as eligibility, hours, cost, and anything else you want to know. Take a tour of the facilities, and talk with the folks in charge.

We think Avedon for All Ages is the best dependent care program around. Let us know what you think.

Sample 10-5

This excerpt from a company's dependent care brochure captures the reader's attention immediately. (How many corporate documents begin with reference to blowing bubbles?) Once the reader is hooked, the brochure provides, in one paragraph, vital particulars: where, who, when, what, and how much.

This is an example of how less is more. Through just 140 carefully chosen words, employees learn a great deal about the new program.

Blowing bubbles. Bifocal lenses. Crayons. Walkers. Comic books. Crochet needles. These intergenerational items are now found in our new dependent center: a combination child and elder care facility.

We have converted our west wing into a room for 50 children and 25 elders. Our doors will open at 8:30 A.M. and stay open until 5:30 P.M. Trained professionals will be there at all times to work and play with your loved ones. Naturally, we provide lunch and snacks. The cost is calculated on a sliding scale, based on your salary. Family members of employees who work more than 30 hours weekly and have been here for at least three months are eligible to participate. And you can join in on whatever they are doing during your lunch hour and breaks, since they are here, on-site.

Sample 10-6

Contrast the friendly, positive tone of Sample 10-5 with this one. Important information is included in this organization's single-page flier promoting off-site dependent care, but it comes across as abrupt.

   If you are interested in taking advantage of our company-sponsored child and/or other dependent care programs, here's what you need to know:

Location:	People Care
	46-89 Tremont Avenue
	Brooksite, New York 58933
Services:	Various activities for elders and preschool children
Eligibility:	Full-time employees with at least 6 months' service
Cost:	Based on what you earn
Hours:	Open from 7:00 A.M. until 6:00 P.M.

For details contact HR at ext. 1865.

Company-Sponsored Activities and Programs

Objective: Advises employees of company-sponsored activities and programs

Purpose: To inform and influence

Readers: Employees interested in various company-sponsored activities

Style: Moderate

Tone: Descriptive, factual, friendly, positive

Format: Quotations; questions and answers; color; illustrations, photographs and other graphics

Contents: Varied, including: health clubs and gyms, weight-loss programs, stop-smoking clinics, country club membership, sports activities, travel services, credit unions, discount tickets.

Sample 10-7

This notice listing the company's recreational activities can be posted on bulletin boards near the cafeteria and outside the HR offices and is printed on neon-colored paper to capture the attention of passers-by.

Although eleven different activities are noted, the contents are not overwhelming; in fact, it is easy to remember all the activities because a list format is used and the activities are logically grouped. For example, memberships are grouped together, as are discounted events.

The tone is friendly and upbeat.

Avedon Activities

We've got it all!

To begin with, we offer . . .

      Health club membership
      Country club membership
      Weight-loss programs
      Stop-smoking clinic
      Discounts and premium seats for sports events
      Discount travel and hotel accommodations
      Discount theater tickets

And that's not all! Throughout the year, there are . . .

      Picnics
      Holiday parties
      Company-sponsored team sports, like softball,
          bowling, and our newest addition, soccer
      Raffles

It just doesn't get any better than this!

Call HR's Avedon Activities Hotline at extension 449 for an up-to-date recorded message about upcoming events, or call extension 443 and talk to an HR representative about any of Avedon's employees' services.

Sample 10-8

This announcement regarding the establishment of a weight-loss program and stop-smoking clinic starts by following up on a promise and reporting the results of a survey. After that, however, no information is offered. Telling employees that there will be awards without describing how the programs work is backward. What must employees do to earn the gift certificates? And what leads HR to believe that employees favor publication of their weight loss in the company newsletter for all to read?

Grade this one an A for its good intentions and a D for its implementation.

November 17, 199X

To: All Employees

From: Paul Converse
         Director, HR

Re: Employee Services

Remember the survey we distributed last month asking how many of you wanted to either lose weight or quit smoking? Well, here are the results: Of the 1,847 surveys that we distributed, 1,694 were returned. Of those, 1,373 of the respondents said that they wanted to lose weight, and 1,112 said they wanted to quit smoking.

Based on these results, we are proud to announce two new employee services: a weight-loss program and a stop-smoking clinic. While the details have not yet been worked out, we anticipate tracking individual progress in our newsletter and offering gift certificates as incentive.

Stay tuned for more information!

Sample 10-9

This memo starts out with the offensive phrase, "As most of you know." It then launches into a self-serving company promotion that continues to the end, referring to management's generosity no fewer than three times! It is enough to make you want to eat something other than turkey for Thanksgiving.

To: Avedon Staff Members

From: Quentin Ribuffo
          Manager, Employee Services

Re: Thanksgiving Dinners

Date: November 18, 199X

As most of you know, it is an annual tradition for Avedon to give all employees, including part-timers and temporaries, a free Thanksgiving dinner. This is an extremely generous act on the part of management. In the past, the package has consisted of enough to feed from six to eight people: a 16–20-pound turkey with all the trimmings, including stuffing mix, cranberry sauce, sweet potatoes, string beans, and apple pie. This year, management will be no less generous and is offering the same dinner, absolutely gratis.

The dinners may be picked up in human resources beginning this Friday. It would be appropriate for you to pick up the phone or drop a line to the president to say, "Thank you for being so generous."

Sample 10-10

This picnic announcement overwhelms the reader with exclamation points. In addition, the words dance around the page in a meaningless pattern. It would have been better to group the food words together, then follow suit with the activities.

Centering the logistics in a box is effective.

Watermelon!

Volleyball!

Hot dogs!

Softball!

Badminton!

Potato Salad!

Salinger Park, Field #4

Saturday, June 23, 199X

12:00 - ?

Bring your family and friends!

Call x8975 and tell us how many are coming!

Hamburgers!

Relay Races!

Soft Drinks!

Desserts!

Prizes!

Piñatas!

Newsletters

Objectives: Keeps employees up-to-date on organizational changes, employee social functions, and personal employee news

Purpose: To inform

Readers: Employees

Style: Moderate to conversational

Tone: Descriptive, friendly, positive, clear, concise

Format: Anything goes, including varied graphics, color, columns, boxes, questions and answers, tables, graphs, charts, and quotations. Text can be traditionally formatted in a full-block style or be given a more creative twist, like the hanging indented format.

Contents: Business news, such as acquisitions; company-sponsored events, such as holiday parties; HR changes, such as new hires and promotions; personal announcements, such as weddings and births

Sample 10-11

Newsline presents a mixed bag of company and personal news in a pleasing and varied format. The use of color on the first page and graphics on the first two pages complement the text effectively.

The text is written in a clear and concise manner. The news is varied, to appeal to a broad range of employees.

Sample 10-11

News Line

| JAN | FEB | MAR | APR | MAY | | JUN | JUL | AUG | SEP | OCT | NOV | DEC |

August 5, 1996

MR. RANCOURTE GOES TO WASHINGTON

DIRECTOR OF MANAGEMENT STUDIES *JOHN RANCOURTE* BROUGHT MEMBERS OF CONGRESS UP TO SPEED ON CORPORATE DOWNSIZING AT A JULY 18 MEETING OF THE CONGRESSIONAL TASK FORCE ON MANUFACTURING.

John spoke to an audience that included members of Congress and congressional aides as well as the press, presenting statistics from XYZ's annual survey on job elimination and job creation.

"Walking up the Capitol steps gives you a certain delusion of grandeur," John admitted. "You find yourself imagining that you have the State of the Union address in your breast pocket."

At the meeting, chaired by Congressman Bob Franks (R-NJ) and titled a "Congressional Forum on Job Security," John concentrated on five points that are generally overlooked in discussions of downsizing:

- More companies are hiring than firing, and more yet are doing both at the same time.
- A majority of major U.S. firms employ more people today than five years ago.

- From mid-1994 to mid-1995, those major firms averaged a net gain of 4.5% in the number of persons they employed.
- Only six percent of the companies eliminating jobs in that period did so due to lesser market demand and no other reason.
- Eighty percent of companies that cut jobs in any given year are profitable in that year.

"Job security and the minimum wage are hot topics on Capitol Hill this summer," John reports. "There'll be more Congressional hearings in both the House and Senate in the fall, and the data from XYZ's 1996 survey will play a part in the debate."

DID YOU KNOW . . .

HOTEL VOUCHERS ARE BECOMING MORE POPULAR?

Few situations allow you security and freedom at the same time. Now, thanks to an increasingly popular invention called the hotel voucher, travelers can have it both ways.

It is most helpful during peak season abroad, when Americans traveling on their own can find themselves without lodging at the end of the day. In many cases, they wind up at the most expensive hotel in town because the staff is apt to speak English and because the bargain places fill up fastest.

Lately, more and more moderately priced hotel chains, as well as independently owned budget lodgings that do joint marketing, accept some sort of book-as-you-go vouchers. These vouchers don't provide guarantees that you can drop by the hotel of your choice at a moment's notice and find a room waiting, especially if, for example, you saunter into Munich during the Oktoberfest.

But when you are meandering around the countryside in a foreign land, they can add a touch of assurance that you will find a warm welcome at an acceptable lodging. Voucher plans can be as different as the hotels, so weigh the benefits carefully. You generally buy the vouchers at a preset rate from your travel agent before your trip. You pay in advance for as many nights as you want. You usually make a firm reservation for your first night abroad. You can make as many advance bookings as you want, but this obviously defeats the purpose of the voucher system.

The point is to be able to fine-tune your itinerary day by day. Sometimes, you have to make a reservation at each subsequent hotel by a certain time: the day you plan to arrive or the day before. But often, one hotel will take care of calling ahead to the next.

A NOTE OF THANKS

THE FOLLOWING IS AN OPEN LETTER FROM THE HOTEL DEPARTMENT STAFF OF GIVERN CITY EXPRESSING THEIR APPRECIATION TO CERTAIN XYZERS.

During the week of July 15-19, the Hotel Department of XYZ Givern began training on the new automated system that was designed to convert them from a manual operating department to a computerized one.

Their note reads, "*Mark Lindenbaum*, Lead Programmer Analyst, *Sam Lipstein, Mary Lima*, and *Rachel Nicole*, Sr. Programmer/ Analysts, Business Systems, under the direction *of Lillian Good*, Manager Business Systems, Information & Technology, developed the system. They not only have brought the department into the 90s but have given it an edge on the 21st century as well. The Hotel Department staff who worked on the design of the system are *Susan Jacobsohn*, Sr. Meeting Coordinator; *Mike Purrillo*, Sr. Meeting Coordinator; and *Consuela Ramirez*, Manager, all of Hotels-GC. *Angie Harton*, Director, Scheduling, was also instrumental in the process. The Hotel Department is very excited about the system and it feels blessed to have had the opportunity to work with such a great group of people from Accounts. They made the whole process a pleasant experience." The department will go on-line with production in the near future.

"The Hotel Department gives special thanks to Mark, Sam, Mary, Rachel, and Lillian for their hard work and time that they invested on this project. Much thanks to *Emily Liu*, Supervisor, Quality Assurance, for her assistance in automating our forms and to *Ann Kobrin*, Database Analyst; *Ted Copper and Rich Ryffel*, Database Administrators, for their database expertise. Most importantly, thank you for your patience. You have taught this department a lot about computers and programs. Each member looks forward to a continuing partnership. Cheers to a great team!"

(continues)

Sample 10-11. Continued.

SEMINAR IDEAS - XYZ GC STYLE

THE "SEMINARS COME FROM THE DARNDEST PLACES" CAMPAIGN IS THE CREATIVE BRAINCHILD OF *ANNE HERDMANN*. DIRECTOR, MARKETING SERVICES. "PROGRAM DEVELOPMENT NEEDED SOME WAY TO ENCOURAGE EVERYONE IN THE COMPANY TO GENERATE SEMINAR IDEAS, " SAID HERDMANN.

Forty-one new seminar ideas have been submitted in the two months since the campaign began. Six of them are scheduled for development.

To generate excitement for new seminar ideas, the Program Development Department turned to the Marketing Department and Herdmann. Through a series of memos and posters, the campaign informed employees that their job and life experiences can yield potential seminars.

Before the campaign, many employees were either unaware they could submit ideas, or wondered if it would be worth the effort. "People would tell me they thought the ideas were to originate from creative teams or the Program Development Department," said Herdmann. "Some just didn't believe that their ideas would be taken seriously."

A follow-up campaign is being considered to keep the message alive. The message? Each employee is key to the success of XYZ/GC: everyone contributes!

NEWS TIP FROM ACCOUNTING

Here is a tip that will take the guessWORK OUT OF WHAT TO DO WHEN XYZers RECEIVE A CHECK FROM A CUSTOMER, A SALES REP, ETC.

Anna Soo, Manager, Check Processing, says, "To avoid passing the check from department to department, send checks of this nature to the Check Processing Department in Accounting, P.O. Box 100, Anytown, CA 00000."

NEED A FALL INTERN?

"NOW IS THE TIME TO PLACE YOUR REQUEST FOR A FALL INTERN," REMINDS *MARGARET BANCROFT,* SR. EMPLOYMENT REP AND *CAROLINE ROBBINS*, SR. HUMAN RESOURCES COORDINATOR, HR.

"If XYZers have special projects, or need assistance completing projects, consider a fall intern to help you.

"The internship program is a 'win-win' arrangement. Managers give interns the opportunity to test academic theories and apply them to special projects . Interns can also contribute new and enlightening perspectives."

To assist Margaret and Caroline in placing the best intern in the right department, send them via E-mail a list of intern projects and requirements or fill out an Intern Request form which can be obtained in the HR Department. This will provide Margaret and Caroline with a better understanding of your needs in order to place an intern with similar interests and academic background who can successfully complete your projects.

INTRODUCING . . .

PLEASE WELCOME THE FOLLOWING NEW STAFF MEMBERS WHO BECAME XYZERS DURING THE MONTH OF JUNE:

In Northwest: *Mukesa Patel*, Assistant Manager, Center Operations, Meeting Operations.

In Southeast: *Charlotte O'Hara,* Administrative Assistant, Product Development.

In Southwest: *Lou Hurwitz*, Jr. Order Entry Specialist, Records Maintenance; *Jane Arnold,* Staff Accountant, Contract Accounting; *Rich Hedge*, Postage/Inventory Analyst, General Ledger.

CONGRATULATIONS TO THOSE XYZERS WHO WERE PROMOTED DURING THE MONTH OF JUNE:

In Southwest: *Harvey Arendt*, Check Applicator Coordinator, Finance; *Melanie*

Hamill and *Faith Jacobs*, Training Specialists, In-Bound Telemarketing;

SEMINAR LEADER RETIRES

"HATS OFF TO DANIEL J. CONNERY, A SEMINAR LEADER WITH THE CENTER FOR MANAGEMENT DEVELOPMENT, WHO RETIRED FROM XYZ ON JUNE 21 AFTER TEACHING FOR 24 YEARS," ANNOUNCES *JULIA BATTEAU*, SENIOR PROGRAM DIRECTOR, CMD SEMINAR ADMINISTRATION.

Dan completed his XYZ career after presenting his last CMD seminar entitled *Improving Your Project Management Skills*, (6503), in the Northeast Center.

Batteau adds, "Dan was one of the pioneers who worked with XYZ to create our very successful curriculum of project management training which began back in 1972. Meeting 6503 was the first project management seminar and is currently one of the top five CMD seminars running today. This seminar alone trains over 2,000 project management professionals annually."

Along with the many thanks and congratulations from the Northeast Management Center staff, seminar participants and other leaders who were teaching at the Center that week, Dan was honored with a plaque by XYZ, which was presented by Julia Batteau, in recognition of his dedication and long-term achievements to XYZ's success.

Batteau said, "Dan is not only a loyal seminar leader but a key contributor to the XYZ family. He'll be missed but we all wish him well in his new life - retirement!"

Sample 10-12

The monthly newsletter for this New York–based, high-tech company averages about fifteen pages. It is produced magazine style on glossy paper and spares no expense in terms of color, graphics, and photographs, which are creatively angled and overlapped, with artistic borders.

The contents are divided into two segments: features about the company and a human interest section, announcing marriages, births, retirements, and the like. Helpful hints of a seasonal nature may also appear. For example, one winter issue contained an article written by a nurse about the flu: what it is, signs and symptoms, who is at high risk, when to call a doctor, and prevention tips. The following sample is an excerpt from that article. It illustrates the clear and concise writing that prevails throughout the newsletter.

Beware of the flu! This viral illness usually attacks between November and April and can be serious—even life threatening if you hesitate to call a doctor when the following occurs:

- Your temperature exceeds 102 degrees for more than 48 hours.
- Your cough lasts more than a week and is accompanied by chest discomfort.
- You have a persistent sore throat.
- You experience shortness of breath.
- You have ear, neck, and sinus pain and/or swollen glands that persist more than a week.
- You have congestion that persists more than two weeks.

Prevention of the flu is easier than you may think. Try washing your hands frequently to minimize the spread of bacteria and disease, increase consumption of foods high in vitamin C, and exercise regularly. If you do become ill, be sure to drink plenty of liquids, since fever and illness can cause dehydration. Also, be sure to eat. If you decrease your food intake, it can add to the stress your body is already undergoing from being sick.

Suggestion Programs and Attitude Surveys

Objective: Encourages employees to contribute ideas that will improve employer-employee relations or productivity and comment on specific work-related issues

Purpose: To inform

Readers: All employees

Style: Open or directed

Tone: Friendly, positive, clear

Format: Boxes to be checked off, items to be circled, comparisons, room to write comments. Restrict the length of the form to one page.

Contents: Address a maximum of three issues, state whether employees may remain anonymous, indicate when and where the forms are to be returned

Sample 10-13

This sample exemplifies an open suggestion program. Management is interested in hearing from employees concerning any work-related question, issue, problem, or opinion. Employees are invited to write down, in essay style, what is on their minds and submit the form to human resources for response. Anonymity is ensured.

Aware that employees may have difficulty dealing with a blank page, this company makes the form palatable, with an inviting drawing of a typewriter and easy-to-write-on lines.

The form is also easy for employees to submit, since it folds into an envelope. The envelope is preaddressed, with postage prepaid, and it is marked "personal and confidential."

Sample 10-13

■ Please **type** your work-related question, concern, problem or opinion in the space below. If you cannot possibly gain access to a typewriter, please **print** your OPEN LINE.

■ The lower portion will be detached before your OPEN LINE is forwarded for action. Your identity will be kept confidential.

■ One subject per form, please.

■ Your answer will be mailed to your home.

Fold along dotted line.

Moisten flap and seal

Date

Fold along dotted line.

Name _____

Home Address _____

City/State/Zip _____

Office Telephone Extension _____

Before your OPEN LINE is sent to anyone, this part of the form will be removed.

Problems and solutions to OPEN LINE may be published in *Newsline*. **Your name will not be used.** If selected, may your OPEN LINE or part of it be used?

☐ Yes   ☐ No

(continues)

Sample 10-13. Continued.

PERSONAL AND
CONFIDENTIAL

BUSINESS REPLY MAIL
FIRST CLASS   PERMIT NO. 7172   NEW YORK, NY

POSTAGE WILL BE PAID BY ADDRESSEE

NO POSTAGE
NECESSARY
IF MAILED
IN THE
UNITED STATES.

Fold along dotted line.

Fold along dotted line.

Fold along dotted line.

Sample 10-14

Sample 10-14 represents a directed suggestion program or attitude survey. Employees are asked to comment on numerous work-related issues by checking off boxes and expressing additional thoughts near the bottom.

The form is overwhelming, with far too many topics crammed into one page. If one main area had been isolated and expanded on, say, communication, the survey would have been more effective.

The lead-in statement is vague as to management's course of action after reviewing the responses.

The questionnaire portion of the form is difficult to read and poorly designed.

Sample 10-14

February 12, 199X

To: Staff Members

From: R. W. Pitchard
             Employee Relations Manager

From time to time, the human resources department surveys the employees of this company to determine what you think about various work-related issues.

Please take a few moments to complete the following questions. Your signature is optional. Return the completed survey to my attention in an interoffice envelope, by February 24. I will collate the responses and report them to you shortly thereafter. Then I will sit down with representatives of management to review your concerns and suggestions.

Thank you for helping us make this a great place to work.

How would you rate the following:

1. The company's general atmosphere ＿＿excellent ＿＿very good ＿＿good ＿＿fair ＿＿poor
2. The sense of company "team spirit" ＿＿excellent ＿＿very good ＿＿good ＿＿fair ＿＿poor
3. Your work load ＿＿satisfactory ＿＿unsatisfactory
4. Working conditions ＿＿satisfactory ＿＿unsatisfactory
5. Health and insurance benefits ＿＿satisfactory ＿＿unsatisfactory
6. Promotion prospects ＿＿excellent ＿＿very good ＿＿good ＿＿fair ＿＿poor
7. Vacation/holidays ＿＿excellent ＿＿very good ＿＿good ＿＿fair ＿＿poor
8. Working relationship with supervisor ＿＿satisfactory ＿＿unsatisfactory
9. Working relationship with co-workers ＿＿satisfactory ＿＿unsatisfactory
10. Number of paid sick days ＿＿satisfactory ＿＿unsatisfactory
11. Treatment of staff versus management ＿＿fair ＿＿unfair
12. Quality of cafeteria food ＿＿excellent ＿＿very good ＿＿good ＿＿fair ＿＿poor
13. Opportunities for cross-training ＿＿excellent ＿＿very good ＿＿good ＿＿fair ＿＿poor
14. Level of interest shown by management in employees ＿＿high ＿＿moderate ＿＿low
15. Communication between management and staff ＿＿satisfactory ＿＿unsatisfactory
16. Level of appreciation in your work ＿＿high ＿＿moderate ＿＿low
17. Your level of motivation ＿＿high ＿＿moderate ＿＿low
18. Present salary ＿＿fair ＿＿unfair
19. Evaluation process ＿＿fair ＿＿unfair
20. Cleanliness of restrooms ＿＿excellent ＿＿very good ＿＿good ＿＿fair ＿＿poor
21. What else would you like us to know?

_____

_____

_____

_____

Name, title, and department (optional)

_____

Sample 10-15

Here is the response to Sample 10-14. It summarizes the results of the survey by reporting the majority of responses to each question, but it does not indicate management plans with regard to areas that employees identified as requiring improvement.

March 29, 199X

To: Staff Members

From: R. W. Pitchard
        Employee Relations Manager

Thanks to all of you who completed the employee survey dated February 12, 199X. We received close to a 90% return.

As promised, here are the overall results:

1. General atmosphere: Very good to good
2. Team spirit: Very good to good
3. Work load: Satisfactory
4. Working conditions: Satisfactory
5. Health and insurance benefits: Fair to poor
6. Promotion prospects: Fair to poor
7. Vacation/holidays: Good
8. Working relationship with supervisor: Satisfactory
9. Working relationship with co-workers: Satisfactory
10. Number of paid sick days: Unsatisfactory
11. Treatment of staff versus management: Unfair
12. Quality of cafeteria food: Fair
13. Opportunities for cross-training: Poor
14. Level of interest shown by management in employees: Moderate to low
15. Communication between management and staff: Unsatisfactory
16. Level of appreciation in your work: Moderate
17. Your level of motivation: Moderate
18. Present salary: Unfair
19. Evaluation process: Unfair
20. Cleanliness of restrooms: Fair
21. Other comments: Generally had to do with expansion on the issues of salary, cross-training, and communication.

It is apparent that we are doing some things very well and need to improve in other areas. Members of management are in the process of reviewing your responses; we will keep you posted.

Thanks again for your cooperation.

Sample 10-16

This is an example of a directed suggestion program requiring little effort on the part of employees yet could yield important information to management. It appears regularly in the company newsletter and, with a maximum of five questions, focuses on a different key area each month. The title is an attention grabber, although it may be a bit too modern for employees beyond the Generation X or "twenty-something" age group.

What's Up With You?

This month's topic: Hours of Work

We're considering introducing alternative working hours as an option to the current Monday–Friday, 9–5 schedule. Of the three following possibilities, which would you prefer?

    1.   <u>Flextime</u>: Each worker puts in the same number of hours each day, with identical core hours, but varying starting and quitting times. _____

    2.   <u>Compressed Workweek</u>: Employees work the required forty hours in four ten-hour days. _____

    3.   <u>Telecommuting:</u> Work at home up to four days a week, linked to the office electronically, with one-two days of work in the office. _____

Results will appear in next month's issue of "Your Company!"

Letters of Congratulations

Objective: Acknowledges outstanding employee accomplishments (e.g., promotions) and personal news (e.g., the birth of a child)

Purpose: To inform

Readers: Individual employee being congratulated

Style: Moderate to conversational

Tone: Friendly, warm, personal

Format: Straight text

Contents: The particular event, why it calls for congratulations

Sample 10-17

This letter of congratulations is written in full-block format. Although the contents are not original, the letter is personalized, referring to the employee's baby by gender and name. Acknowledging the employee's spouse is another nice touch.

January 12, 199X

Ms. Geraldine Henderson
2344 Corona Court
Plankton, NJ 45367

Dear Gerry:

On behalf of everyone at Avedon Industries, congratulations on the birth of your daughter, Dawn Marie. We know how much you wanted a girl; you must be thrilled.

How is Howard holding up? We hear he's already changing diapers and warming bottles!

We look forward to meeting the newest member of the Henderson family soon.

Best regards,

Gina Mendeli
Manager, Employer/Employee Relations

Sample 10-18

This letter of congratulations inappropriately alludes to the employee's return to work. Without this sentence, the letter, written in a semiblock format, is effective.

February 19, 199X

Ms. Patricia Watkins
99 Sourdough Lane
Newton, Minnesota 76756

Dear Patricia:

Everyone in the accounting department has asked me to convey their congratulations on the birth of your baby. We all want to know what name you've selected, how much he weighed, and whether he looks like you or John.

When you're feeling up to it, call me with the answers to these questions so I can pass on the information. At that time, you can also let me know about your plans for returning to work—we need you!

Again, congratulations and best wishes.

Sincerely yours,

Justin Baker
Manager, Accounting

Sample 10-19

This thoughtful letter of congratulations is addressed to an employee who recently became a father. The company recognizes that birth acknowledgments should not be exclusively for women employees. Adoptions should also be recognized.

March 11, 199X

Mr. Walter Atkinson
89 Putnam Blvd.
Sunny Plains, Nebraska 33565

Dear Walter:

    Congratulations to you and your wife, Mary, on the birth of your son, Jason. We are all happy for you and look forward to seeing pictures of the baby.

    We hope he enjoys playing with the toys we're sending along.

Sincerely,

Susan Mendehlson
Sr. HR Representative

Sample 10-20

The message in this letter of congratulations is simple, direct, and sincere.

November 23, 199X

Ms. Victoria Dardinelle
52 Wolpert Place
Cognac, Texas 45467

Dear Victoria:

Congratulations on earning your masters' degree. We all know how hard it has been for you to combine a full work load with school, especially during finals.

I understand that you are planning to take five vacation days beginning Monday; sounds as if you timed it just right!

Again, congratulations.

Yours truly,

Samuel Yonkers
Director, Marketing

Sample 10-21

The intent of this letter is ambiguous. Although it is directed to a recently promoted employee, it focuses on the manager's hiring abilities.

August 21, 199X

Ms. Linda Pendagrass
90 Evergreen Lane
Lake Hurley, Michigan 76757

Dear Linda:

Congratulations on your promotion to the position of senior accounts receivable clerk. I knew from the outset that you would move up the employment ladder quickly. When I hired you, I could tell that you weren't one to stand still. In fact, I wouldn't be surprised to see you post for another promotion in a short while!

Regards,

Joanna Barnes
Accounting Manager

Letters to Sick Employees

Objective: Extends best wishes for a speedy recovery

Purpose: To inform

Readers: Sick employee

Style: Moderate, personal pronouns

Tone: Warm, sincere, empathetic

Format: Straight text

Contents: Acknowledges employee's illness

Sample 10-22

Although brief, the letter is adequate. It expresses concern for the employee, wishing him a speedy recovery.

January 30, 199X

Mr. Barry Whitehorne
One Cherry Lane
Watertown, California 90789

Dear Barry:

I am sorry to hear of your prolonged bout with the flu. I wish you a speedy recovery and hope that you will be able to return to work soon.

Sincerely,

Josh Markus
Sr. HR Representative

Sample 10-23

The last thing a hospitalized person needs to worry about is the quality of that institution's care. This supervisor was thoughtless in failing to consider how the recipient might react when reading that a fellow employee had bad experiences in the same hospital.

October 9, 199X

Ms. Kelsey Brown
875 Cocoa Boulevard
Tundra City, Arizona 73812

Dear Kelsey:

Everyone here in the records department feels awful about your being rushed to the hospital yesterday with a ruptured appendix. It's too bad you couldn't tell the ambulance driver to take you to South Shore Community Hospital instead of Brookdale Hospital. Josie from HR was in Brookdale last year and has oodles of horror stories to tell about her stay there.

Anyway, I'm sure everything will be all right and that you will be back at work real soon!

Best regards,

LouAnn Landsman
Supervisor, Records Maintenance

Sample 10-24

The message in this letter is warm and generous. The recipient is likely to react positively to the sentiments expressed and believe that the writer is genuinely concerned.

September 11, 199X

Ms. Carmen Flowers
44 Sunset Place
Fort Williams, Virginia 59988

Dear Carmen:

On behalf of the entire department, please accept my sincerest wishes for a speedy recovery from your surgery. We all miss you, and hope you are able to return to the office soon.

Give me a call when you are up to receiving visitors. I know many of your colleagues would like to stop by.

Meanwhile, if there is anything you need or want, let me know, and I'll do my best to get it for you.

Best regards,

John Hennis
Employment Manager

Letters of Condolence

Objective: Expresses sympathy for the loss of a loved one

Purpose: To inform

Readers: Employee who has experienced the death of someone close, usually a family member

Style: Moderate, personal pronouns, natural

Tone: Empathetic, compassionate, sincere

Format: Straight text

Contents: Acknowledges employee's loss

Sample 10-25

This expression of sympathy carries condolences too far by suggesting that the employee take as much time as necessary to recover. Most companies have policies governing the maximum number of days allowed for the death of a loved one. Although reference to the loss of the writer's spouse is inappropriate, offering a "shoulder" is a generous gesture.

April 21, 199X

Mr. Steven Marshall
71 Welcott Court
Caravel, Montana 43989

Dear Steve:

   Please accept my deepest condolences on the passing of your wife. I understand that this is an extremely difficult time for you and want you to take as much time as you need to cope with your devastating loss. I know what you are going through; my husband passed on two years ago.

   I am here for you if you want to talk.

Most sincerely,

Regina Walsh
HR Director

Sample 10-26

This is an honest and sincere expression of sympathy.

December 3, 199X

Ms. Deirdre Perkins
10 Clemins Court
Newbridge, Utah 67686

Dear Deirdre:

I don't really know what to say to express how sorry I am over the death of your father. I know you two were very close and that you were planning a visit with him over the holidays.

If I can be of help to you in any way during this difficult time, please let me know.

Sincerely,

Henry Jones
Communications Coordinator

Sample 10-27

This letter goes beyond the standard expression of sympathy by suggesting that the employee contact the company's EAP for bereavement counseling.

November 1, 199X

Ms. Rhonda Fitzgerald
666 Wanamaker Lane
Winston, Idaho 55078

Dear Rhonda:

    All of us at Avedon Industries were very sorry to learn of your mother's death. Please accept our sincere condolences and let me know if I or anyone else can be of help to you.

    You may also want to call the EAP hotline at 555-HELP and talk with a counselor who specializes in bereavement.

    Again, our deepest condolences.

Very truly yours,

Patrick Dullas
Employer/Employee Relations Specialist

Letters for Retirement

Objective: Expresses thanks for the work an employee has performed

Purpose: To inform

Readers: Employee who is retiring

Style: Moderate, personal pronouns

Tone: Descriptive, distinct, clear, concise, positive

Format: Straight text

Contents: Acknowledges employee's length of service and outstanding contributions to the organization

Sample 10-28

This is intended to be a retirement letter for Morgan Wittfield, yet it starts by discussing the letter writer. There is some acknowledgment of the employee's achievements in the first paragraph, but then the writer refers to what the recipient obviously knows—her plans on retiring—thus detracting from the employee's contributions.

May 15, 199X

Ms. Morgan Wittfield
531 Goldenrod Landings
Brazelton, Massachusetts 11312

Dear Morgan:

I joined this company five years ago armed with two degrees and thinking I knew a great deal about human resources. After just six months of working with you, I realized just how little I actually knew. To this day I continue to be amazed at the broad base of knowledge you have and how adept you are at applying it. Particularly impressive is how you are able to recall the names and titles of employees you hired as far back as twenty years ago.

Well, after more than two decades with us, and nearly thirty years in the field of human resources, you have chosen to retire and pursue your avocation of physical anthropology in the Peten jungle of Guatemala. What a change that's going to be!

All of us wish you the very best in your retirement and new adventures.

Best regards,

Peter Langly
HR Manager

Sample 10-29

This concise, clearly written letter expresses personal regrets over the retiree's departure and identifies one particularly outstanding contribution.

June 20, 199X

Mr. Shepherd Fieldings
12 Gray Boulder Path
North Bridges, Maine 44565

Dear Shep:

I want you to know how deeply you will be missed when you retire at the end of this month after twelve years of selfless service. Your contributions to this company have been noteworthy, especially your handling of the outplaced employees during our massive downsizing two years ago.

I wish you a retirement filled with good health and happiness.

Sincerely,

Roger Gardner
President

Sample 10-30

This retirement letter is abrupt, stiff, and formal. Apparently the writer does not know the retiree personally or anything about his accomplishments. Sending no letter at all would have been preferable.

September 11, 199X

Mr. Jack Ridge
12 Piper Road
Stonehill, New York 11798

Dear Jack:

This is to thank you for your 10 years of service to this company. We appreciate your contributions and regret losing such a valuable employee.

We wish you the best in your retirement.

Very truly yours,

Jefferson Ramsey
Vice President—HR

11

Writing Employee Handbooks and Human Resources Policy Manuals

Employee handbooks and HR policy manuals share the following objectives and uses:

- To serve as written declarations of a company's commitment to fair employment practices and equal employment opportunity.
- To express the basic philosophies of senior management.
- To serve as basic tools of communication.
- To provide employers with a systematic approach to effective employer-employee relations.
- To outline company rules and requirements.
- To clarify an organization's expectations of its employees.
- To identify lines of authority and levels of responsibility.

In addition, an HR manual serves as a training resource for newly hired or recently promoted managers, reducing the risk of poor HR-related decisions.

Handbooks also offer a brief history of the organization and a description of its primary products or services, outline the benefits and privileges of working for the organization, and identify the employer's obligation to employees with regard to continued employment.

Since HR manuals and employee handbooks have many similarities, containing several of the same topics, they are often prepared simultaneously. This dual-purpose mission should be accomplished with caution, however, since HR manuals are geared for managers as a guide to daily interaction with employees, and handbooks serve primarily employees for use as a description of company rules, expectations, and benefits. Hence, although many of the same topics may appear in both documents, the specific contents and emphasis will vary. The two should be compatible, not identical.

Every organization, regardless of its size, structure, or employee composition, should adhere to a write-review-rewrite approach to developing HR manuals and employee handbooks:

1. *First draft.* Focus on overall content, and do not labor over specific language. Your goal at this stage is to identify topics for inclusion, organize your thoughts, and focus on the objectives.

2. *Review stage.* Make certain the language is clear, concise, complete, and consistent. Also, define the style, design, and layout. Consider preparing the contents of both the manual and the handbook on paper that can easily be replaced in anticipation of updates. Hence, a looseleaf notebook is most practical.

It is recommended that manuals be prepared on $8^1/2$- by 11-inch paper. The design of the handbook allows for greater flexibility, with most being $8^1/2$ by 11, $7^1/2$ by 11, $5^1/4$ by $8^1/2$, $4^1/2$ by $6^1/2$, 4 by 6, or $3^1/2$ by 7 inches. Some companies opt for a small $3^1/4$- by $4^3/4$-inch format. The text may carry across the entire page or appear in columns— generally two per page.

A format consisting of some predetermined combination of heads and subheads, different type sizes, varying fonts, underlining, boldface type, italics, white space, color, illustrations, borders, boxes, photographs, lists, comparisons, and questions and answers should be adhered to throughout both documents to give the reader a sense of consistency.

Decide, too, on the arrangement of topics and page numbering system you want to use. There are two common arrangements for topics: (1) alphabetical, useful in small companies with a limited number of topics; and (2) functional, which groups topics under broader titles. The most widely used page numbering methods are consecutive and decimal. The latter is tied in with each major section (e.g., 1.1, 1.2, 1.3, . . . , 2.1, 2.2, 2.3). Companies that use a functional arrangement of topics generally select a decimal page numbering system. Alphabetical listings tend to go hand in hand with consecutive page numbering.

3. *Rewrite stage.* This is the time for fine tuning. Have you varied the pace of your sentences? Steered clear of unnecessarily complex words? Used a consistent tense throughout? Avoided clichés and limited the use of jargon? Is your language nonsexist? Have you avoided ambiguous terms? Is your tone positive? Have you used the active voice? Have you checked the accuracy of all grammar, spelling, and punctuation? Have you distinguished between words that denote as opposed to connote?

Usually three drafts will be required at the rewrite stage before the handbook and manual contents can be considered complete.

Throughout all three stages, it is a good idea to work as part of a team. Representatives from HR, senior management, line management, and outside consultants can offer a variety of perspectives and insights that will contribute to the finished product. The team approach is also useful when manuals and handbooks are reviewed for updating (every six to twelve months is recommended) and revamping (every five years is recommended.)

Following are some effective and ineffective handbook and manual samplings. The contents have not been evaluated.

Sample 11-1

This 5¼- by 8½–inch employee handbook is bound, negating any chance of periodic updates and replacements. The pages are numbered consecutively. There are twenty-nine topics. One of them, benefits, has eighteen subtopics. The topics are listed in random order, and there is no table of contents. Employees will have difficulty finding items of interest.

The information is arranged in straight-text form. The only visual break is provided by boldface heads, in the same type size and font as the text.

There is varied pace in the length of some sentences. The messages under each topic are clear and concise, albeit short. The passive voice prevails, making the overall tone of the handbook neutral at best.

Some of the information is ambiguous. For example, the first topic, "Working Hours," says that normal working hours are from 8 A.M. to 5 P.M., Monday through Friday. That implies that there are other options, although none are listed.

The grammar, spelling, and punctuation have been carefully checked.

Sample 11-1

WE'RE GLAD YOU'RE HERE

We WELCOME you as a new member of our team and will do our best to make your career with us pleasant and mutually beneficial.

We hope this booklet will help to familiarize you with the Company's policies and answer questions you may have about our Company. If not, please feel free to talk to your immediate Supervisor or our Human Resources Department.

We hope you will enjoy being part of our team and find working for our Company "A Source of Pride."

OURS IS A GREAT HISTORY

[The company uses the remainder of the page to trace its history from its origin in 1899 to the present day.]

1. **Working Hours**

   Normal working hours are from 8 AM - 5 PM with 1 hour for lunch, Monday through Friday.

2. **Reporting Absence**

   In the event of absence, call your Supervisor as close to 8 AM as possible.

3. **Attendance**

   A record of attendance is maintained. If you are absent because of illness, your Supervisor is authorized to approve payment for the days you are absent within the limits of established Company policy. Your Supervisor may also refuse to authorize payment when there is reason to doubt the validity of the absence. Your attendance record is reviewed along with performance reviews.

4. **Dress Code**

   Every Friday or the day before a holiday at the end of the week is designated as "Product Day", and employees may wear clothing offered by our divisions. We expect all employees to display good taste in wearing professional attire appropriate for a corporate office on all other work days.

5. **Recording Time Worked**

   Maintenance personnel punch a time clock as a record of their working hours. All other non-exempt employees will make daily entries on time sheets covering a two-week period. These time sheets will be signed and submitted to the immediate Supervisor by the Monday immediately following the end of a regular two-week pay period.

6. **Maintenance of Work Area**

   Appearance of desk top and adjacent work area is the employee's responsibility. Desk tops should be cleared of all papers each night.

7. **Care of Equipment**

   Contact the Office Services Department for all office equipment repairs except for PC's. Call the Business Systems Department for PC repairs.

8. **Smoking**

   We maintain a smoke-free working environment at Corporate Headquarters. Smoking will be restricted to a designated room in the building. The company will reimburse an employee the cost up to the amount of $100.00 of an approved smoking cessation program if they desire to try to eliminate the habit and strive for good health.

9. **Drugs and Alcohol**

   This Company maintains a strong commitment to its employees to provide a safe drug-free, alcohol-free work place and to establish programs promoting high standards of safety and health. We expect every employee to abide by the guidelines stated in the Company's Drug and Alcohol Abuse Policy.

(continues)

Sample 11-1. Continued.

10. Supplies

Office supplies may be requisitioned in the stockroom. Employees are not to store large quantities of office supplies in their desk drawers. Office supplies should not be used for personal projects.

11. First Aid

Remedies for simple headaches as well as minor cuts and bruises are available in the copy room cabinet, the medicine cabinet in the supply room, and in the garage.

12. Injuries

Office Services should be notified immediately in case of an injury or accident. We have trained personnel throughout the building who can offer assistance.

13. Bulletin Boards

Notices regarding Government Laws, Job Postings, Holidays, Company Product Sales, etc. are placed on the bulletin boards. Employees are encouraged to read the bulletin boards, located in both kitchens and at the side entrance to the building. All notices should be given to Office Services for proper posting.

14. Parking Areas

Adequate parking spaces are available for employees. Reserved spaces at the rear and on the northwest side of the building are for use only by assigned vehicles. Employees should at no time park in the Visitors Parking Lot in front of the building. In the event of snow, any car left at the office overnight should be parked on the upper lot and car keys given to Office Services.

15. Paychecks

A. Paychecks are distributed every other Friday. The check received includes payment for time worked up to 5 o'clock that day. Any necessary payroll adjustments are made in the ensuing pay period. Direct Deposit is also available to all employees upon request.

B. Payroll deductions are made as follows:

1. Medical – 1/2 amount from first pay of the month; 1/2 amount from second pay of the month.

2. Long Term Disability Insurance – Full amount from first pay of month.

3. Accidental Death & Dismemberment/Supplemental Group Life Insurance – Full amount from second pay.

4. As an additional service to employees, payroll deductions for Government Savings Bonds, Credit Union and United Way Fund contributions are available.

C. When an employee's vacation is during a regular pay week, the employee may do the following:

1. Have the check held until their return or,

2. Have the check mailed to their residence or,

3. Request their check be deposited into their bank by the Payroll Department. A deposit slip must be given to the Payroll Department before the employee's vacation period.

16. **Overtime**

   A. Overtime is considered to be work performed in excess of the basic work week and must have the prior approval of the immediate Supervisor. For each hour worked beyond the normal 40 hour week, non-exempt employees receive one and one-half times their regular hourly rate of pay. The regular hourly rate is the weekly salary divided by 40.

   B. Holidays, vacation, death in the immediate family and jury duty will be counted as time worked for the purpose of computing overtime premiums. Illness of the employee or illness in his/her immediate family, office closing due to special days off, weather, power failure, etc., will not be counted in computing overtime. Overtime payments will be included in the first paycheck following the pay period in which the overtime was actually earned.

17. **Performance Reviews**

   A. Normally, non-exempt employees will receive a performance review six months from their date of employment. Subsequent reviews will be made on an annual basis.

   B. The amount of merit increase is established by the Compensation Department and represents a prescribed percentage of the employee's present salary. The results of the Supervisor's review will be discussed with the employee prior to any salary adjustment.

18. **Promotions**

   It is the practice of the company to fill vacant jobs through promotion or transfer, whenever possible. When an opening occurs, the records of present personnel are reviewed to determine if anyone has the necessary requirements. Promotions may be considered justification for a salary adjustment.

BENEFITS

19. **Fringe Benefits**

   A. **Health Care**

      There are three health plans available for employees and their dependents. Coverage is selected by the employee with costs handled through payroll deductions. Refer to the Health Care Plan Booklets for complete details.

   B. Sick Pay

      Non-exempt employees are eligible for five paid sick days per year. No payment will be made for unused sick days, no carry-over permitted for unused sick days.

(continues)

Sample 11-1. Continued.

C. Short Term Disability Insurance

The STD Plan covers all full-time salaried employees. The plan provides for continuing income if the employee is unable to work as a result of illness or injury. The Company pays the entire cost of the plan. Refer to the Plan Booklet for details.

D. Long Term Disability Insurance

LTD Insurance is available to all full-time salaried and sales employees. Premiums are paid by the employee through payroll deductions. For additional information, refer to the Group Voluntary Long Term Disability Insurance Plan Booklet.

E. Life Insurance

A three month waiting period is required for non-exempt employees. Each employee is provided with a Company paid Life Insurance policy. The face value of the policy is one and one half times the employee's annual salary to a maximum of $50,000. Supplemental Insurance is available at additional cost to the employee.

F. Accidental Death and Dismemberment Insurance

AD & D Insurance is available to all full-time salaried and sales employees under the age 70. Employees may elect to cover their spouse and dependent children. The amount of coverage and corresponding premium are selected by the employee. Employee's coverage may be changed or a dependent's coverage may be added at any time. For a complete explanation of requirements and coverage, refer to the Group Voluntary Accident Insurance Plan Booklet.

G. Business Travel Accident Insurance

An additional insurance coverage provided for all full-time employees is the Business Travel Accident Insurance policy. Participation is automatic and the Company pays the entire cost of the plan. Coverage is provided for injuries resulting from an accident while traveling on company business. Refer to the Plan Booklet for details.

H. Pension

Pension benefits are completely paid for by the Company. An employee earns a vested interest after completion of five years of service. Refer to the Pension Booklet for complete details.

I. Tax Advantaged Savings Plan (401K)/Employee Stock Ownership Plan (ESOP)

Salaried and sales employees with 12 months of continuous service are eligible to participate. You may have between 2% and 10% in pre-tax earnings withheld. The Company matching contribution is entirely in Our stock, "ESOP Convertible Preferred". Matching contribution is 50¢ on the dollar on employee contributions of up to 6%. Per cent of salary includes base pay, overtime, and incentive bonus. Vesting in Company contributions takes 60 months. For a complete explanation of contributions and benefits, refer to the Plan Booklet.

J. Holidays

There are nine paid holidays per year, with no waiting period for new employees. They are: New Year's Day, Good Friday, Memorial Day, Independence Day, Labor Day, Thanksgiving Day, the day after Thanksgiving, Christmas Eve, and Christmas Day.

K. Vacations

1. Employees will be allowed time off for vacation according to the following schedules:

   - 1 week after 6 months
   - 2 weeks after 1 year of employment
   - 3 weeks after 10 years of employment
   - 4 weeks after 20 years of employment

2. After the completion of one full year of employment, personnel may schedule vacations at any time between January 1 and December 31 of a given year.

3. All vacation scheduling must have the approval of the Department Head. Normally, employees are required to schedule their vacation time for one week periods. Therefore, if any other arrangements are desired, such as individual vacation day periods, it requires the approval of the Department Head.

4. No pay will be given for unused vacation and no days may be carried over from year to year.

L. Jury Duty

An employee who is called for Jury Duty is paid at the normal rate regardless of any juror's pay received.

M. Death in Family

Time off with pay will be granted up to three working days when death occurs in an employee's immediate family. Immediate family is defined as spouse, parent, child, brother, sister, parent-in-law, and any relative permanently residing in the employee's household. One day off with pay is granted for the death of a spouse's brother or sister or for a grandparent or grandchild of either the employee or the employee's spouse.

N. Federal Credit Union

New employees are eligible immediately. Refer to booklet for more information.

O. Employee Educational Assistance Program

1. All permanent, full-time employees with 12 months of continuous service who wish to further their career development through job-related courses are eligible to receive educational assistance with the approval of the Department Head. Please see Human Resources Department for the educational assistance forms and for more information on the policies and procedures.

(continues)

Sample 11-1. Continued.

2. The Company will not be responsible for any commitments that are made by the employee and/or the Supervisor before getting all the required Management approvals on the official "Educational Assistance Application" form.

3. Employees are responsible for payment of all course expenses. After presenting evidence of satisfactory completion of the course (C or better), reimbursement will be made for:

   a. 100% of all tuition fees
   b. 100% of all mandatory fees including registration and lab fees
   c. 100% of all required course textbooks.

P. Matching Grant Program

To aid and support education and public television, the company will match contributions by eligible employees to appropriately accredited Colleges, Universities, and Public Television stations.

All permanent, full-time employees with one year continuous service are eligible to participate. The company will match dollar for dollar an individual's contribution to an accredited institution from a minimum of $50 to a maximum of $10,000 per calendar year.

Q. Keystone Community Blood Bank

Annual fee paid by the company. Refer to Keystone Community Blood Bank brochure for more details.

R. Exercise Facility

Employees may use the exercise facility at the designated time periods for their gender.

20. Leave of Absence

A leave of absence is an approved absence from work of one or more weeks, without pay, over and above the regular vacation and sickness allowances. The Department Head must approve any requested leave. The employee's benefit coverages will continue through the approved leave. However, the Company cannot guarantee holding open a position for an extended leave of absence.

Family and Medical Leave

FMLA requires "covered" employers to provide up to 12 weeks unpaid, job-protected leave to "eligible" employees for certain family and medical reasons. Employees are eligible if they have worked for an employer for at least one year and for 1,250 hours over the previous 12 months.

Should you have occasion to request FMLA, please see your Human Resources Representative to complete the proper forms.

21. Military Service

If you are a full-time employee and are required to serve in a Reserve or National Guard unit for two week training periods, the Company will grant the necessary time off with pay and it will have no effect on time off for regular vacations. A military leave of absence will be granted for the length of service in the Armed Services of the United States, including the time during which re-employment rights exist under the law. Group insurance will terminate upon induction or enlistment and be reinstated without a waiting period on the day the employee returns to work in the service of the Company.

22. Employee Orders - Subsidiary Merchandise

Division catalogs will be kept in Office Services for employees' use. Orders will be written on an Employee Order Form and submitted to Office Services for processing. Merchandise and invoices will be sent directly to the employee at the Corporate office address. It is the responsibility of the employee to pay the invoice directly to the division.

COMMUNICATIONS

23. Copying Procedures

In order to avoid waste, control costs and eliminate unnecessary filing, the employee should make every effort to keep copies to a minimum.

24. Mail Procedures

All domestic mail should be sent first class. Air mail postage should only be used for correspondence destined for delivery overseas. It is the policy of this office not to forward any 3rd class, or "junk" mail to subsidiary offices. In preparing subsidiary correspondence the employee should place the mail into an envelope, clearly marking it, with the individual's name, division name and location. To avoid incorrect mailing, do not use the company stationery envelope when sending mail to the divisions.

25. Personal Mail

The mailing of personal packages is discouraged by Management. If necessary, however, all personal packages should be so noted before given to the Stockroom or Mail Clerks. All postage for personal mail will be paid by the employee. You should be aware that U.P.S. will accept packages from this office only with our return address. Consequently, the individual cannot use their home address when mailing a personal package by U.P.S.

26. Telephone Usage

A. In order to reach an individual within this office, simply dial the three digit number noted on your office directory. To obtain a local outside line, dial 9 and wait for a dial tone. To obtain a long-distance outside line, dial 7 plus area code and number.

B. Whenever possible, any personal long distance phone calls should be charged to your home telephone number.

27. Petty Cash

The petty cashier will cash personal checks for employees, but this **privilege must not be abused.** A limit of $200 dollars per check (made payable to the company) has been established and will be strictly enforced.

(continues)

Sample 11-1. Continued.

28. Business Travel Advance/Expense Report

Please see the Travel and Expense Policy.

29. Subscriptions

A. Employees will be provided with the necessary newspapers, trade journals, magazines, and bulletins with which to effectively accomplish the responsibilities of their position.

B. Personnel shall obtain authorization for subscriptions from their supervisor. Requests for subscriptions should be placed with Office Services and final approval will be given by the Corporate Secretary.

EQUAL OPPORTUNITY/AFFIRMATIVE ACTION EMPLOYER

We are an equal opportunity employer. It is our policy to hire those applicants who possess the necessary skills, education and experience, regardless of race, color, religion, creed, age, sex, national origin, ancestry, physical ability, marital status or military background. This policy also applies to all promotions, transfers, dismissals, advertising for employment and establishment of pay rates.

We will aggressively seek qualified women and minorities to fill positions within our Company.

ADA

We treat every person as an equal. We do not make any decisions based on a person's race, sex, age, religion, national origin or disability. The Company is also an Affirmative Action employer and actively seeks to encourage the employment and promotion of qualified individuals.

HARASSMENT

It has long been the policy of the Company – and it will continue to be the Company's policy – that all employees shall have the opportunity to perform their work in an atmosphere and environment free from any form of unlawful discriminatory or retaliatory treatment or physical or mental abuse, including, but not limited to, harassment based on race, color, religion, sex, national origin, citizenship, age, or disability.

In keeping with this policy, the Company will not tolerate any form of harassment of any of its employees based on race, color, religion, sex, national origin, citizenship, age, or disability. By way of example, conduct will be considered harassing, and therefore a violation of this policy if:

1. Submission to the conduct is made either an explicit or implicit condition of employment;

2. Submission to or rejection of the conduct is used as the basis for an employment decision affecting the harassed employee; or

3. The harassment substantially interferes with an employee's work performance or creates an intimidating, hostile, or offensive work environment.

Any employee who feels he or she has suffered any form of harassment should report such incident to his or her Supervisor or to any member of the Human Resources Department without fear of reprisal. In the alternative, the employee may discuss the matter with his or her Supervisor or Department Head.

Such a complaint will be treated confidentially and will be handled independently of the Company's complaint procedure. A prompt and thorough investigation of any such complaint will be discreetly carried out, and appropriate action will be taken after an investigation. Any manager, supervisor, agent, or other employee who has been found, after a thorough investigation, to have harassed another employee will be subject to appropriate discipline. Such discipline may range from a warning in his or her file, up to and including termination.

The making of accusations which are known by the accusing person to be false is a form of misconduct likely to result in serious impairment of the Company's effort to administer this policy properly and effectively for the benefit of all employees, and, accordingly, such misconduct may result in discipline, up to and including termination.

[SEE EQUAL EMPLOYMENT OPPORTUNITY POLICY FOR LIST OF OTHER FEDERAL GOVERNMENT AND STATE AREAS OF PROTECTION]

OPEN DOOR POLICY

Problems are bound to arise in any relationship. Most problems can be settled satisfactorily by a discussion with one's immediate Supervisor. If a problem does arrive, or you feel you have a complaint, you are encouraged to tell your Supervisor about it. A discussion with your Supervisor is usually the best and quickest way to settle a problem. However, should you have personal problems that you would not feel comfortable discussing with your Supervisor, the Human Resources Department is always open to handle such matters in a confidential manner.

YOUR HUMAN RESOURCES DEPARTMENT

The Human Resources Department is responsible for interviewing and selecting new employees. Final selection is always made by Department Heads.

The Human Resources Department supervises employee records, educational benefits, employee services and coordinates employee benefits. For this reason, it is important that you inform the Human Resources Department of any appropriate change of name, address, beneficiary or phone number.

(continues)

Sample 11-1. Continued.

(Tear out - To go in personnel/payroll file for each associate)

I have read, understood and agree to the terms and conditions set forth in the Associate Handbook dated May 199X.

_____

Name (Print)

_____   _____

Signature   Date

Sample 11-2

This sample shows excerpts from a twenty-page employee handbook. The complete handbook is is 7½" × 11" and features photos of nearly 200 employees, scattered throughout the pages. The pictures are all head shots, against a gray or blue background. Some are group photos, and everyone is smiling. (The photos are not reproduced here to protect the privacy of the individuals involved.)

The table of contents sets out the handbook's primary segments: corporate philosophies, general information, pay procedures, benefits, communication resources, time off, career development, and professionalism. Each segment is subdivided into six to ten topics.

The contents are clear, concise, complete, and consistent. Charts clarify topics that may be difficult to digest, such as vacation plans, bonus days, and sick time. Personal pronouns provide a friendly, positive tone.

An employment-at-will statement clearly identifies the handbook as a set of guidelines, not a binding contract. Employees are asked to sign and return the statement.

Note: In the actual manual, small black-and-white head shot photographs of employees are found alongside the text.

Sample 11-2

Our employee policies and benefit programs are constantly under review, and they may be changed from time to time. None of the policies or benefits described in this Handbook are intended by reason of their publication to confer any special rights or privileges upon specific individuals or to entitle any person to any fixed term or conditions of employment.

It is expressly understood that your employment is for no fixed period of time and that it may be terminated by the employee or the Organization at will. The Organization reserves the right to modify or cancel certain of the personnel policies or benefits described in the Handbook. You will be notified of such changes as soon thereafter as practicable. All statements of coverage are subject to the terms, conditions, restrictions, and eligibility requirements set forth in our Summary Plan Description, which is the final word in terms of eligibility and coverage.

We hope you make frequent use of your Handbook. Refer to it for information about the Organization and its policies. Questions concerning the information in this Handbook or situations not covered in this Handbook should be discussed with your immediate supervisor or manager.

Table of Contents

(continues)

Sample 11-2. Continued.

Corporate Principles and Philosophy

Our Mission

[Company mission statement]

Our Values

Values we hold essential are the dignity of the individual, the integrity of the workplace, and our belief in the need to exceed customer expectations at every point of contact.

Equal Employment Opportunity/Affirmative Action

It has been and will continue to be the policy and practice of the Organization not to discriminate against any applicant, employee, or customer because of race, color, religion, sex, age, disability, national or ethnic origin, veteran status, or any other basis prohibited by state or local law. This policy extends to every phase of the employment process including: recruiting, hiring, training, promotion, job assignment, compensation, benefits, transfers, reductions in force, terminations, recalls, and Organization-sponsored educational, social, and recreational programs.

We will provide reasonable accommodations for qualified job applicants, staff members, and customers with disabilities, provided such disabilities have been brought to our attention.

Harassment

The Organization is committed to providing a work environment totally free of harassment. Harassment can occur with a single incident, or through a pattern of behavior where the purpose or effect is to create a hostile, offensive, or intimidating work environment. Harassment can result from a broad range of actions which might include, but are not limited to, the following:

- Physical or mental abuse
- Racial insults
- Derogatory ethnic jokes
- Religious slurs
- Display of obscene or offensive materials
- Unwelcome sexual advances
- Requests for sexual favors

Our policy against harassment extends to prohibiting the acts of non-employees which result in harassment of employees in the workplace. Our policy also prohibits harassment by our employees of non-employees in the workplace.

Solicitation/Distribution

Solicitation of employees by other employees is prohibited when either employee is on working time (working time does not include break or meal period). Solicitation by nonemployees is prohibited at all times. Distribution of unauthorized literature is prohibited in working areas at all times.

Ethics

The Organization adheres to the highest standard of conduct so as to foster fair and honest relationships among staff members, as well as with customers, suppliers, and the communities in which it maintains a presence. All activities are conducted in strict observance of both the letter and the spirit of the law.

All persons representing the Organization must maintain its standards of conduct by exercising judgment and diligence in the performance of duties, and by the avoidance of a conflict of interest. All relationships must meet both legal requirements and the test of honesty and integrity.

All persons representing the Organization must conduct themselves so as to avoid any action or behavior that would bring embarrassment to it.

Policies and procedures of organizational units may supplement but not contradict this policy.

Gifts from Suppliers

Staff members must decline all offers of gifts or gratuities, except trinkets of no market value, made by a past, current, or prospective vendor or made on the vendor's behalf to an employee's family.

Proprietary Information

During employment it is expected that certain confidential information concerning the Organization's activities, services, and operating practices may come to the employee's attention. The employee agrees that he/she shall not, either during the term of employment, or at any time after termination, divulge or disclose to any person, firm, or corporation any confidential information or facts concerning the operation or affairs of any of the Organization's activities, which may have been acquired in the course of, or as incident to, his/her employment, whether for his/her own benefit or whenever the disclosure of which could be calculated to cause damage or loss, or could be considered to be detrimental to the interests of the Organization.

General Information

Classification of Staff Members

A regular full-time staff member is on the payroll 52 weeks of the year, works at least 35 hours per week, and is entitled to the Organization's employee benefits.

A regular part-time staff member is on the payroll 52 weeks per year and works at least 20 hours per week with proportionate time for vacation and proportionate pay for each hol-

(continues)

Sample 11-2. Continued.

iday, based on the standard number of hours worked per week. Other benefits may be prorated.

A temporary employee is eligible for statutory benefits, and may participate in selective health screening benefits as determined by each location.

Personal Safety

We make every effort to provide safe and secure places of employment for our staff members. All staff members, of course, have a responsibility for their own safety and are required to observe the operating guidelines established for each location.

Personnel Records

Staff members have the opportunity to review their personnel file with a Human Resources representative present. Consult your supervisor or the *Policies* manual for additional information.

Hours of Work

The normal work week consists of 35 hours, Monday through Friday, 9:00 a.m. to 5:00 p.m. One hour for lunch may be taken any time between 12:00 noon and 2:00 p.m. Flexible work arrangements are offered where practical and at the discretion of the manager.

Attendance

If it is necessary for you to be absent, it is your responsibility to notify your supervisor no later than one half hour after your normal starting time, explaining the reason for your absence and advising when you expect to return to work.

A doctor's certificate will be required if the period of absence extends for five or more consecutive work days.

Supper Allowance

The Organization provides a supper allowance to full-time staff members who work at least two hours overtime beyond the normal working day. This allowance applies only if the distance from the office to home makes it impracticable for the staff member to have dinner at home and return to the office within a reasonable time.

Pay Procedures

Payday

Payday is every other Thursday. The pay period includes the prior week worked and the current week through Friday. If a payday falls on a holiday, paychecks will be distributed on the last work day prior to the holiday.

Direct Deposit

Regular full-time and regular part-time staff members may elect to have their paychecks deposited directly into their checking or savings accounts, provided that the individual staff member's bank offers a direct deposit plan. Forms may be obtained from the Human Resources Department.

Overtime

Only non-exempt staff members are eligible for overtime pay. Overtime hours at work must be scheduled in advance with the approval of the appropriate department head. The pay rate for non-exempt staff members for time worked in excess of 35 hours up to and including 40 hours will be paid at the rate of straight time. Scheduled hours worked in excess of 40 hours will be paid at the rate of time and one-half.

Holiday Pay

Pay for holiday hours is considered hours worked in the determination of overtime pay. Non-exempt employees required to work on a holiday will be paid at the rate of straight time, in addition to holiday pay. Should the number of hours worked on a holiday bring the total weekly hours over 40, time and one-half will be paid for all hours worked in excess of 40.

Vacation Pay

When computing vacation pay, the base salary or wages in effect at the time of vacation shall apply. Regular part-time staff members will receive paid vacation in accordance with the eligibility requirements and vacation allowance schedule but on a prorated basis governed by the average number of hours worked per week.

Vacation pay is not automatically paid in advance. When a payday falls within the vacation period, a regular full-time or regular part-time staff member may draw in advance the amount due on that payday. A request for advance paycheck must be submitted to the Payroll Department 4 weeks in advance. Salary for the remainder of the scheduled vacation will be paid on the first payday following the staff member's return to work. Staff members may not elect to receive pay instead of earned vacation; nor may they be requested to forgo vacation with the promise of receiving pay instead.

(continues)

Sample 11-2. Continued.

Required Deductions

According to the law, deductions from your salary must be made for Social Security, Medicare, and/or federal taxes and appropriate state and local taxes. The amount deducted is determined by your salary, marital status, residence, and the number of exemptions you declare on income tax withholding forms.

Benefits

Health Insurance and Pension Benefits

The Organization offers **Major Medical Health Insurance** to staff members and their eligible family members. As an alternative to Major Medical Health Insurance coverage, you may have the option to enroll in a Health Maintenance Organization (HMO) depending on where you live. We provide Short Term Disability, Long Term Disability, Group Life Insurance, Dependent Life Insurance, Business Travel Accident Insurance, Accidental Death and Dismemberment Insurance, Dental Insurance, and a Pension Plan to staff members.

Most of your insurance and all of your pension benefits are paid for by the Organization. In addition, we contribute an amount equal to your FICA deductions to Social Security and Medicare. As overall changes occur in insurance and pension benefit plans, announcements are made to the staff, and revised pages are distributed for *Your Benefits* binder. The Organization also contributes to Unemployment Insurance and Workers' Compensation Funds.

Employee Assistance Program

The Employee Assistance Program (EAP) is a confidential assessment and referral program. This program provides a limited number of counseling sessions paid for by the Organization to help staff members to overcome personal problems.

Health Programs

The blood donor drive, influenza inoculation, and hypertension screening programs are administered annually in house where possible. Additionally, the Organization conducts "Whole Health Workshops." Led by health-care specialists, these presentations address various health-related topics and issues. Videotaped presentations are available for all locations.

Savings Plans

Savings Account. An employee may authorize the Payroll Department to make deductions from each paycheck and deposit the funds in a savings account in his/her name with a local savings bank. Arrangements have been made with a bank in each of the major business locations.

U.S. Savings Bonds. An employee may authorize payroll deductions to be taken in order to purchase series EE U. S. Savings Bonds. They are available in denominations of $100, $200, $500, $1,000, $5,000, and $10,000. The purchase price is equal to one-half the face value of the bond.

Savings and Investment Plan (SIP). Eligible employees may participate in the SIP, which allows you to save money for retirement on a pre-tax basis up to certain prescribed limits. Generally, the Organization matches part of your savings.

Because this program is intended to help supplement retirement income, withdrawals are limited under IRS regulations.

Achievement Awards Program

The Achievement Awards Program is designed to reward those staff members who enhance the Organization's internal and/or external image through outstanding performance **beyond the scope of expected job responsibilities.** This program is open to every staff member. Nominations can be made either by a co-worker or a supervisor/manager and are judged by the Achievement Awards Committee.

Informal Recognition Award

This award is for managers to recognize an individual staff member on an immediate basis for an accomplishment or contribution that has had a positive impact on the Organization, but which does not meet the criteria for the more formal Achievement Awards Program.

Scholarship Program

The Organization offers a competitive scholarship program to encourage the children of employees to continue their education in college. The program is administered through the Human Resources Department. The Scholarship Committee is composed of prominent educators who select the recipients of the scholarship award.

(continues)

Sample 11-2. Continued.

Communication Resources

Improving our internal communications is an ongoing concern. We have a number of tools to ensure that communications flow across our geographic and functional boundaries.

Newsletter

Our internal newsletter provides staff members with up-to-date organizational information such as senior management planning reports, new program developments, policy changes, and news from all areas of the Organization.

The President's Letter

The President's Letter is an occasional direct communication from the President and Chief Executive Officer to all staff members. It is used to discuss matters of interest and/or importance to the entire staff.

Job Opportunities

Staff members learn of open positions as they occur through the Job Opportunities posting.

Check Points

Our quarterly internal benefits newsletter is designed to help staff members become educated consumers of both insurance benefits and health care. It gives the latest information regarding our benefits.

Telephone Directory

The standard directory is revised several times each year. Entries are arranged alphabetically with a section listed by department/division to be used as a reference aid.

Bulletin Boards

Bulletin boards are maintained for the purpose of posting job opportunities, legal documents, and upcoming social events.

Grievances

Every staff member shall have the right and opportunity to be heard fully and without prejudice.

If a problem exists and a solution is not agreed upon by the staff member and the immediate supervisor, the staff member may contact the next level manager to review the problem. If the staff member still feels that the problem has not received proper consideration, the staff member may request a conference with a Human Resources representative.

A staff member may contact the Human Resources Department in confidence at any time.

OPEN LINE

OPEN LINE is an anonymous upward communications program for all staff members. *OPEN LINE* forms are available in wall-mounted holders near the main copying machines and at other appropriate locations. If you have a concern or a problem you are unable to resolve or a suggestion to offer, you may want to use the *OPEN LINE* program. When you send in your form, which is a self-mailer, the *OPEN LINE* Administrator will detach the lower portion, which identifies you, and then pass your typed message along to the President and Chief Executive Officer, who will respond or assign it to the appropriate senior manager for action. A written response to your concern will then be sent to your home by the *OPEN LINE* Administrator. The *OPEN LINE* Administrator is not a member of the Human Resources Department or the Senior Management Group.

Time Allowance

Vacations

The Organization recognizes the physical and psychological benefits of vacations and provides vacation time to all regular full-time and part-time staff members.

The amount of vacation a staff member receives shall be in accordance with the following schedule, which is prorated for regular part-time staff members:

GRADES 2 THROUGH 16

Employment date/ Length of service	Vacation allowance
First working day of January through May 31	5 days after 6 months employment; 10 days for each succeeding calendar year
June 1 through December 31*	10 days after December 31 **and** completion of 6 months of employment
Completion of 4 years' service by December 31	15 days beginning the following year
Completion of 14 years' service by December 31	20 days beginning the following year

*Staff members hired or rehired after May 31 will not be eligible for vacation during that year

(continues)

Sample 11-2. Continued.

GRADES 17 AND ABOVE

Employment date/ Length of service	Vacation allowance
First working day of January through May 31	10 days after 6 months' employment; 15 days for each succeeding calendar year
June 1 through December 31*	15 days after December 31 **and** completion of 6 months of employment
Completion of 4 years' service by December 31	20 days beginning the following year

*Staff members hired or rehired after May 31 will not be eligible for vacation during that year

Once eligibility requirements have been met, vacation may be taken at any time during the calendar year, subject to the approval of the immediate supervisor. Every effort will be made to accommodate individual choice of vacation time, so staff members should plan well in advance to allow for the needs of the individual and the needs of the Organization to be fully taken into account.

Staff members may carry over up to 10 unused vacation days, which must be used during the first 6 months of the next calendar year, or remaining days will be forfeited.

Holidays

We generally offer a total of 11 paid holidays each year to all regular full-time staff members. The Human Resources Department issues a schedule announcing which days are officially designated as holidays, and a copy is sent to each staff member.

In addition to designated holidays, other holidays and/or optional holidays may be offered to reach the total of 11 days. A staff member should make arrangements with his/her supervisor to take an optional holiday at least one (1) week in advance of the day selected. Optional holidays may not be carried over into the following year, nor will pay be granted instead of an optional day.

Those days designated as optional holidays will be granted to regular full-time staff members hired prior to December 1 of the current year.

Career Development

Performance Planning and Appraisal System (PPAS)

The Organization relies upon the performance of its staff members for its success and, therefore, places a high priority on the performance and development of all individual staff members. The Performance Planning and Appraisal System (PPAS) is a consistent, organization-wide method of performance planning and appraisal which managers and supervisors use as the basis for:

- Training and development
- Performance improvement plans
- Performance evaluations
- Merit increases and promotions

This system is designed to encourage you to produce the best results in your job—which will ultimately provide our customers with the best products and services available.

For further information, please refer to the *Performance Planning and Appraisal Guidebook* or discuss it with your supervisor.

Merit Increases

Staff members are appraised annually for merit increase eligibility purposes. Whether or not an increase is granted, a completed Performance Planning and Appraisal System (PPAS) form must be submitted to the Human Resources Department.

Education

It is our policy to provide appropriate job-related training and development opportunities to all staff members. To this end, we encouraged regular full-time staff members to participate in approved educational courses related to their self-development and career progress.

Approved courses of study may include undergraduate, graduate, and degree-granting programs, and non-credit programs offering specialized instruction. The Organization offers tuition reimbursement to staff members who participate in the Educational Assistance Plan. However, in order for individual credit courses or degree programs to qualify for reimbursement, they must be relevant to the job currently held. In no way may these activities interfere with the staff member's proper performance of regular assigned job duties. Criteria and procedures pertaining to each form of study are further explained in the *Policies* manual.

Promotion

Employment and promotional opportunities exist for qualified staff members based on merit, regardless of race, color, religion, sex, age, disability, national or ethnic origin, or veteran's status. Positions are filled by promotion from within the Organization wherever possible.

(continues)

| Sample 11-2. Continued. |

Job Posting

Open positions listed in **Job Opportunities** are posted on the job opportunity board located in the Human Resources Department and at other assigned locations. Exempt level positions are posted at all locations; non-exempt positions are posted locally.

If an employee meets the requirements of a posted position, and has been in his/her current position for at least 6 months, he/she may bid on a position by obtaining an internal application from the Human Resources Department. This internal application must be completed and received by the Human Resources Department no later than 5:00 p.m. on the last day of the posting. Internal applications are held in strict confidence. External recruiting may occur simultaneously.

A Human Resources representative will interview all internal job applicants to determine their suitability for referral to the requisitioning department. If the Human Resources representative finds that the candidate does not meet the job requirements, the candidate will be informed and no further action will be taken. For qualified candidates, the Human Resources representative will arrange for an interview with the requisitioning department.

Final selection will be made by the department, dependent upon the candidate's conformance with the job specifications and past performance.

Professionalism

Telephone Usage

While personal phone calls are not encouraged, we recognize that there are occasions when a call from the office is necessary, such as in cases of emergency and for calls that simply cannot be made at night. When a strictly personal, non-business telephone call is necessary, staff members may place the call from an office phone; however, staff members are expected to reimburse the Organization for excessive charges.

In answering the telephone, whether your own or a co-worker's, promptness, consideration, and courtesy are extremely important. Staff members are expected to answer a ringing unattended telephone, and assist the caller to the best of their ability. Remember, you are speaking for your company, your department, and yourself.

Answer the telephone promptly and identify yourself by name and department, if appropriate. If you answer a call for another staff member who is not immediately available, offer to be of help by taking a message. If a call comes through on your line in error, transfer it to the correct extension.

Reimbursement of Business Expenses

Expense reports are to be submitted on a frequent basis (no less than once a month) by staff members who incur expenses regularly. Staff members who incur expenses intermittently should submit expense reports within one (1) week from the date the expense is incurred. For further information regarding reimbursement of business expenses, see the *Policies* manual or consult your supervisor.

Leaving Your Work Area

If you will be away from your work area for a long period of time, inform your supervisor (or someone in your department if your supervisor is not available) where you can be reached and when you plan to return.

Courtesy and Appearance

A pleasant manner and courtesy to our co-workers or building employees or the general public is an important part of our job and part of being professional. Guidelines for appropriate dress may vary from department to department in consideration of the type of work involved; however, we are expected to always maintain a neat appearance.

ACKNOWLEDGMENT

I have received and read the Handbook. I have specifically read and understand the Statement of Equal Employment Opportunity, Harassment, Ethics, and Proprietary Information policies.

I understand that the contents of the book do not constitute a binding contract, but rather comprise a set of guidelines concerning the Organization. I understand that these guidelines are not intended by reason of their publication to confer any special rights or privileges upon specific individuals or to entitle any person to any fixed term or condition of employment. I also understand that no supervisor or manager has the authority to enter into a contract with me, binding upon the Organization, unless such contract is in writing and signed by the President and Chief Executive Officer or his delegate. I understand that the Organization may modify any of the provisions in this book at any time.

_____

Dated

_____

Name (please print)

_____

Signature

Sample 11-3

This sample is from a 5¼- by 8½-inch employee handbook. Each page consists of straight text in a semiblock format. The type is small and tiring to read. There are underlined heads, although not delineated by boldface type, different point sizes, or varying fonts. Other than skipping a space between paragraphs, there is no white space.

The text contains personal pronouns, and the message comes across as sincere.

Some of the language is sexist (e.g., referring to the supervisor and president as "he").

Complaints

In order to ensure that employees receive fair treatment and are given an opportunity to communicate problems and complaints, we have developed a complaint procedure to be used by everyone. Most of us have a question or complaint at some time. If you do, the only way we can answer your question or solve your problem is for you to tell us about it and talk it over with us.

If you have a question or complaint, you should first talk it over with your supervisor. Your supervisor knows more about you and your job than any other member of management, and he is in the best position to handle your problem properly and satisfactorily. He will do his best to satisfy you, and in most cases, he will be able to solve your problem.

If you are not satisfied with the answer you get from your supervisor, you should discuss the matter with the personnel office. The personnel director will review the matter and do whatever he can to resolve your problem.

If you still feel that you have not gotten your problem resolved to your satisfaction, you may then submit the matter in writing to the president of the company. He

is interested in making sure that your complaint gets settled satisfactorily. In doing so, he will investigate the case, determine the facts, and give his decision to both you and your supervisor.

If your complaint involves any type of unlawful discrimination or harassment, you may take your problem directly to the personnel director rather than going to your supervisor. We will do everything we can to ensure that everyone is treated fairly.

Employee Suggestions

New ideas are important in any progressive organization. In your everyday work, you may think of changes which will improve efficiency or otherwise benefit both you and the company. We welcome and appreciate any suggestions that you have that will improve the way in which we operate. Please submit all suggestions in writing to the personnel department, or put them in the suggestion box provided.

Sample 11-4

This company intersperses drawings and cartoons throughout the employee hand-book to break up the text. The twenty-nine page booklet, in a 4- by 6-inch format, has an average of one illustration for every two pages. Following the two-page text are other illustrations.

There are some pretentious words, like *auspices,* in the first sentence under "Company Publication." Clichés are also tossed in, such as "leave the comfort of their homes."

Company Publication

This book is written and published under the auspices of the Personnel Dept. for the benefit of all employees. Your contributions are welcomed and encouraged.

The company newspaper appears every month, and is designed to keep you up-to-date about a wide range of topics and personalities, as well as company policies and views, that will be of interest to everyone.

The Show Must Go On

You are an important part of our company . . . and your absence from work throws a monkey wrench into the department in which you work. If you are sick, or unable to work because of some emergency situation, it is important that you call as soon as possible, or within one hour after you were scheduled to report to work. If you cannot make the call, it is important to have a member of your family telephone the company. The reason for your absence would be given, as well as some indication as to when you will be able to return to work.

If you are absent for three consecutive work days without notifying the company, you will be considered to have quit without notice.

Working Hours

The company normally operates on a 40-hour week with a half-hour for lunch.

Your supervisor will advise you of your starting time, rest periods, lunch periods and quitting time. We ask that you be mindful of your individual work schedule, since your co-workers will be depending on you.

Winter Storm Procedure

If snowy or icy weather forces the closing of the plant, the announcement to shut down the plant for the day will be made as early as possible over local radio stations...so First Shift employees will not have to leave the comfort of their homes. When possible, these announcements are made as early as 5:30 A.M., while Second Shift cancellations are announced over the radio by 2:00 P.M. and Third Shift cancellations are announced by 10:30 P.M.

Smoking...and No Smoking

Because of the nature of our business, we have to be extremely careful about smoking in and around the plant. A serious fire can destroy our jobs.

So please, in the interests of job protection, safety and cleanliness, observe the "No Smoking" signs. Smoke only in authorized areas, which have been provided for your convenience.

[1]

Solicitation and Distribution

Our company policy prohibits any solicitation during working time of either the employee soliciting or the employee being solicited. Additionally, any distribution of literature is prohibited during working time or at any time within work areas.

One exception to this policy is the United Way/Combined Health Appeal Campaign. The company is a strong supporter of the United Way, and does permit solicitation of pledges during working hours, provided the solicitor has been authorized to act in that capacity on behalf of the United Way.

Temporary Assignment

When, a regular employee is temporarily assigned (more than eight hours) to a job with a higher rate of pay than his classified job rate, he or she will be paid the higher rate. When this temporary assignment is to a lower rated job, the employee will be paid his or her present classified rate.

Lost & Found

If you lose something, or find an item of possible value, please notify the Personnel Department as soon as possible.

Lockers and Coat Racks

Lockers are assigned to you whenever possible, but remain the property of the company and are subject to periodic sanitary and security inspections. Coat racks are available at convenient locations in the plant and are at your disposal. Under no circumstances should you leave money or other valuables in your locker or coat because of the temptation this may present to the occasional dishonest person.

Telephones Mean Business

The telephone is a very important sales tool. Customers call in orders, prospects make inquiries, and customers are satisfied through the use of company telephones. It's obvious that they must be available for business at all times to keep from turning away or offending customers. Customers make sales, and sales keep us on the job.

You are welcome to make personal calls at the pay phone booths before or after work, on your breaks or at lunch time - but do not tie up the company's lines with private calls during the plant hours except for real emergencies. Ask your friends who persist in calling you to cooperate in this matter. In cases of emergency, we will, of course, assist you in making whatever calls are necessary, and we will relay important messages to you.

[2]

(continues)

Sample 11-4. Continued.

Your Time Record

The badge which you have been issued is your assurance that you will receive accurate payment for time worked, since the badge itself is the official record from which your pay is figured.

This badge is part of what we call "The Link System," and the system will be described to you in detail by your supervisor.

Your Link System badge becomes, in effect, your time card. Ring your badge in at the beginning of your work day, at the beginning of your lunch break, at the end of your lunch break...and at the end of your work day.

Ringing in the badge of another employee, or having someone else ring in your badge, is forbidden and would subject all involved employees to possible dismissal.

Because of their importance, Link System badges are not to be removed during the work day, or taken home. They must be displayed on your person at all times.

Salaried personnel use the more traditional time cards, and the company's rules for punching the card in and out are exactly the same as those that apply to badges. Supervisors will be required to sign these time cards before they can be processed through payroll.

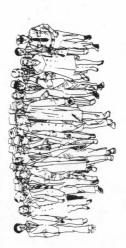

Visitors

Our visitors, no matter how much we like them, do disrupt business. Unless there is an emergency involved, remind your friends and relatives not to disturb you while you are on the job.

If visitors do call on you at the plant on an important matter, you will be paged and asked to come to the Personnel Dept.

Keep The Record Straight

Accurate employment records are important to assure you of all your benefits and to comply with government regulations. Keep your confidential records up-to-date by notifying the Personnel Department of:

1. Change of address and phone number.
2. Change of person to be notified in case of accident.
3. Change in your legal name.
4. Change in your number of income tax exemptions.

24

5. Change in your marital status.
6. Change in your insurance beneficiary.

If We Part Company

If circumstances are such that you must leave, please tell your supervisor or department head well in advance so he can make the necessary arrangements.

Also, check in your equipment and tools and return your badge to the Personnel Department. Your final check will be mailed to you.

We expect at least one week's notice prior to the date of your departure. Check with the Personnel Dept. regarding your vacation status and your continuance in the various insurance programs.

Bulletin Boards

The company utilizes bulletin boards throughout the plant as a means of keeping you informed on important matters. It is suggested that you make a practice of reading the notices posted on these boards daily to be properly informed.

Bulletin boards are provided for employees wishing to post personal notices. If you wish to have a personal notice posted, it must be presented to the Employee Relations Department for authorization prior to posting.

Seniority

Seniority refers to the amount of uninterrupted time you have worked for the company. It gives you protection and certain preferences when decisions must be made in regard to promotion, reduction in the workforce and determination of eligibility for various benefits.

Some things to remember about seniority are:

1. New employees are considered probationary until they have completed 3 months of employment. During this period they will have no seniority benefits.

2. Promotions are given to the most senior qualified employee when skill, ability and work records are comparable.

3. In the event of a required reduction in the work force or layoff, temporary, probationary, and part-time employees are released first. If further reduction is necessary, such layoffs are made on the basis of plantwide seniority in the affected departments, provided those who remain are qualified to do the work that is required.

4. Employees whose jobs are eliminated during a period of reduction in work force, but who are not laid off because of seniority, shall be assigned to available jobs on the basis of skill, ability and seniority. The company will enter into reasonable training programs to maintain seniority order so that new or recalled skills necessary to perform a new job assignment can be acquired at standard levels inside of four weeks.

5. Recall from layoff is made on the basis of seniority, provided the most senior employee on layoff is qualified to do the available work.

[4]

Sample 11-5

This sample is from a handbook with more than fifty pages in the form of a looseleaf binder, with six colored tabs dividing the sections: Policies and Procedures, Fringe Benefits, Health Insurance, Life Insurance, Disability, and Pension Plan. The format is a mixture of heads and subheads, boldface type, varying fonts, different type sizes, photographs, lists, and questions and answers. This variety is especially effective in breaking up the text throughout the drier sections, such as those pertaining to insurance, which read like a technical or legal document.

With so much of the text devoted to insurance-related topics, perhaps these areas should have been placed in a separate handbook.

Sample 11-5

Dental Expense Coverage

Q: **Do I receive the same amount of reimbursement for all dental work?**

A.   **The** amount of reimbursement depends on the type of work you have done. There are two primary classifications for reimbursement: 80 percent and 50 percent:

- 80 percent reimbursement:

    Charges for routine oral examination including diagnosis, x-rays, and prophylaxis, but not for more than one exam per insured individual for any six-month period.

    Extractions, fillings (not gold), root canal work, peridontal treatment and drugs requiring a dentist's prescription.

    Oral surgery.

    Repair of dentures and bridgework.

- 50 percent reimbursement:

    Inlays, crown, and gold fillings.

    Initial installation of, or addition to, full or partial dentures or fixed bridgework required as the result of the extraction of one or more injured or diseased natural teeth while insured, provided that the denture or bridgework includes the replacement of a tooth so extracted, and is performed within 12 months after such extraction.

    Replacement or alternation of full or partial dentures or fixed bridgework required as the result of the following events occurring while insured provided that replacement or alternation is completed with 12 months of the injury or oral surgical treatment:

    - accidental injury necessitating oral surgical treatment, or

    - oral surgical treatment involving the repositioning of muscle attachments, or the removal or a tumor, cyst, torus, or redundant tissue.

    Replacement of a full denture required as the result of structural change within the mouth provided that the replacement is made more than five years after the date of the installation of the dentrures and two years or more after the person becomes insured under the plan.

Covered charges do not include any expenses which exceed the regular and customary charges for services, supplies, and treatments or their fair and reasonable value.

Q.   Are there dental services that are not covered?

A.   Covered dental charges shall not include expenses for services, supplies, and treatment:

- Unless they were prescribed as necessary by a dentist.

- For orthodontic treament.

- For dentistry for cosmetic purposes, including the alteration or extraction and replacement of sound teeth to change appearance.

Sample 11-6

This introduction to a policies and procedures manual explains the purpose of the manual and how it is to be used. Managers and supervisors are advised that all policies are to be implemented without discrimination.

The message is straightforward and clear. Personal pronouns lend warmth.

Sample 11-6

January 199X

To Our Managers and Supervisors:

As an organization grows in size and complexity, the uniform interpretation of management objectives becomes increasingly important. One tool for achieving this uniformity is the translation of company goals and objectives into specific programs, policies, and procedures. Nowhere is this more important than in matters directly affecting the employees of an organization. For this reason, we have prepared the Policies and Procedures Manual.

As managers and supervisors, it is your responsibility to fully utilize the skills and potential demonstrated by the people you supervise. This requires the application of consistently sound employer/employee relations practices in all dealings with staff. Our manual is designed to assist you in this responsibility by providing complete, current, and easily accessible information as a basis for dealing with all matters of

cont'd . . .

Sample 11-6. Continued.

policies and procedures accurately and in a uniform manner. Should you require elaboration or clarification of any item contained herein, you are encouraged to contact the Personnel Department.

The statements in this manual have been formulated to provide equal employment opportunity for all persons in every aspect of the employer/employee relationship. This includes recruiting, selection, hiring, working conditions, benefits, compensation, training, career paths, promotions, transfers, performance evaluations, and termination of employment. Any and all actions taken with regard to any employer/employee matter will be implemented without discrimination.

You will receive revisions and additions to this manual as necessary. Please keep your copy up to date by adding or substituting new material upon receipt.

The Personnel Policies and Procedures Manual has been written for your use. I believe it will answer many of the questions you may presently have in your day-to-day dealings with employees and make some of your daily decision-making tasks less burdensome. Most importantly, by keeping well informed, your management/employee relationships will be strengthened, thereby making you more effective managers and supervisors.

Sincerely,

Chief Executive Vice President

Sample 11-7

This sample is from an 8½- by 11-inch looseleaf policies and procedures manual, divided into nine sections: EEO and Affirmative Action, Recruitment and Employment Practices, Salary Administration, Benefits Administration, Training and Development, Disciplinary Action, Employee Grievance Procedure, General Information, and Forms. The setup for each section (except for the one containing forms) is identical: section title and number, subject, and page number. The format is also the same: underlined capitalized heads, bullets and underlined lowercase letters for subheads, and single-spaced text with double and triple spaces between paragraphs. While not terribly creative, the document is appropriately structured and makes for easy reading. Each section contains a policy statement, managerial-supervisory responsibilities, and guidelines for administration, providing uniformity.

The manual implements the four C's throughout: the language is clear and concise, the information is complete, and the tone and style are consistent. The sentence pace is varied; this is significant, since the manual is over two hundred pages. The use of clichés, jargon, and connotations is limited, and the language is nonsexist.

That personal pronouns are lacking, as is the active voice, lends a formal tone to the document.

Sample 11-7

DISCIPLINARY ACTION

Section: 6.1
Subject: ADMINISTRATION OF DISCIPLINE

THE PURPOSE OF DISCIPLINE

When discipline is applied to an employee for breaking a rule or committing an offense, the purpose is
to restore him/her to complying with established
standards not to punish merely for the sake of pun-
ishment. Discipline then should be corrective, not
punitive.

MANAGERIAL/SUPERVISORY RESPONSIBILITIES

A study of arbitration cases reveals that the main
causes for discipline breakdowns can be traced to
bad communications, poor training, and inconsistent
and vascillating leadership. In this regard, the
following list of managers' and supervisors' responsibilities serves as a guide to help prevent discipline problems from occurring:

- Clearly communicate applicable
  rules and regulations.

- Maintain a highly motivated work
  environment.

- Be sensitive to employee needs and
  concerns.

- Respond to employee suggestions.

- Encourage upward mobility.

- Provide employees with proper tools
  with which to perform their jobs.

- Encourage the development of existing skills and training to acquire
  new skills.

- Maintain a system of open, two-way
  communication.

DISCIPLINARY ACTION

Section: 6.1
Subject: ADMINISTRATION OF DISCIPLINE (Cont'd)

- Clearly communicate job expectations.

- Make certain employees and jobs are appropriately "matched."

- Apply discipline in a consistent manner.

- Know each employee's skills, interests, and potential, and treat each employee as an important individual.

- Set a proper example.

- Coach and counsel employees as appropriate (coaching involves ongoing, day-to-day communication; counseling involves the addressing of specific problems when they occur, not at the employee's next scheduled performance appraisal interview).

(continues)

Sample 11-7. Continued.

Section: 6.2
Subject: GENERAL GUIDELINES
_____

- In any disciplinary matter, managers and supervisors must remember that the steps outlined below are for a repeat of the same infraction.

- A manager or supervisor cannot "back document." Documentation and discipline must occur at the time of the infraction in order to be valid.

- The seriousness of an offense; the frequency of its occurrence; its effect on productivity, other employees, and the company as a whole; an employee's overall employment history; and all contributing circumstances will determine the degree of discipline to be administered.

- Managers and supervisors are cautioned against acting hastily. Administering discipline is a very serious matter. Be certain all the facts have been gathered and objectively evaluated before deciding on a course of action.

- Any type of disciplinary action taken against an employee should be based upon just cause fully attributable to the employee.

- Managers and supervisors must be certain to apply the disciplinary guidelines uniformly and without bias.

- Managers and supervisors are urged to consult with Personnel before taking any action.

DISCIPLINARY ACTION

Section: 6.2
Subject: GENERAL GUIDELINES (Cont'd)

DISCIPLINARY STEPS

The following steps are intended for use as a
guide. Certain occurrences, i.e., acts of
physical violence, proven theft, etc., may warrant
suspension or immediate dismissal. Hence, issuing
a verbal warning followed by two (2) written warnings would not pertain. On the other hand,
excessive tardiness or absenteeism would require
following the steps outlined.

Once again, managers and supervisors are urged to
confer with Personnel before administering any
disciplinary action.

Step 1. First Offense - Verbal Warning

Often, a verbal warning clarifies misunderstood
directions, eliminates certain assumptions, and
resolves any conflicts which may exist.

Verbal warnings should always be conducted in
private. The manager or supervisor should explain,
clearly and concisely, the purpose of the meeting.

This explanation should include defining the
alleged infraction, the date(s) the infraction is
to have occurred, the specific nature/source of
information leading to the belief that the infraction had occurred (if not personally observed), and
any other pertinent data. The employee must then
be permitted ample time to discuss/refute what has
been said.

Managers and supervisors are urged to "block" a
sufficient period of time for this meeting. Since
verbal warnings frequently serve to negate the need
for additional disciplinary action, the time required for a thorough verbal warning session is a
worthwhile investment.

(continues)

Sample 11-7. Continued.

DISCIPLINARY ACTION

Section: 6.2
Subject: GENERAL GUIDELINES (Cont'd)
_____

An "informal" record of this meeting should be
made for reference in the event of a second
infraction of the same offense. This notation
should not be placed in the employee's file.
Verbal warnings may not be officially documented.

Verbal warnings should be given as soon after an
offense occurs as possible.

Step 2. Second Offense - Written Warning

If the same infraction should occur following a
verbal warning, the employee should be issued a
written warning.

The written warning is a statement of what
occurred, who was involved, when and where the
infraction took place, and why it warrants disciplinary action. The contents should contain
facts only.

Employees must be given an opportunity to read the
contents of the written warning and make any comments they wish. They should also be urged to sign
the written warning, indicating that they have seen
and read the warning and understand its contents.
Signature does not necessarily mean agreement, only
understanding. Refusal to sign should be so noted.

Employees should be given a copy of the warning and
be told that a copy will be placed in their
personnel file. Written warnings will remain on
file for a period of six (6) months. Managers and
supervisors are urged to discuss the seriousness of
the situation with the employee and explain that
continuation of such behavior could affect promo-
tional/transfer opportunities, future salary
increases, and may ultimately result in termination
of employment.

All meetings involving written warnings should be
conducted in private as soon after the occurrence
as possible. A representative from Personnel
should be present at the meeting or available for
advice.

DISCIPLINARY ACTION

Section: 6.2
Subject: GENERAL GUIDELINES (Cont'd)

Step 3. Third Offense - Written Warning

Depending on the nature of the infraction, a third
occurrence may result in a second written warning.
Should this happen, the guidelines described under
Step 2 above will apply.

Step 4. Fourth Offense - Termination

Following a verbal warning, written warning(s), or a
suspension, an employee may be terminated for repeat of the same infraction. This is termination
for cause and means, among other things, that the
employee is not eligible for rehire or certain
termination benefits. A written statement summarizing the termination should be prepared by the
manager or supervisor and placed in the employee's
file. A representative from Personnel should be
present during this meeting or available for
advice.

(continues)

Sample 11-7. Continued.

DISCIPLINARY ACTION

Section: 6.3
Subject: SUSPENSION _____

Under certain circumstances, such as, suspected
dishonesty or theft, an employee may be suspended.
The employee must be informed, during a ''closed
door'' meeting, of the reason for the suspension
and be made aware of the seriousness of the
situation.

Managers and supervisors are urged to have a representative from Personnel present at this meeting or
available for advice. A statement summary of the
meeting should be written and placed in the employee's personnel file. A copy should also be given
to the employee.

Suspensions will usually be for a duration of from
one (1) to three (3) working days, depending on the
seriousness of the infraction.

DISCIPLINARY ACTION

Section: 6.4
Subject: CAUSES FOR DISCIPLINARY ACTION

The following is a list of certain acts which would
be considered causes for disciplinary action.
Managers and supervisors are cautioned that this
list is not meant to be all inclusive. If uncertain
as to whether or not the administration of discipline is in order, contact Personnel before taking
any action.

- Habitual/excessive tardiness;

- Habitual/excessive absenteeism;

- Unexcused absences;

- Insubordination;

- Falsification of records;

- Theft;

- Threats and/or actual acts of
  physical violence;

- Willful violation of known company
  rules;

- Destruction or abuse of company
  property;

- Misuse of checking privileges;

- Possession and/or use of alcohol
  and/or controlled substances
  during working hours;

- Reporting to work in an intoxicated
  condition;

- Tending to personal matters during
  working hours;

- Gambling on company property;

- Interfering with the work of other
  employees.

(continues)

Sample 11-7. Continued.

DISCIPLINARY ACTION

Section: 6.5
Subject: DOCUMENTATION
_____

The importance of written documentation cannot be
overemphasized. Every conversation/meeting between
a manager or supervisor and an employee, beyond the
verbal warning stage, regarding actual or possible
future disciplinary action <u>must</u> be documented.

<u>GUIDELINES</u>

- Written documentation must be
  objective, specific, and factual.

- The "basic questions" of who? what?
  where? when? and why? should be
  addressed.

- Statements must be exclusive of any
  bias, opinion, or conjecture.

- Words and phrases that are subject to
  interpretation, such as "uncooperative,"
  "disrespectful," and "bad attitude"
  should be avoided. Wherever possible,
  actual statements made by the parties
  involved should be recorded, as well as
  a description of the events leading to
  the need for disciplinary action.

- Recommended steps for improvement should
  be noted.

- The tone of the document should be
  corrective, not punitive.

- The employee should be asked to sign the
  document, indicating understanding of
  contents. He/she should also be permitted to attach comments.

- Employees should be given a copy of the
  written document and informed that a copy
  will be included in their personnel file.

- Managers and supervisors are cautioned
  against "back documentation." Documentation must occur at the time of the
  infraction in order to be valid.

Sample 11-8

The policies and procedures manual for this small, growing company is in notebook form. It is divided into six sections, identified by name and number: (100) Employment Practices, (200) Salary Administration, (300) Benefits, (400) Disciplinary Action, (500) Training and Development, and (600) General Information. Each section is subdivided, and each of these subdivisions is assigned a number (e.g., 500-1 is the Training and Development Policy, 500-2 is the segment on Special Training Programs, and 500-3 is the organization's Tuition Refund Policy).

The sample that follows is Section 600, General Information, with sixteen subdivisions. The topics are listed in the Contents but are not arranged alphabetically or according to any other identifiable method. The sixteen topics do not contain the same categories. Some identify a specific policy and procedure; others note management's responsibility; still others are purely informative.

The language is generally nonsexist and easy to understand, although the grammar and punctuation could have been checked thoroughly, and there are occasional inconsistencies between voice and tense. The section and subject boxes were left blank on the first page of 600-13. The document is wordy in spots (e.g., in 600-6, *during the course of* could have been replaced with *during*). Personal pronouns are used irregularly; there is a mix of active and passive voice.

Some of the information is incomplete. For example, the policy on "Death in Family" does not specify the number of days an employee is entitled to take off.

Sample 11-8

	PPM No. 600-1
	Page 1 of 2

POLICIES AND PROCEDURES MANUAL	Section: GENERAL INFORMATION
	Subject: MEDICAL SERVICES

EMPLOYEE ILLNESS OR INJURY

If an employee becomes ill or is injured on the job, the Personnel Department should arrange for transportation, at the company's expense, to send the employee home and may ask another employee to accompany the patient.

Whenever possible, the employee should be given the opportunity to call his or her own physician.

AMBULANCE SERVICE

When ambulance service is required for an employee, the Personnel Department should call the local Police or Fire Department Emergency service.

SENDING AN EMPLOYEE TO THE HOSPITAL

If ambulance service is not required, but hospital attention is indicated, the patient may be sent to the hospital by taxi or driven as arranged by the Personnel Department.

Whenever an ill or injured employee is sent to a hospital, he or she should be accompanied by another employee. Personnel should provide the escort with sufficient funds to cover anticipated expenses and necessary information such as Group Medical Plans identification information. The escort should remain with the patient until admission to the hospital has been completed and then relay to the Supervisor/Manager, as soon as possible, any information regarding

PPM No. 600-1
Page 2 of 2

POLICIES AND PROCEDURES MANUAL	Section: GENERAL INFORMATION
	Subject: MEDICAL SERVICES

the patient's condition. Personnel should communicate with the employee's family. If the hospital releases the patient, the escort should accompany the employee home.

WORKMEN'S COMPENSATION

It is the Manager/Supervisor's responsibility, after appropriate medical attention is provided, to assist Personnel in preparing the required Accident/Illness report. The Personnel Department will prepare and send any supplemental reports to the Workmen's Compensation insurance carrier as required. Reports will also be prepared in compliance with the Occupational Safety and Health Act (OSHA).

(continues)

Sample 11-8. Continued.

	PPM No. 600-2
	Page 1 of 2

POLICIES AND PROCEDURES MANUAL	Section: GENERAL INFORMATION
	Subject: EMPLOYEE COMMUNICATION

NEWSLETTER

An employee newsletter will be developed by the Personnel Department in the near future. Its purpose will be to keep employees informed of various activities, including news of job opportunities, recent promotions, etc. It will also serve to stimulate employee interest in the organization and provide information about different departments.

Individuals interested in contributing their services to this project are invited to contact the Personnel Department.

MANAGEMENT'S RESPONSIBILITY

Although the newsletter is very important and satisfies certain needs, oral communication continues to be the most effective means of communication. Only the Supervisor or Manager can adequately fulfill this responsibility and to do so he or she must become "communications-conscious." Information received in meetings, through memoranda, or in consultation with higher management should be evaluated for employee interest content and passed along as suitable. Never assume that employees are not interested in the "big picture." Try to keep them informed on departmental and company-wide progress and problems. A demonstrated willingness to communicate can have a great impact on employee morale.

PPM No. 600-2
Page 2 of 2

POLICIES AND PROCEDURES MANUAL	Section: GENERAL INFORMATION
	Subject: EMPLOYEE COMMUNICATION

BULLETIN BOARDS

Bulletin boards are located at various accessible locations throughout the organization. These boards are monitored by Personnel and are for the benefit of all employees. Any notice or announcement must be approved by Senior Management before being put up on a bulletin board.

EFFECTIVE COMMUNICATIONS

Since effective communications require an upward flow of information as well as downward, it is very important that each Supervisor and Manager have an attitude that encourages freedom of expression on the part of employees. Only as employees make known their problems and suggestions can there be full understanding and cooperation between management and staff.

(continues)

Sample 11-8. Continued.

| | PPM No. 600-3 |
| | Page 1 of 1 |

| POLICIES AND PROCEDURES MANUAL | Section: GENERAL INFORMATION |
| | Subject: COUNSELING EMPLOYEES |

POLICY

Most employee counseling should take place at the Supervisory/ Managerial level and above, particularly when the topic for which counsel is needed is job-related. Personnel stands ready to participate should you or the employee feel that a third party is needed. This is in no way intended to usurp or to circumvent supervisory authority. There may be occasions when, due to personalities involved, counsel outside of the department would be in order. In addition, every individual should have the "right to be heard."

PPM No. 600-4
Page 1 of 1

POLICIES AND PROCEDURES MANUAL	Section: GENERAL INFORMATION
	Subject: DRUG/ALCOHOL ABUSE

POLICY

The possession, use, or sale of any narcotics or alcoholic beverage on premises, or while employees are engaged in company business, will be grounds for disciplinary action, including possible termination.

PROCEDURE

If it is determined that an employee is in possession of, using, or selling any narcotics or alcoholic beverage, it should be reported to the Personnel Department immediately. While each case will be reviewed individually and all circumstances will be considered, it is probable that the employee will be urged to seek professional help. Failure to do so or a second infraction may result in termination of employment.

MANAGER'S/SUPERVISOR'S RESPONSIBILITY

While Managers/Supervisors are urged to develop effective communications with their employees and should counsel them in areas of job-related problems, it must be recognized that drug and alcohol abuse are very serious matters and require the assistance of experts. Hence, Managers/Supervisors are cautioned against trying to resolve matters involving drugs or alcohol by themselves. Instead, they should report any occurrences to the Personnel Department who will proceed to seek expert advice.

(continues)

Sample 11-8. Continued.

	PPM No. 600-5
	Page 1 of 1

POLICIES AND PROCEDURES MANUAL	Section: GENERAL INFORMATION
	Subject: OUTSIDE EMPLOYMENT

<u>POLICY</u>

Employees may be employed in work outside of their regularly scheduled job as long as that additional work does not interfere in any manner with their job accomplishment at the company.

<u>CONFLICTS OF INTEREST</u>

Known conflicts of interest on the part of employees will not be tolerated. Employees may be asked to discontinue any such conflict, with refusal to do so resulting in possible termination.

	PPM No. 600-6
	Page 1 of 1

POLICIES AND PROCEDURES MANUAL	Section: GENERAL INFORMATION
	Subject: EMERGENCIES

MANAGER'S/SUPERVISOR'S RESPONSIBILITY

The primary responsibility for the continued conduct of business during the course of emergencies must necessarily rest with the Supervisor or Manager in charge of each department. The effects of these problems can be minimized by the utilization of good supervisory practices on a regular basis. For example, a continuing program of training and job rotation overcomes the limitations of specialization. Accurate personnel records provide current addresses and telephone numbers. An emergency plan establishes priorities for each departmental function and essential activities that must be continued.

EXTREME EMERGENCIES

An emergency may develop beyond the point that will permit you to deal with the problems in accordance with the preceding statements. In these cases special plans and guides will be devised by Senior Management to provide standards applicable to the company as a whole.

(continues)

Sample 11-8. Continued.

	PPM No. 600-7
	Page 1 of 1

POLICIES AND PROCEDURES MANUAL	Section: GENERAL INFORMATION
	Subject: EMPLOYEE DEATHS

MANAGER'S/SUPERVISOR'S RESPONSIBILITY

Word of an employee's death should be communicated to the Personnel Department as quickly as possible. As soon as it is available, this initial notification should be followed up with the details of the funeral arrangements and other pertinent information.

DEATH BENEFITS

Flowers or other appropriate expressions of sympathy will be sent on behalf of staff. Personnel will set the procedure in motion for the payment to the employee's beneficiary of any benefits due under insurance and retirement programs. A representative of the Personnel Department will contact the beneficiary and make arrangements to visit the beneficiary to assist in the prompt and orderly processing of benefits.

These actions on the part of Personnel will, of course, be in addition to any voluntary expressions of sympathy and offers of assistance to the deceased employee's family on the part of the Supervisor/Manager and co-workers.

PPM No. 600-8
Page 1 of 1

POLICIES AND PROCEDURES MANUAL	Section: GENERAL INFORMATION
	Subject: DEATH IN FAMILY

MANAGER'S/SUPERVISOR'S RESPONSIBILITY

Managers/Supervisors should contact Personnel immediately upon receiving information concerning the death of a member of an employee's family. Furnish the name of deceased, relationship to employee, date of death, and funeral arrangements.

EXPRESSION OF SYMPATHY

In the case of the death of a member of the employee's immediate family, the company will arrange to send flowers or other appropriate expression of sympathy on behalf of the staff. A letter of condolence may also be sent to the employee by Senior Management.

The foregoing is in addition to whatever expressions of sympathy may be voluntarily extended by the employee's co-workers.

DEFINITION OF "IMMEDIATE FAMILY"

An employee's immediate family is defined as legal spouse, parent, grandparent, child, brother, sister, and any other relative who is a member of the employee's household.

(continues)

Sample 11-8. Continued.

	PPM No. 600-9
	Page 1 of 1

POLICIES AND PROCEDURES MANUAL	Section: GENERAL INFORMATION
	Subject: VISITORS IN WORK AREA

<u>POLICY</u>

Unless approved by Senior Management, visitors will not be permitted to enter company buildings.

PPM No. 600-10
Page 1 of 1

POLICIES AND PROCEDURES MANUAL	Section: GENERAL INFORMATION
	Subject: PERSONAL APPEARANCE AND CONDUCT

POLICY

The company has no intention of attempting to control the appearance of any of its employees. However, it does require that employees maintain good hygiene practices and appropriate dress habits in accordance with the work they are performing, and in conjunction with OSHA and other safety requirements.

MANAGER'S/SUPERVISOR'S RESPONSIBILITY

It is the Manager's/Supervisor's responsibility to make sure that the conduct and appearance of employees under his or her supervision are in good taste. Personnel may be consulted for assistance in resolving any problems in this area.

(continues)

Sample 11-8. Continued.

	PPM No. 600-11
	Page 1 of 1

POLICIES AND PROCEDURES MANUAL	Section: GENERAL INFORMATION
	Subject: TELEPHONE USAGE

POLICY

Telephone facilities are for business purposes and must be limited to such. Telephones should not be used for personal communications except in case of emergency or absolute necessity. Similarly, employees should discourage having persons call them from outside the office. At no time is an employee permitted to charge a personal telephone call to the company.

MANAGER'S/SUPERVISOR'S RESPONSIBILITY

Managers/Supervisors must see that telephones are not used for personal calls except in cases of emergency. In such an instance, the employee should be encouraged to keep the call short.

| PPM No. 600-12 |
| Page 1 of 1 |

| POLICIES AND PROCEDURES MANUAL | Section: GENERAL INFORMATION |
| | Subject: BREAK PERIODS |

Coffee breaks have become a ''work habit'' and are viewed as a morale builder. They reduce fatigue, improve quality of work, increase productivity, and improve concentration. Wherever the work schedule permits, two (2) break periods of ten (10) minutes in duration may be given per shift.

Schedule breaks so as to permit adequate coverage to provide efficient work continuation. The break period is included as working time and is provided solely for the purpose of rest and relaxation. Employees must not be permitted to leave the premises for the purpose of taking a break. It is not to be construed as time off. Employees may not be permitted to apply time usually granted for the purpose of a break to other purposes. For instance, employees may not waive the break period and leave ten minutes early or report ten minutes later. The break period is intended as an interruption in the work schedule for the purpose of rest and refreshment only.

(continues)

Sample 11-8. Continued.

	PPM No. 600-13
	Page 1 of 1

POLICIES AND PROCEDURES MANUAL	Section: GENERAL INFORMATION
	Subject: SMOKING

<u>MANAGER'S/SUPERVISOR'S RESPONSIBILITY</u>

The Manager/Supervisor is responsible to see that employees who smoke observe the usual precautions for safety and orderliness and that they are considerate of their co-workers who do not smoke. Common sense and courtesy are normally the best guides.

PPM No. 600-14
Page 1 of 1

POLICIES AND PROCEDURES MANUAL	Section: GENERAL INFORMATION
	Subject: EXIT INTERVIEWS

PURPOSE

In order to continue to improve on the quality of employer/employee relations, it is essential that management have a clear understanding of why employees voluntarily leave our company to seek employment elsewhere. Even if an employee is being terminated, it is important to determine how he or she felt while employed. For this reason, it is urged that every employee who leaves for any reason be given an exit interview.

PROCEDURE

The Personnel Department will conduct exit interviews, using exit interview questionnaires as a guide. Terminating employees should be made to understand that the information being requested will not, in any way, be used against them. The purpose described above should be explained to them to eliminate any hesitation to be totally frank and honest.

In addition to responding to the questions on the questionnaire, departing employees should be encouraged to add any additional comments they may have regarding benefits, working conditions, compensation, job environment, etc. Hence, the questionnaires should be viewed as guides, and not all inclusive.

The completed exit interview questionnaires should be placed in the terminated employee's personnel folder. It is the responsibility of the Personnel Department to pursue any "patterns," which may be revealed departmentally or organizationally.

(continues)

Sample 11-8. Continued.

	PPM No. 600-15
	Page 1 of 2

| POLICIES AND PROCEDURES MANUAL | Section: GENERAL INFORMATION |
| | Subject: SAFETY |

GENERAL

Each Supervisor and Manager is responsible for making certain that employees under his or her supervision/management are provided a safe and healthful workplace. This is not only a legal obligation, but a moral one as well.

In this regard, and in compliance with the Occupational Safety and Health Act (commonly referred to as OSHA), the Manager/Supervisor must be aware of all health and safety hazards and must initiate and follow up action to correct such hazards.

PERSONNEL DEPARTMENT RESPONSIBILITIES

Personnel is responsible for maintaining records of occupational injuries and illnesses and for preparing reports as required by OSHA.

MANAGER'S/SUPERVISOR'S RESPONSIBILITIES

Supervisors should report material hazards immediately for correction. Mechanical hazards, for example, would be reported to the company holding the service contract for a particular piece of equipment. Managers/Supervisors should also advise employees that they, too, are charged with compliance with all safety standards, rules, and regulations.

	PPM No. 600-15
	Page 2 of 2

POLICIES AND PROCEDURES MANUAL	Section: GENERAL INFORMATION
	Subject: SAFETY

Inform employees of the protection provided them by OSHA. Prominently display the Labor Department's informational poster, "Safety and Health Protection on the Job," on the bulletin board as required by OSHA.

For detailed information regarding OSHA, contact the Engineering Department.

(continues)

Sample 11-8. Continued.

	PPM No. 600-16
	Page 1 of 1

POLICIES AND PROCEDURES MANUAL	Section: GENERAL INFORMATION
	Subject: REIMBURSING MOVING EXPENSES

When an executive is recruited from an area distant from his or her new job location, the company will pay reasonable moving expenses. At least two (2) estimates for the cost of moving must be submitted for approval by Senior Management. Reimbursement for moving expenses will be charged to the operating expenses of the department/division to which the new executive is to be assigned.

Sample 11-9

This sample of a tuition refund plan is from a manual that identifies both a policy and a procedure for each topic. This approach provides clear guidelines.

The policy describes the purpose of the tuition refund plan, identifies its components, and specifies the basis for reimbursement. Eligibility is defined, followed by the procedure employees are to follow for course approval and reimbursement. The result is a descriptive, distinct document written in a straightforward style.

Double spacing throughout and the choice of fonts make reading somewhat difficult; the format is an odd mixture of full block and semiblock.

Sample 11-9

POLICY

As part of our employee development program, we have established a Tuition Refund Plan to help employees pay for the cost of courses, classes and workshops as they relate to their present work or future goals within the company.

The Plan applies to study programs offered by accredited or reputable educational organizations. This includes high school GED classes, Bachelor's and Master's degree courses, workshops and seminars, correspondence and programmed instructional courses.

For formal high school and college courses, reimbursement will be 100% of the amount paid for instruction or tuition, providing the employee receives a passing grade, if the grading system is "pass or fail," or a letter grade of "C" or better. Reimbursement does not cover textbooks, transportation, equipment, graduation fees, or meals. There is no reimbursement for failing grades or letter grades "C-" or lower.

Job-related workshop and seminar costs will be 100% reimbursed. Reimbursement includes workshop or seminar fees, the cost of lodging, travel, meals and phone calls to the office. Travel arrangements must be made through the company travel bureau. Meals will be reimbursed up to $50 per day for each day requiring an overnight stay. $25 will be allotted for the last day of a workshop.

For correspondence and programmed instructional courses, reimbursement will be 50% of the cost of required written instructional materials.

Tuition refunds will be granted only for courses approved by the employee's manager and HR director <u>before</u> the employee begins the course or training.

ELIGIBILITY

All employees working a minimum of 30 hours per week, who have been employed for a minimum of one year, and have received a satisfactory or higher rating on their most recent performance appraisal are eligible.

Employees who terminate their employment before the course, class or workshop is completed are not eligible for reimbursement.

PROCEDURE

Employees should submit the following to their manager:

(continues)

| Sample 11-9. Continued. |

1.   A course description

2.   Information about the educational organization

3.   A memo detailing why and how the course would be
     beneficial

If approved, managers should submit these three items, as well
as a note indicating approval, to the HR director.

The manager will notify the employee in writing upon approval
by the HR director. Within 30 days of completing the course, the
employee is required to submit a Tuition Reimbursement Form,
and evidence of his or earned grade, when applicable, or a
workshop certificate of completion, to the HR director.

   Reimbursement will be processed within two weeks of
receipt.

Sample 11-10

This dress code policy begins by stating the effective date as being "immediately." A specific date would be more meaningful. There are clichés, jargon, and repeated phrases. The occasional use of personal pronouns makes it read more like an employee handbook than a manual. On the plus side is the partial list of items considered inappropriate attire. Also to its credit is the fact that the dress code does not distinguish between attire for men and women.

Sample 11-10

Policy:	Dress Code
Effective Date:	Immediately
Pertains To:	All Employees

The dress code for all employees in all positions in all departments at corporate headquarters will henceforth be in accordance with senior management's standards and expectations, which are as follows:

Monday - Thursday:

Employees are expected to wear traditional business attire, including a suit or blazer with trousers or skirt, or a dress with a jacket. Employees are expected to wear appropriate shoes to complement their attire. That goes for jewelry, too: do not wear anything that will get in the way when you are working or is too much of an attention-getter. Employees are expected to practice good grooming and good hygiene.

Friday:

When employees do not have meetings with clients or vendors, they may dress "down" on Fridays. This means you may (but, of course, do not have to) wear:

- Casual slacks
- Sweaters
- Sports shirts
- Casual shoes
- Skorts

Don't get too carried away, though. Here is a partial list of items that are considered inappropriate at all times:

- Jeans
- Open-toed shoes
- Sneakers
- Bare legs
- Bare midriffs
- Shorts
- Cut-offs
- Leggings
- Stirrup pants
- Tank tops

<u>Procedure</u>

Employees who do not dress appropriately may be subject to our disciplinary process.

Index

Italicized numerals indicate that the material is contained in a figure.